Fruits & Vegetables

Fruits & Vegetables

CONSULTANT EDITOR
Judy Moore

Published by Fog City Press
814 Montgomery Street
San Francisco, CA 94133 USA

Reprinted 2006

FOG CITY PRESS
CHIEF EXECUTIVE OFFICER John Owen
PRESIDENT Terry Newell
PUBLISHER Lynn Humphries
MANAGING EDITOR Janine Flew
ART DIRECTOR Kylie Mulquin
COVER DESIGN John Bull
PICTURE EDITOR Tracey Gibson
EDITORIAL COORDINATORS Paul McNally, Kiren Thandi
PRODUCTION MANAGER Louise Mitchell
PRODUCTION COORDINATOR Monique Layt
SALES MANAGER Emily Jahn
VICE PRESIDENT INTERNATIONAL SALES Stuart Laurence
EUROPEAN SALES DIRECTOR Vanessa Mori

LIMELIGHT PRESS PTY LTD
PROJECT MANAGEMENT Helen Bateman/Jayne Denshire
PROJECT EDITOR Lynn Cole
PROJECT DESIGNER Katie Ravich
CONSULTANT EDITOR Judy Moore

A catalog record for this book is available from the
Library of Congress, Washington, DC.

ISBN 1 876778 96 2

Color reproduction by Bright Arts Graphics (S) Pte Ltd
Printed by LeeFung-Asco Printers

Printed in China

A Weldon Owen Production

Contents

How to Use This Book

This valuable guide will lead you gently through the process of planning and caring for your garden. Whether you are a novice or a more experienced gardener, you'll discover how to get the best results from your soil, whatever the size or design of garden you have chosen.

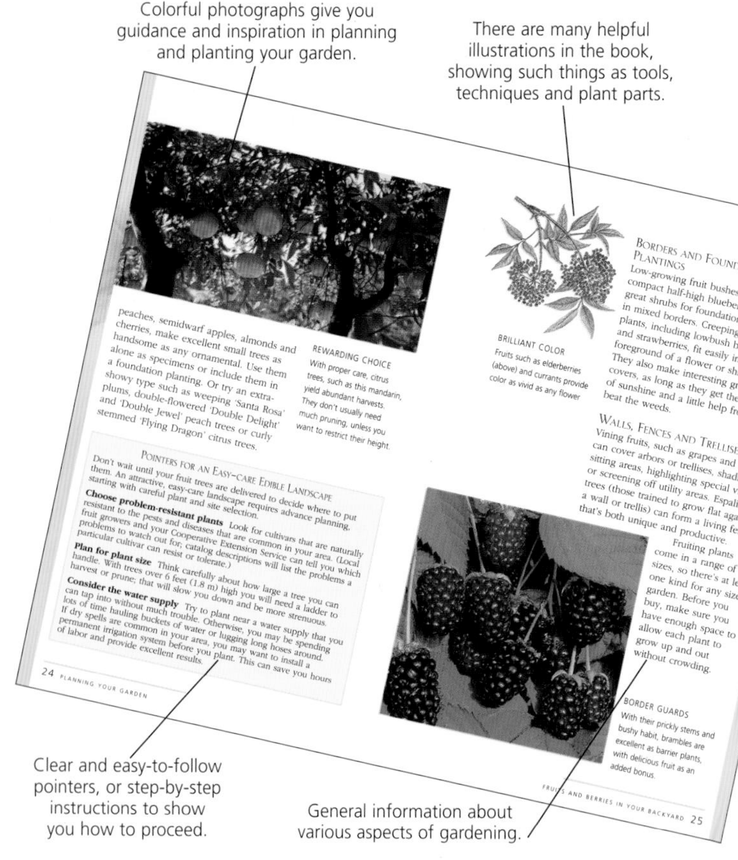

Colorful photographs give you guidance and inspiration in planning and planting your garden.
There are many helpful illustrations in the book, showing such things as tools, techniques and plant parts.
peaches, semidwarf apples, almonds and cherries, make excellent small trees as handsome as any ornamental. Use them alone as specimens or include them in a foundation planting. Or try an extra-showy type such as weeping 'Santa Rosa' plums, double-flowered 'Double Delight' and 'Double Jewel' peach trees or curly stemmed 'Flying Dragon' citrus trees.
REWARDING CHOICE
With proper care, citrus trees, such as this mandarin, yield abundant harvests. They don't usually need much pruning, unless you want to restrict their height.
POINTERS FOR AN EASY-CARE EDIBLE LANDSCAPE
Don't wait until your fruit trees are delivered to decide where to put them. An attractive, easy-care landscape requires advance planning, starting with careful plant and site selection.
Choose problem-resistant plants Look for cultivars that are naturally resistant to the pests and diseases that are common in your area. (Local fruit growers and your Cooperative Extension Service can tell you which problems to watch out for; catalog descriptions will list the problems a particular cultivar can resist or tolerate.)
Plan for plant size Think carefully about how large a tree you can handle. With trees over 6 feet (1.8 m) high you will need a ladder to harvest or prune; that will slow you down and be more strenuous.
Consider the water supply Try to plant near a water supply that you can tap into without much trouble. Otherwise, you may be spending lots of time hauling buckets of water or lugging long hoses around. If dry spells are common in your area, you may want to install a permanent irrigation system before you plant. This can save you hours of labor and provide excellent results.
24 PLANNING YOUR GARDEN
BRILLIANT COLOR
Fruits such as elderberries (above) and currants provide color as vivid as any flower
Fruiting plants come in a range of sizes, so there's at le one kind for any size garden. Before you buy, make sure you have enough space to allow each plant to grow up and out without crowding.
BORDER GUARDS
With their prickly stems and bushy habit, brambles are excellent as barrier plants, with delicious fruit as an added bonus.
FRUITS AND BERRIES IN YOUR BACKYARD 25
Clear and easy-to-follow pointers, or step-by-step instructions to show you how to proceed.
General information about various aspects of gardening.

Photograph of individual plants, showing what they look like when grown in the right conditions.

Botanical name

Family name

Refer to the Zone Maps starting on page 308.

Common name

Berberis spp.

BERBERIDACEAE

HARDINESS
Zones 3–9.

HEIGHT
3–12 feet
(90–360 cm)

SPREAD
3–12 feet
(90–360 cm)

COMMENTS
Common barberry *Berberis vulgaris* and other species, including raisin barberry *B. asiatica* and Nepal barberry *B. aristata*, are used for their fruits.

BARBERRY

BARBERRIES PRODUCE RED, YELLOW OR BLACK BERRIES; BOTH THE FLESH AND SKIN OF THE BERRIES ARE EDIBLE. THE FLAVOR IS USUALLY TART, BUT IN SOME SPECIES THE FRUITS HAVE ENOUGH SUGAR TO BE DRIED INTO "RAISINS."

Position Barberries prefer full sun and moist, well-drained soil. (Evergreen species are generally less hardy than deciduous species.)

Cultivation Set out container-grown plants anytime the soil isn't frozen, or plant bareroot shrubs in spring or autumn, while they are still dormant. Space plants 3–12 feet (90–360 cm) apart, depending on how big the particular species gets.

Pruning Cut a few of the oldest stems to the ground in winter. Also shorten spindly stems and thin out suckers if the stems are crowded.

Propagation Mix seed with moist peat moss and refrigerate it for 2–3 months before sowing in a warm, bright place. Or dig up and transplant suckers from the base of a bush.

Pests and diseases Generally no significant problems.

Harvesting and storage Harvest the berries after they are fully colored. Make the fruit into conserves, jams or pickles for storage, or dry them and store in airtight jars.

248 PLANT DIRECTORY

Carissa macrocarpa

APOCYNACEAE

HARDINESS
Zone 10.

HEIGHT
2–18 feet
(60–540 cm), but cultivars vary in their eventual height and spread.

COMMENTS
Natal plum fruit is usually cooked into jellies, sauces and pies.

NATAL PLUM

THE ROUNDISH FRUIT OF NATAL PLUM IS THE SIZE OF A PING-PONG BALL, WITH A CRIMSON SKIN AND STRAWBERRY-RED FLESH. THE WHOLE FRUIT IS EDIBLE; SOME PEOPLE PREFER TO REMOVE THE SMALL SEEDS.

Position Plant in full sun or partial shade in well-drained soil. Natal plum withstands salt spray and is moderately drought-tolerant.

Cultivation Set out container-grown plants anytime, spacing them roughly 10 feet (3 m) apart, depending on the eventual size of the particular cultivar. Natal plum generally needs cross-pollination, so plant at least two seedlings or cultivars. Hand-pollination often helps when fruiting is poor. In areas where Natal plum is not hardy, grow it indoors in a container.

Pruning Prune only as needed to shape the plant and to remove dead or crossing branches. You can even shear this plant as a hedge.

Propagation Take cuttings of semi-woody shoots, or layer a branch from an established plant.

Pests and diseases Generally no significant problems.

Harvesting and storage For fresh eating, pick fruit when fully ripe (fully colored); pick fruits slightly underripe for cooking. Plants produce fruit almost year-round, so pick it as you need it.

FRUITS 249

Each section is color-coded for easy reference.

General information about planting, propagating and caring for your plants to get optimum results.

Part One

Planning Your Garden

CONSIDER YOUR CLIMATE

More than any other single factor, climate influences the selection of plants you can grow. The term describes the interaction of air temperature, moisture, wind and other factors.

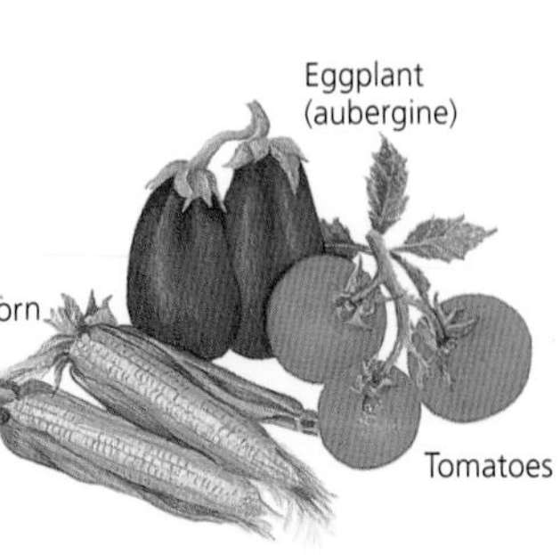

The climate of your locality also depends on its latitude, altitude and proximity to mountains and bodies of water. The temperate zone, where most of us live, is characterized by alternating periods of moderately wet and dry weather, with predictable winds. Fortunately, most of the vegetables you are familiar with are well suited to this temperate climate.

Often within larger temperate zones there are "mini-regions," which may differ from the average by being drier, wetter, cooler or warmer than the surrounding areas. If you live in one of these extreme locations, seasonal conditions will be affected and you will have to adapt your plans to meet the rigors of the local weather patterns.

OBSERVE SUN AND SHADE PATTERNS

Most crops require ample sunlight to yield a generous supply of produce. Start your sun-and-shade survey as soon as you can—today, if possible. Try to watch the light patterns through one whole growing season before doing any planting. A site that is sunny in early spring or autumn may be in deep shade by midsummer. On one sunny day a

WARM-WEATHER CROPS

Bell pepper (capsicum), cantaloupe (rockmelon), carrot, corn, cucumber, eggplant (aubergine), lima bean, okra, parsnip, peanut, potato, pumpkin, rutabaga, snap bean, summer squash, sweet potato, Swiss chard (silverbeet), tomato, watermelon.

month, for at least several months before planting, watch your proposed sites through the day. Record when the sun first strikes the ground and when shadows take its place.

Your fruits and vegetables have three basic, climate-dependent requirements: a suitable temperature range, a favorable frost-free period and an adequate supply of moisture. Monitor the weather in your area, and be prepared to take action if your plants aren't getting the conditions they need to grow to their best.

Outside their preferred temperature range, plants may die or become dormant, which means that the chemical

RAISED BEDS

These are the ultimate in outdoor, custom-built plant containers. They require an initial investment of energy, but you'll save both time and labor later. Raised beds are very productive and working them is easier on your back.

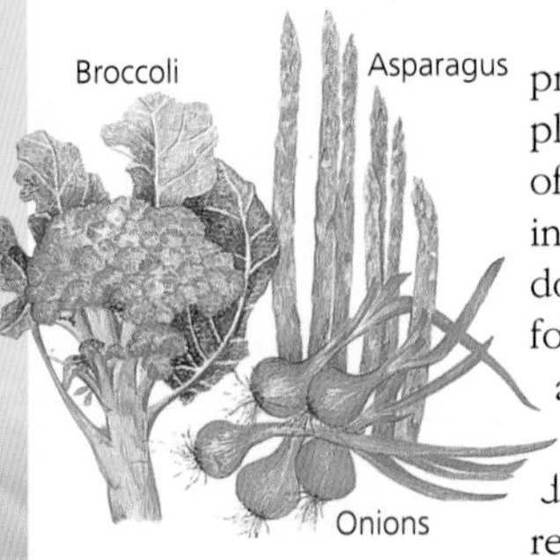

processes that normally occur inside the plant have slowed to a temporary stage of rest. For example, potato tubers left in the ground in autumn will remain dormant until the soil warms them the following spring. Some gardeners are able to "overwinter" autumn-planted spinach. The young plants remain dormant during the cold season, then resume growing as temperatures rise in the spring. These clever gardeners harvest the earliest crops in their area.

Cool-weather Crops

Arugula (rocket), beet, broccoli, brussels sprouts, cabbage, cauliflower, chicory, Chinese cabbage, collard, corn salad (lamb's lettuce, mâche), escarole, kale, kohlrabi, lettuce, mustard, onion, pea, radish, spinach, turnip.

Growing Season

In temperate climates, the growing season begins after the last frost of the cold season, and ends when frosts begin again in autumn. But gardening activity begins before the technical start of the growing season and continues beyond the end. Frost occurs when the air temperature falls below 32°F (0°C) during the night, after dew has formed. The result is a lacy, white coating of water crystals on leaves the following morning. Frost damage may seem to be limited to the surface, but the plant's interior is also affected. Sensitive plants may die when exposed to frost in the spring or autumn. Hardier vegetables, such as those belonging to the cabbage family, will tolerate some frost damage.

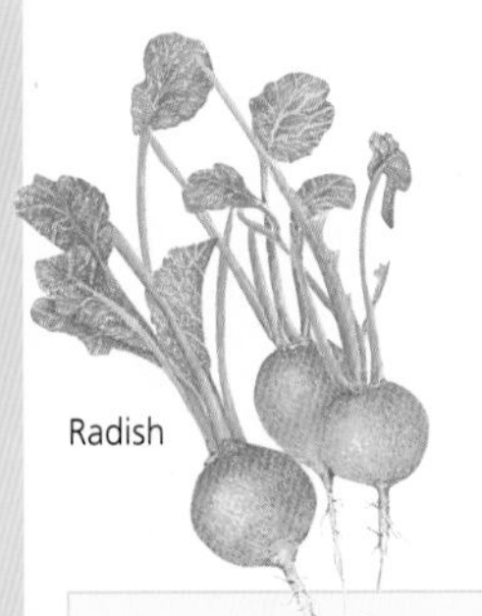

Shade Crops

There are a few vegetables that can tolerate partial shade. Choose crops that fit your conditions from the following list: arugula (rocket), cabbage, corn salad (lamb's lettuce, mâche), endive, horseradish, lettuce, pea, radish, rhubarb, spinach, Swiss chard (silverbeet).

PRODUCTIVE AND BEAUTIFUL

This mixed cottage garden demonstrates what can be done with a relatively small, but well-sited, space.

Garden Planning

POTS OF GOODNESS

For a small household, just a few heads of cabbage and some fresh salad greens, planted successively in containers, may be all that you need. This is far better than building a garden that is too big and that will be a chore for you to look after.

When planning your garden, think about how much time you want to spend in it. The amount of work your garden requires will depend on its size and will vary with climate and seasons.

Site Selection

Consider also how much fresh produce you want. You may need only a small vegetable garden near the kitchen to meet your day-to-day demands for organically grown vegetables. Or you may decide to dedicate a substantial area to growing fruits and vegetables so that you'll have enough produce to freeze or store for later consumption.

Topography

Slopes and contours influence the way you arrange your garden. The idea is to minimize the loss of soil through erosion and maximize water retention. If you must plant on a slope, place the rows or beds across the slope. If rows run up and down the slope, water will trickle down the slope instead of penetrating the soil to reach plant roots. It will also carry the precious topsoil away. Also avoid gardening in low-lying areas, where poor air circulation makes your plants more susceptible to disease.

Since most vegetables need at least 1 inch (2.5 cm) of water each week, be prepared to water your vegetable patch during dry periods. Make sure you can reach the site with a garden hose or irrigation pipe, or be prepared to carry water by hand. Avoid gardening in low areas prone to flooding, and on high areas with too much drainage.

Obstacles and Access

Locate your garden in a place that's easily accessible, both to you and to vehicles that will deliver materials you may need later, such as soil or compost. Avoid areas that have had heavy foot or vehicle traffic, because this activity compacts the soil and damages its structure. Paths should be wide enough for a wheelbarrow or cart. As you choose a site, look for hidden

Hints on Crop Rotation

Wait 3–5 years before growing the same, or closely related, vegetables in the same spot.

Include soil-improving crops such as rye or clover between early and late crops, or between autumn and spring crops.

Grow legumes, such as clover or peas, the year before grasses, such as corn.

Grow light feeders (such as root crops) before heavy feeders (tomatoes, peppers, cabbages and most leafy vegetables).

Make heavy compost applications to heavy feeders during the growing season.

Make light compost applications to light feeders during the growing season.

HIGH YIELDS

Before planting a fruit and vegetable garden on this scale, think about how much produce you actually need. Freezing and bottling are time-consuming and must be done when the crops are ready, whether or not that fits in with your schedule.

obstacles such as septic systems, tree roots, shallow boulders and utility lines, and avoid these areas.

Light

Most plants need 6–12 hours of sunlight each day. Pick a site well away from shade trees and buildings that cast shade for more than half the day. If you have a city garden nestled among tall buildings, you may be limited to shade-tolerant plants. Given a favorable position, the soil in your garden will warm quickly and you may be able to plant early.

A SIMPLE PLAN

With structured beds, organizing crop rotation is fairly easy. Each year, move your crop over to the next bed in the sequence. Set aside a separate bed for perennials, such as asparagus and rhubarb. Sketch a plan of the bed each year so you're not relying solely on your memory.

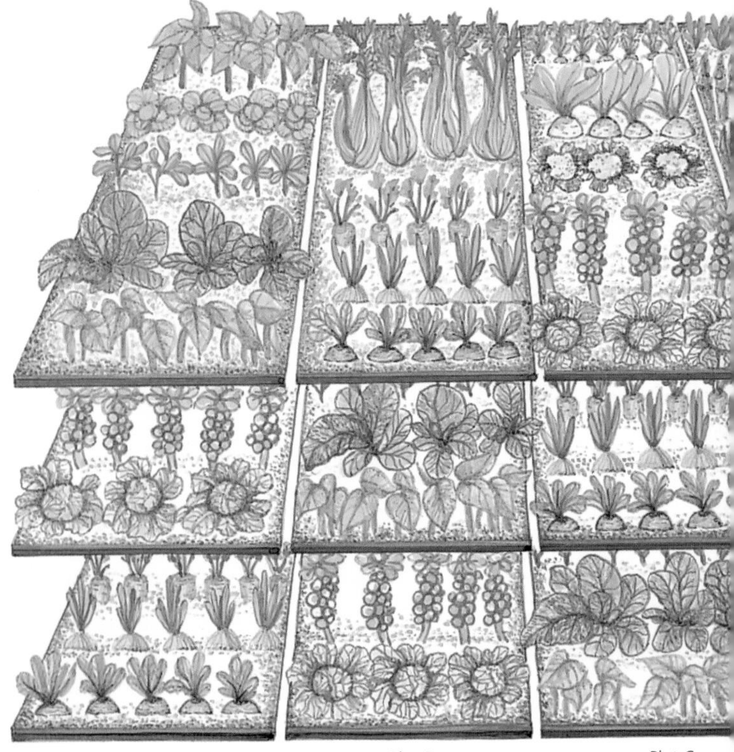

Plot A Plot B Plot C

DEMARCATION

This ornamental red cabbage would make an attractive border to separate sections of your garden.

Plot D

Turn Lawn into a Vegetable Garden

Use a spade to remove the sod. Slip the blade forward just under the surface to slice through the roots.

Or solarize the area to kill both grass and weeds by covering it with clear plastic for several months during summer.

Or simply mulch the area thickly. It may take a month or two to smother the grass completely. Then dig over the area.

ESPALIER FEATURE

Perhaps the ultimate in space saving, espalier training can also provide your ripening fruit with additional warmth from a sunny wall.

WIRE CAGES

An alternative to staking for plants such as tomatoes is this cage system. You can also grow vining crops such as cucumbers or gourds this way, with the cage upright, or turn the cage on its side and secure it with several stakes. Plant inside the cage; the vines will loop around and form a horizontal tube. This works well for heavier crops, such as melons.

Means of Support

Training plants to grow vertically, instead of horizontally, saves space and makes cultivating and harvesting easier. Because fruits aren't in contact with soil, they're less likely to succumb to soilborne pathogens. Staked plants are also very tidy and leave you more room for special techniques such as interplanting and companion planting. You can purchase stakes made of wood, metal, plastic or bamboo in a variety of heights to fit the needs of the plant.

No matter what method you use, have your support system in place before you plant. Vines such as peas and beans attach themselves by wrapping tendrils or twining stems around the support. Plants such as tomatoes or bell peppers (capsicum) need help. Tie loosely to the stake with scraps of soft cloth or cotton rope.

Trellising Brambles

Start by setting sturdy 6-foot (1.8-m) posts every 20 feet (6 m) along the planting row. Then construct the trellis in one of these configurations.

A T-trellis makes picking easy for summer-bearing red, black and purple raspberries, as well as blackberries. Add a cross arm to the top of each post and another arm about halfway down the post. Run wires between the ends of opposite arms. After cutting out the fruited canes after harvest, tie the remaining shoots to the bottom wires. When the shoots are tall enough, tie them to the top wires, too.

A hedgerow trellis holds up bramble canes together between the wires. Put one cross arm about three-quarters of the way up each post so it resembles a T. Run wire along the end of each cross arm to support both sides of the plants.

STOUT STAKES

Staking improves plant health, since better air circulation promotes drying and lessens the chance of disease. Sturdiness is more important than the appearance of the stakes, since your plants will become heavy with fruit as the season progresses.

TRAINING WIRES

This simple structure provides wires or strings for plants such as beans and cucumbers to climb up. Just remember not to place it where the growing plants will cast shade over their smaller neighbors.

Fruits and Berries in Your Backyard

CONTAINERS

Decks, patios and balconies can be fruitful when you grow suitable edibles in containers. Strawberries look superb cascading out of hanging baskets or strawberry pots. Dwarf citrus, apple and peach trees are also good candidates for container culture.

It's surprising that fruiting plants have been neglected so long for landscapes. Most have two irresistible features: attractive flowers and edible fruits.

Many have other features as well, such as showy autumn color or interesting bark. The options for including edibles in your yard are limited only by the space available. Here are some ways to use these beautiful and productive plants.

Shrubs and Hedges

Fruit- and nut-bearing bushes, such as some hazelnuts, Manchurian bush apricots, elderberries, currants and highbush blueberries, form large shrubs substantial enough to edge the boundary of your property, mass into an informal hedge or naturalize. Prickly shrubs, such as raspberries, blackberries, citrons and gooseberries, make a barrier that the neighborhood children, dogs and other animals won't be quick to push through.

Shade Trees

If you're starting a new landscape or renovating an old one, consider growing an edible plant as a shade tree. Walnuts, pecans and other full-sized fruit and nut trees provide height and shade plus a useful crop. Short fruit trees, such as

APPLE BLOSSOM WALK

A shady path is a striking feature in a large garden.

REWARDING CHOICE
With proper care, citrus trees, such as this mandarin, yield abundant harvests. They don't usually need much pruning, unless you want to restrict their height.

peaches, semidwarf apples, almonds and cherries, make excellent small trees as handsome as any ornamental. Use them alone as specimens or include them in a foundation planting. Or try an extra-showy type such as weeping 'Santa Rosa' plums, double-flowered 'Double Delight' and 'Double Jewel' peach trees or curly stemmed 'Flying Dragon' citrus trees.

Pointers for an Easy-care Edible Landscape

Don't wait until your fruit trees are delivered to decide where to put them. An attractive, easy-care landscape requires advance planning, starting with careful plant and site selection.

Choose problem-resistant plants Look for cultivars that are naturally resistant to the pests and diseases that are common in your area. (Local fruit growers and your Cooperative Extension Service can tell you which problems to watch out for; catalog descriptions will list the problems a particular cultivar can resist or tolerate.)

Plan for plant size Think carefully about how large a tree you can handle. With trees over 6 feet (1.8 m) high you will need a ladder to harvest or prune; that will slow you down and be more strenuous.

Consider the water supply Try to plant near a water supply that you can tap into without much trouble. Otherwise, you may be spending lots of time hauling buckets of water or lugging long hoses around. If dry spells are common in your area, you may want to install a permanent irrigation system before you plant. This can save you hours of labor and provide excellent results.

BRILLIANT COLOR

Fruits such as elderberries (above) and currants provide color as vivid as any flower.

Borders and Foundation Plantings

Low-growing fruit bushes, such as compact half-high blueberries, make great shrubs for foundation plantings or in mixed borders. Creeping fruit-bearing plants, including lowbush blueberries and strawberries, fit easily in the foreground of a flower or shrub border. They also make interesting groundcovers, as long as they get their fair share of sunshine and a little help from you to beat the weeds.

Walls, Fences and Trellises

Vining fruits, such as grapes and kiwis can cover arbors or trellises, shading sitting areas, highlighting special views or screening off utility areas. Espaliered trees (those trained to grow flat against a wall or trellis) can form a living fence that's both unique and productive.

Fruiting plants come in a range of sizes, so there's at least one kind for any size garden. Before you buy, make sure you have enough space to allow each plant to grow up and out without crowding.

BORDER GUARDS

With their prickly stems and bushy habit, brambles are excellent as barrier plants, with delicious fruit as an added bonus.

Part Two

Taking Care of the Soil

Knowing Your Soil

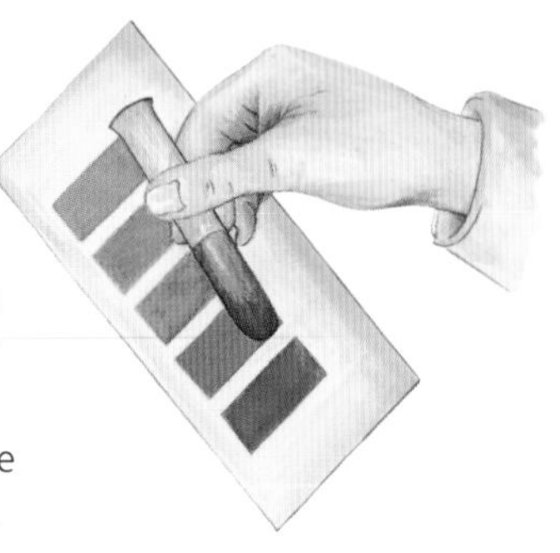

Good soil is the gardener's key to success. Since it influences your plants' growth, health and yield, it deserves your first consideration. The golden rule is to treat your soil well.

Soil Composition

Soil is actually a mixture of minerals, water, air and organic matter. Average soil contains about 45 percent mineral matter, 25 percent air, 25 percent water, and 5 percent organic matter.

Soil texture refers to the fineness or coarseness of your soil's mineral matter. Texture is determined by the relative proportions of sand (very coarse), silt and clay (very fine); it influences fertility, water retention and air circulation within the soil. The ideal garden soil is a loam, composed of about 40 percent sand, 40 percent silt and 20 percent clay. The spaces between soil particles, called pore spaces, hold water, air and dissolved nutrients. If the spaces are large, as between sand particles, the soil is unable to retain sufficient water or nutrients.

The way sand, silt and clay particles join together is called soil structure. Both sand and compacted clays have no structure. In between these extremes, various proportions of sand, silt, clay and organic matter are arranged as larger pieces, called aggregates. Soil structure is especially important because it influences pore spaces, which in turn influence

HOME LITMUS TEST

Using a kit like the one above is an easy way to get a rough idea of your soil's acidity or alkalinity. Put some soil in the clean container and stir in distilled water. Let it stand for an hour, then place a strip of litmus paper in the mixture and leave it in for at least 60 seconds. Remove the paper and rinse with distilled water. Match the color of the paper to the chart that came with the kit.

water content and drainage, movement of air in the soil and the release of nutrients. The ideal soil has a crumbly, granular structure that allows water to drain and oxygen and carbon dioxide to move freely from the air into the pore spaces. A light, loose soil structure is known as "friable." Adding organic matter will improve the structure of all soil types.

Air and Water in the Soil

Plants take in the oxygen they need from the air in the soil, so it is critical for healthy soil and vigorous plant growth. Oxygen is also critical for the well-being of soil organisms, such as earthworms. Air also contains gaseous nitrogen, which specialized bacteria convert into a form that your vegetables can use.

A steady supply of water is vital for the health of almost all plants. Plant roots absorb water and dissolved minerals from pore spaces in the soil. A good garden soil will hold enough water for plant growth while letting excess water drain down to deeper layers. While most vegetables prefer well-drained soil, there

Check Your Soil pH

Soil pH, the relative measure of how acid or alkaline your soil is, can affect nutrient availability for plants. It is measured on a scale from 1.0 (strongly acid) to 14.0 (strongly alkaline). Most plants thrive within a range of 6.0–7.0, from slightly acid to neutral. Nutrients tend to be most accessible to plant roots at this pH range. If you suspect your soil is extremely acid or alkaline, it's wise to have it properly tested. If the results confirm your suspicions, you can make small changes to your soil's pH by incorporating compost or soil amendments, such as powdered sulfur to lower pH or ground limestone to raise it. A soil test report will recommend the types and quantities of amendments to use. But the best solution is to select plants that do well in your natural conditions.

HEALTHY SOIL

Good granular soil is a pleasure to work with. Careful digging and regular additions of organic mulch will keep it healthy.

are a few, such as celery and watercress, that can tolerate more moisture. Raised-bed gardening can help if you need to improve the drainage of your garden beds (see page 13).

Organic Matter

Soil organic matter refers to the decomposing remains of plants and animals. Organic matter is important because it attracts and holds important plant nutrients in the soil. It is critical for soil structure because it provides the "glue" that holds individual particles of minerals together as aggregates. When organic matter has decomposed, its stable remains are called humus. The organic matter content of your soil is influenced by many factors, including climate, vegetation, drainage, soil organisms and cultivation. Generally, wetter climates and healthy populations of soil microbes help create soil with a high content of organic matter. Higher annual temperatures, less vegetative growth

Little Helpers

Your allies in the battle for good soil structure are the small creatures that crawl through your soil. Earthworms are perhaps the most famous soil builders. Their tunneling loosens and aerates tight soil, and the organic matter they drag down encourages stable soil granules. Rodents churn the soil as they dig and mix organic matter into the subsoil. Plant roots also improve soil structure by adding organic matter below the surface as they break down. Plus, the tiny passages left by the decayed roots allow water and air easier access to lower soil layers, in turn encouraging even better microorganisms and plant growth.

PROTECT YOUR SOIL

Good soil looks dark and has a crumbly texture, with visible organic matter.

and more cultivation lessen the ability of soil to accumulate organic matter.

Soil Nutrients

The amount and type of soil nutrients that are available to your plants depend on the interaction of many factors, including soil texture, structure, moisture, organic matter and pH. Fine texture, loose structure, ample moisture, high organic matter content and near-neutral pH are all conditions that make the most nutrients available to your plants.

DO NO HARM

Before you start digging in spring, or after heavy rain, wait until the soil has dried out a bit, or you will damage its structure.

A Hands-on Test for Soil Texture

To check if your soil is sandy, silty or clayey, take a chunk of soil about the size of your thumb. Moisten it enough so that you can roll it into a ball. Flatten the ball between the pad of your thumb and the side of your bent index finger. Push your thumb forward repeatedly, pressing the soil outward to form a ribbon. The longer the ribbon, the more clay is in the soil. A heavy clay will make a ribbon 1 inch (2.5 cm) long; a sandy soil might not make a ribbon at all. To confirm your findings, put the ribbon in your palm and add enough water to make a runny paste. Rub the index finger of your other hand around in the slop in your palm. If it feels gritty, the soil is sandy. If it's smooth, the soil is silty. If it's on the sticky side, you've got clay.

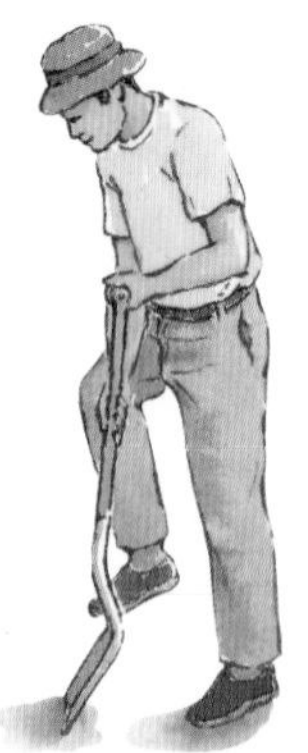

SPARE YOUR BACK

Here are some tips that can help save your muscles next time you turn the soil. First, insert the spade into the soil so the blade is straight up and down. Now:

1. Keeping your back straight and your foot on the upper edge of the spade, use your weight to push the spade into the soil.
2. Bend both your waist and knees as you slide the spade under the soil, then straighten up to lift the load.
3. Turn your whole body before depositing the dirt—don't just twist your torso as you fling the soil to the side.

It's easy, in your rush to finish up, to ignore pain. But pain has a purpose: It's telling you to take a break. You'll get more done and feel better if you take regular breaks, before you start to feel pain.

To check the nutrient content of your soil, it may be worthwhile to have a lab test your soil before you plant your crops. It's often a good idea to test the soil in a newly created bed, or in a bed that has been producing for many years. You can get your soil tested by your local Cooperative Extension office or a private soil-testing lab. They will provide you with a statement indicating any nutrient deficiencies or excesses, along with recommendations for fertilizers to add to correct the imbalances. Make sure you ask for recommendations for organic fertilizers. You may want to test the soil again in a few years to monitor the results of your gardening practices and make any necessary adjustments.

When to Work the Soil

Each time you work the soil, you have a chance to either destroy or maintain good structure. If you dig when it's too wet, the soil forms clods that are hard to break apart once they dry. And walking around on wet soil while you're digging promotes compaction, another factor that can ruin good soil structure. If you work the soil when it's too dry, the clumps of soil disintegrate, leaving powder that can blow away in the wind or be carried off by the next rainfall.

Even if you don't affect structure, there are other good reasons to avoid working very wet and very dry soils. Wet soils stick to everything—your shoes, your tools and the dog keeping you company. Dry, crusty soils make it hard to push a spade into the ground, so digging is twice as much work as it needs to be.

Should You Dig in Spring or Autumn?

In most cases, your odds of finding soil in just the right condition for digging are better in autumn than spring. Rains are usually less frequent then, so the soil gets more time to dry out after soakings. If the soil is too dry, you can just water it and wait a day or two.

Autumn tilling is a bad idea if you garden on a slope because it exposes loose soil to erosion. Because slopes drain faster than level soils, you may be able to work them in spring when other soils are still too moist. If you do till in the autumn, cover the soil with a thick layer of straw or another light mulch that you can rake off in spring. Or protect the soil by growing a cover crop in the winter months.

SIMPLE READINESS TEST

To check when the soil is at the right stage for digging, pick up a handful of soil and squeeze it. Open your hand. If the soil stays in a firm ball in your palm, it's too wet to work. If it falls apart, it's too dry. If it holds together until you poke it with your finger, it's just right.

Compost

Composting is an excellent way to manage yard and kitchen wastes and make your own fertilizer. It is a good source of organic matter and nutrients for plants.

Compost improves soil structure and water retention and research shows that it contains beneficial microorganisms that suppress plant pathogens in soil.

How to Make Fast, Hot Compost

1. Start saving all the organic wastes you normally throw away—leaves, grass clippings, kitchen scraps, rotted straw and other organic wastes. Decomposition is most efficient if materials are shredded. You can use a leaf-shredding machine, but a lawn mower will shred leaves and other light materials to a good size for mulching. Woody prunings, tree bark and newspaper should be shredded to fine pieces. Avoid adding oils, meat scraps and bones

BREWING COMPOST TEA

To make a good liquid fertilizer, put a shovelful of compost in a cheesecloth or burlap bag. Tie the bag closed and suspend it in a container of water. Keep it covered for a few days. Once it has steeped, use the liquid to drench the soil at the base of plants you want to fertilize. Or dilute the liquid with water until it is the color of weak tea, then spray it on plant leaves. Because the nutrients are dissolved in water, the plants can take them up immediately for a quick burst of energy. (Reuse the "tea bag" several times, then add the soaked compost to the garden.)

RECYCLING SCRAPS

Keep a small trash bin handy to your kitchen to collect compostable food scraps.

Fast, Hot Compost

Build up the layers of your compost heap with equal amounts of high-carbon and high-nitrogen materials (see page 37).

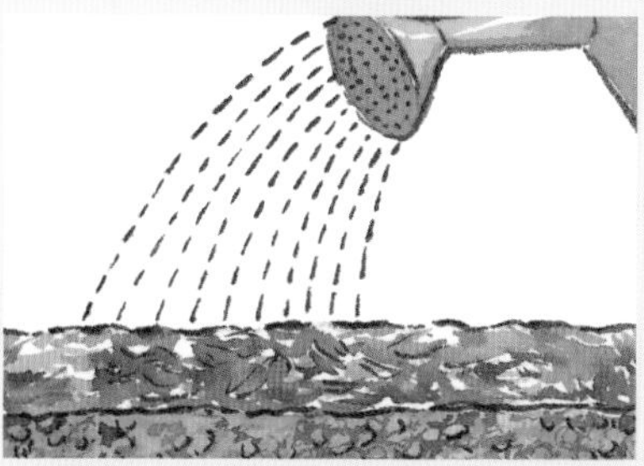

Sprinkle water generously over each layer to keep the pile moist and encourage decomposition of the materials.

Aerate the compost pile by turning it over every couple of days with a garden fork. This hastens microbial activity.

Compost for Busy People

For easy access, put your compost pile on a level, well-drained spot close to the vegetable garden. Some gardeners build elaborate, multi-chambered compost bins, but you can just dump your stuff in a pile. Besides kitchen scraps, toss in pulled weeds (if they don't have seeds) grass clippings, fresh cow or horse manure, sawdust, shredded paper from the office shredder and just about any plant or plant derivative. Don't add diseased plants because the bacteria, fungi or viruses might survive and spread.

Turn the pile every so often with a pitchfork; the more often you turn it, the more air gets in and the faster the soil organisms can break it down. If you're chronically pressed for time, buy a cheap pitchfork and leave it near the compost pile so you can turn the pile when the mood strikes, not at those less-frequent times when you remember to bring the good fork from the shed. When your compost is dark and crumbly (in a few weeks or months), it's ready to use.

because they attract scavenging animals and slow the decomposition process. Do not add human or pet feces, or pesticides, or pesticide-treated grass clippings.

2. Choose a spot near the vegetable garden for composting and store ingredients in piles or bins. Containment is not important, but walls will keep the area neat and

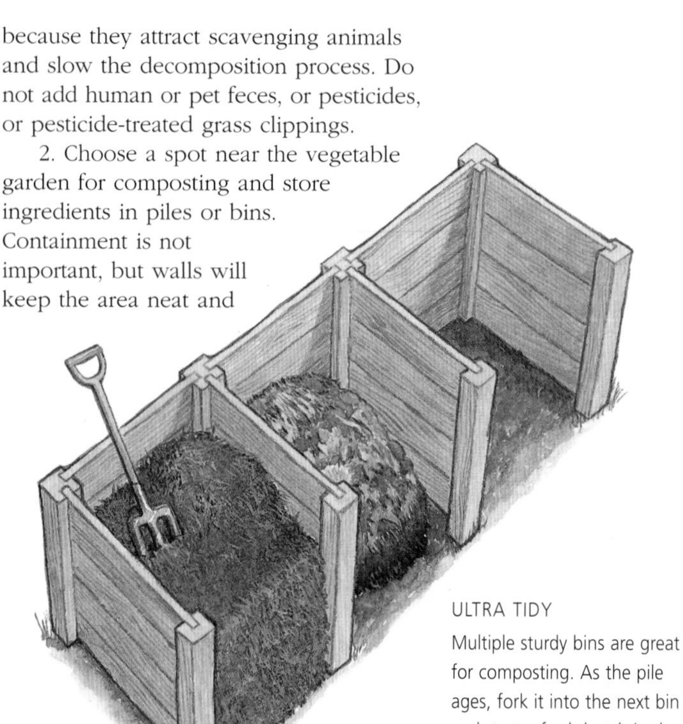

ULTRA TIDY

Multiple sturdy bins are great for composting. As the pile ages, fork it into the next bin and start a fresh batch in the first bin. Put a sliding door on each bin if you wish.

Compost Troubleshooting

If your compost pile doesn't heat up, add more high-nitrogen material (see page 37). If the pile is dry, add water, or try turning the pile.

If the pile smells bad, add more high-carbon material (see page 37). If it is too wet, turning may help to add more air.

If the finished compost is covered with seedlings, your compost has not heated up enough and seeds of weeds and other plants have survived. Either avoid adding materials with seeds or make sure they're in the center of a hot compost pile.

If woody stems, prunings and dry leaves have not broken down, try shredding or chopping them into smaller pieces before adding them to a new pile. Adding more high-nitrogen ingredients can help balance these high-carbon materials.

TOPDRESSING

Apply compost to a depth of 1–2 inches (2.5–5 cm) over the surface of your garden each year or use it to mulch rows of plants. If soil tests indicate a nutrient imbalance, sprinkle the appropriate fertilizers over the soil before adding the compost, or add fertilizer to the compost itself. You can dig the compost in, or leave it on top as a mulch.

the dog out. Or purchase a ready-made compost bin or tumbler.

3. You'll need enough raw materials to make a pile roughly 3 feet (90 cm) on each side; smaller piles won't heat up as efficiently. Build the pile by stacking the materials layer upon layer, using any kind of garden fork. Alternate materials that are high in carbon (brown, woody materials such as sawdust, straw and newspaper) with layers of material high in nitrogen (green, sloppy materials such as fresh grass clippings, kitchen scraps, weeds and manure).

Use about equal volumes of each. A pile with too much carbon remains cool and breaks down more slowly. Too much nitrogen can create odor problems. As you work, add several shovelfuls of garden soil to inoculate the pile with the right decomposer organisms. Just sprinkle soil on top of alternate layers. You can add dry mineral fertilizers, too, if your soil needs them. If you are adding insect-infested plant material to your pile, make sure you put it in the center, where temperatures will be high enough to kill the pests.

4. Keep the pile moist, but not soggy. As you build the pile, sprinkle the layers with water if the materials are dry. Keep the layered pile covered with a tarpaulin to help maintain the right amount of

TURN, TURN, TURN

Forking over the compost pile helps the microbes with their task. A hot compost pile can be ready to use in 2–6 weeks. You'll know it's ready when the temperature has stabilized and the individual materials you added at the beginning are no longer recognizable.

WORM FARMS

Worm castings are a rich source of organic matter. Buy a commercial worm bin and follow the instructions that come with it to keep your worms healthy and ensure a constant supply of this powerful soil supplement.

moisture. Conditions that are too wet or too dry will change the rate of decomposition, and your compost might not be ready when you want it.

5. To work properly, organisms that hasten decomposition require oxygen. The simplest way to aerate the pile is to turn it every day or two. Invert the pile, one forkful at a time, with your garden fork, next to the original pile. Materials originally on the outside should end up in the middle. Fluff the pile as you go, sprinkling with more water as needed.

Aeration hastens microbial activity, which increases the temperature of the pile. Turning every day or two helps maintain a constant temperature. Use a compost thermometer to monitor the temperature, which should stay below 160°F (71°C), since higher temperatures will kill important decomposer organisms. If the pile gets too cool, turning it will raise the temperature. If the temperature gets too high, let the pile stand for a few days without turning it over, or add a small amount of water.

TYPES OF WORM FARMS

Basically a worm farm is a simple box with a drainage system to collect liquid waste. Several designs are commercially available, but you could also make your own. Buy worms that are bred for worm farms.

Fertilizers

Plants need 16 chemical elements for healthy growth, some in greater amounts (macronutrients) than others (micronutrients or trace elements). Each of these elements performs a particular role.

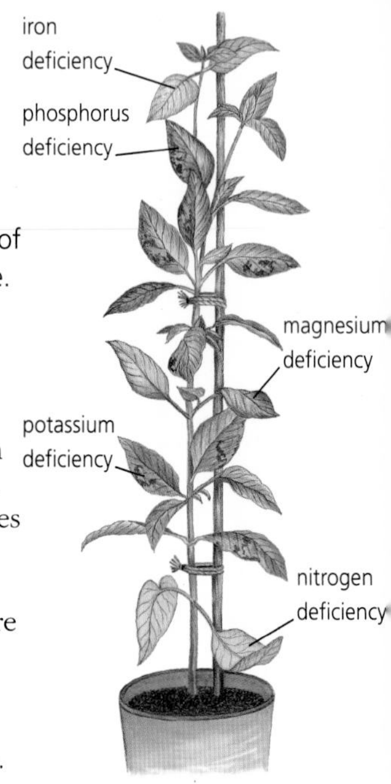

Fertilizers or Amendments?

A fertilizer is a material that contains significant amounts of the chemical elements that plants need to grow, such as nitrogen, phosphorus and potassium. It may also contain material that improves the soil, such as organic matter. But its primary function is to add nutrients. Bloodmeal, bat guano and greensand are examples of organic fertilizers.

An amendment improves the soil physically, usually its structure or drainage, or enhances microbial activity. It may contain some nutrients, but not enough to be called a fertilizer. Compost, grass clippings, lime and peat moss are examples of soil amendments. The material you use depends on what effect you want. Fertilizers provide a general nutrient boost during the growing season and are useful for correcting specific nutrient deficiencies. Amendments are important for long-term soil health, because they add organic matter and humus. Work these in before planting, or use as mulches, but don't count on them to provide enough nutrients to support heavy-feeding plants. Build up soil humus and use a balance of fertilizers and amendments and your plants will have all the nutrients they need.

DEFICIENCIES

Thankfully, plants rarely show all these nutrient deficiencies at once. If you see any of these symptoms, try a seaweed spray for a quick fix, then amend the soil with compost or a supplement for a long-term solution.

A BEAUTIFUL CROP

These rutabagas (right) look as if they have everything they need to thrive.

DEEP, RICH COLOR

The dark green of these cabbages indicates that they are getting enough nitrogen.

Nitrogen for Lush Leaves

If you've ever fertilized a lawn, you know what a dramatic effect nitrogen has: It gives plants a deep green color and stimulates leafy growth. It is one of the three primary macronutrients that plants need and is probably the nutrient you'll have to add most often, because it easily washes out of the soil.

Most of the nitrogen in the soil is bound up in organic matter. It is slowly released and converted to a form plants can use, which is dissolved in the water held between soil particles. Unlike many nutrients, the form of nitrogen dissolved in the soil solution leaches readily from the soil. That's why nitrogen is often in short supply, especially in quick-draining sandy soils or in those where it is removed by vigorous plants.

Good Organic Sources of Nitrogen

Alfalfa meal (ground alfalfa hay) contains about 5 percent nitrogen as well as potassium. Bloodmeal contains 13 percent nitrogen. Cottonseed meal contains about 6 percent nitrogen as well as some phosphorus. It is often used on acid-loving crops such as blueberries. Fish emulsion, made of fish byproducts dissolved in water, is about 5 percent nitrogen. Spray it on leaves or water it into the soil at the base of the plant. Fish meal consists of dried, ground fish parts; it's a balanced fertilizer that contains 5 percent nitrogen, 3 percent phosphorus and 3 percent potassium. Guano is aged, dry bird or bat droppings mined from roosts and caves. It contains 10–15 percent nitrogen. Because it contains calcium, it raises the soil pH.

GREEN MANURE

Dig a crop of clover into your soil. As it decays, it will release nitrogen in a form accessible to other plants.

Adding Extra Nitrogen

You can add nitrogen to the soil in several ways. If you have naturally fertile soil, it's enough just to add compost or manure each year to replace the nitrogen that plants remove. These balanced materials will provide a steady supply of nitrogen to growing plants throughout the season.

If your plants need extra nitrogen, you can use a more concentrated source. Depending on the fertilizer you choose, the nitrogen may be available right away, but it may last only a short while or be released gradually over a long period. See "Good Organic Sources of Nitrogen" (opposite) for materials you can add.

Growing a green manure crop of clover, alfalfa, lespedeza or some other legume is a useful way to add extra nutrients to the soil in your vegetable garden. Legumes host beneficial soil bacteria on their roots. These bacteria draw nitrogen gas from air in the soil and convert it to a form that both they and the plants can use. When you work legumes into the soil, the decaying roots release nitrogen other plants can absorb.

AN EXCEPTION

If you add nitrogen to pea and bean crops, you may actually reduce your harvest.

HOLD THE NITROGEN

To get the best yield of beautiful tomatoes from your plants, hold off on the nitrogen. It promotes the growth of lush leaves at the expense of the fruit.

Phosphorus for Roots and Fruits

Plants need large amounts of phosphorus, which, like nitrogen, is one of the primary elements. Crops use it to produce flowers, fruits and to form seeds. It also helps them mature, counteracting the effects of too much nitrogen. Roots, especially the fibrous roots that spread out to absorb water and nutrients, need phosphorus to develop. Phosphorus makes stems strong and improves the quality of your vegetables; it also improves their resistance to disease. A lack of phosphorus limits how well your plants are able to absorb other nutrients, especially nitrogen.

A VITAL ELEMENT

For great crops, remember that phosphorus plays a crucial role in forming healthy roots and strong stems. It also helps in seed formation. Where there is a deficiency, fruits and seeds set and mature late.

Supplying Phosphorus

Most soils are low in phosphorus, and most of the phosphorus that is there is not available, especially in soils that are very acid or alkaline. In soils with an extreme pH, the phosphorus reacts with chemicals in the soil, such as iron, calcium, aluminum and manganese, to create compounds that plants can't absorb. So, if you add phosphorus to very acid or alkaline soil, much of it binds to these chemicals.

To make more phosphorus available to plants, adjust the pH to near neutral (see page 29). In acid soils, this means adding lime. In alkaline soils, add sulfur. The pH changes slowly, so test your soil once or twice each year for several years, taking samples in the same month each time. Next, add a phosphorus fertilizer, both to increase the supply in the soil and to replace the phosphorus that crops remove (see "Good Organic Sources of Phosphorus" below). Since microorganisms help make phosphorus more readily available, add phosphorus to your compost rather than directly to the soil.

Because phosphorus doesn't dissolve readily, it doesn't move down through the soil, so dig it in where it's needed, in the root zone. It's best to correct major phosphorus deficiencies before planting, especially for more permanent features such as trees. When it is cold, even soil that has plenty of phosphorus may not supply your plants with what's needed. In permanent plantings, rake off heavy mulches in spring to help soil warm up. Try a temporary black plastic mulch to warm the soil before planting vegetables.

SURE SIGN

Among common signs of phosphorus deficiency is a purplish cast to the leaves, especially on seedlings. Plants may be stunted, including the roots, and the leaves may have yellow streaks. Other signs are skinny, brittle stems.

Good Organic Sources of Phosphorus

Animal manures contain phosphorus, nitrogen and potassium. Poultry manure has the highest content of phosphorus at about 14 percent total. About 2 percent is available at any time. Bonemeal, made from ground animal bones, has 11 percent phosphorus. Steamed bonemeal is a more available source of phosphorus than raw bonemeal, but both release phosphorus more quickly than rock phosphate. Fish emulsion and liquid seaweed give a quick shot of phosphorus when sprayed on plants or watered into the soil. The effect isn't long lasting but can be a big help for young plants forming roots, plants setting fruit and plants showing symptoms of a phosphorus deficiency. Rock phosphate is less expensive than bonemeal, but it takes longer to release its phosphorus. The more finely ground the rock, the more quickly the phosphorus is released. Rock phosphate is about 32 percent total phosphate, but only about 3 percent is available at any one time.

Good Organic Sources of Potassium

Finely ground, potassium-rich granite powder, mined from quarries, contains about 4 percent total potassium, which it releases slowly. Greensand, a slow-release source, with 7 percent potassium, is mined from ocean beds that have lifted and dried over time. Langbeinite (also sold as Sul-Po-Mag) is a source of quick-release potassium containing about 22 percent potassium. It also adds magnesium and sulfur to the soil without altering the pH. Kelp meal, which is dried, ground seaweed, contains 2–3 percent potassium in a relatively available form, as well as beneficial trace minerals.

Potassium for Healthy Growth

Although potassium doesn't get as much attention as the other primary nutrients, plants use as much of it as they do nitrogen and about four times as much as they do phosphorus. Potassium makes plants vigorous by helping them to develop strong root systems and resist disease. It regulates how plants absorb nitrogen, sodium and calcium. Potassium

Telltale Signs

If plants don't get enough potassium, they will be stunted and yield poorly, unlike true dwarf cultivars. Potassium deficiency can cause leaves to develop irregular yellow splotches, starting at the bottom of the plant and working upward. In more severe cases, leaves are dry and scorched at the edges. Be aware, however, that other problems can cause similar symptoms.

also balances the tendency of nitrogen to cause leafy growth and of phosphorus to encourage fruiting. Plants use potassium in photosynthesis and it is part of the process that moves newly photosynthesized sugars from the leaves to the roots, then converts them to starches.

HEALTHY CROPS

A good balance of soil potassium will promote strong, healthy growth in all your crops. It is especially important in tuber formation, and crops such as potatoes (below) require high amounts of this element to form starches.

Keeping a Proper Level

Most soils, except those composed mostly of sand, are high in total potassium. The problem is that, like phosphorus, much of it is unavailable. Some 90 percent is in rock minerals, such as mica and feldspar, which resist weathering. Fortunately, if you add potassium to the soil, plants can absorb it readily until it is leached away.

The trick to keeping potassium at the right level is to apply it twice a season, half a dose each time, rather than putting it on all at once. This way, your plants get just what they need.

ZINC DEFICIENCY

Although not required in large amounts, an absence of trace elements such as zinc can cause problems. Above we see the typical yellowing between dark green veins and the leaves starting to roll along the edges that indicate a lack of zinc.

Secondary Macronutrients

Besides nitrogen, phosphorus and potassium, plants need large doses of calcium, magnesium and sulfur. **Calcium** helps plants absorb nitrogen and create proteins. Without it, new leaves and end branches are deformed; the upper leaves curl upward and turn yellow around the edges, then dry and fall off. Stems are hard and roots are brown and stubby. Blossom-end rot, where the bottom of fruits turn brown or black, is a common symptom of calcium deficiency in tomatoes and bell peppers (capsicums). Drought can cause calcium deficiency because plants can't absorb it from the dry soil. Excess potassium can also limit available calcium.

Limestone is the main source of calcium. Limestone also neutralizes soil acidity, making it a useful addition to acid soils but something to avoid on alkaline soils. Add gypsum to alkaline soil that is calcium-deficient. Calcium is also found in fertilizers that supply other nutrients, such as rock phosphate, bonemeal, kelp meal and wood ashes.

Magnesium is part of the chlorophyll molecule, which makes plants green and is essential for photosynthesis. Without it, plants are chlorotic—the leaves are pale with dark green veins. Correct a magnesium deficiency in an acid soil by adding dolomitic limestone, containing magnesium carbonate. In alkaline soils, use Epsom salts, which is magnesium sulfate.

Sulfur is part of the proteins that plants build. Plants with a sulfur deficiency are small, pale and spindly. Sulfur also makes soils acid. Deficiencies are rare. Adding ample quantities of organic matter will usually supply all the sulfur your plants need. To lower your soil's acidity, use sulfur dust, also known as flowers of sulfur.

MAGNESIUM DEFICIENCY

Mottling and dead spots on leaves, which may be brittle and curl up, indicate a lack of magnesium. Fruit matures late or not at all. Deficiencies are more common late in the season and in soils with too much potassium or calcium.

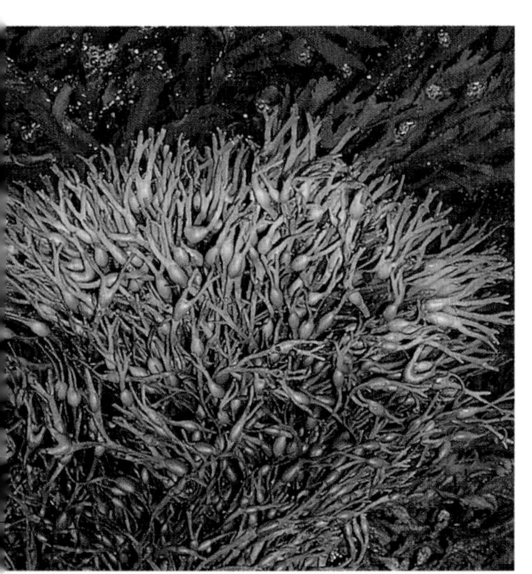

SEAWEED

In its fresh form or prepared as an extract, seaweed is an excellent source of calcium and trace elements, or micronutrients, such as iron, zinc, copper and boron.

Mulches

Mulching retains soil moisture, controls weed growth, provides a barrier against soilborne diseases, protects soil from erosion and keeps your harvest clean. Its importance cannot be overestimated.

Organic Mulch

Organic mulches are plant residues, such as compost, bean hulls, grass clippings, shredded leaves, newspapers, pine needles, sawdust, straw and wood chips. Their decomposition enhances soil productivity, enriches the soil with nutrients and supplies organic matter.

Organic mulches encourage and shelter beneficial organisms at the soil surface and just below it. Thick layers of mulch act as a cushion, reducing soil compaction. And at the end of the season, you don't have to remove them, because they decompose naturally. Ideally, organic mulch should be applied before

SHREDDED LEAVES
Run autumn leaves through a shredder to make a lightweight insulating mulch that is just the thing for protecting late-season crops.

GRASS CLIPPINGS
Use both fresh and dry grass clippings, hay or similar material to mulch around all kinds of plants. Because they contain balanced amounts of carbon and nitrogen, they won't draw nitrogen from your soil as they break down.

annual weeds (such as lamb's-quarters) have a chance to germinate and the perennials (such as quack grass) emerge.

The plants you choose to grow and the location of your garden determine when and how you should apply mulch. Vegetables such as peas and spinach will appreciate early mulching, which can help keep the soil cool. Early mulching is also a good idea in dry climates, since it traps the moisture from spring rains. On the other hand, if you are planting heat-loving crops such as eggplant (aubergine), it's better to wait until the soil has warmed up before you apply the mulch. Mulching later in the season is also useful in wet areas, because the soil will have dried out a bit.

Build a mulch layer 4–12 inches (10–30 cm) thick. Use less material in wet climates, and more in dry climates. Keep the mulch about 4–8 inches (10–20 cm) away from plant stems to promote surface aeration, which helps lessen the chance of disease and problems from slugs and snails.

Bark Mulches

Wood chips may contain wood that has been treated with chemicals that could harm plants. If you chip your own bark, let it sit outside for a few months before using it, so that any natural substances harmful to plants are leached out. Turn the pile every few weeks to keep chips from going "sour." Cypress bark can be toxic to young plants.

TWICE AS EFFECTIVE

Compost works best when it is topped with a thin layer of a longer-lasting mulch, such as shredded bark, wood shavings or similar materials.

LANDSCAPING FABRICS

Black plastic and similar material used as a mulch should be put in place early in the season. Apply it several weeks before planting, to warm the soil. Landscaping fabrics can go on anytime before planting. Cut away holes for planting.

ORGANIC LITTER

Organic mulches enrich your soil as they break down. They also provide the kind of environment that worms, friendly bacteria and other beneficial garden creatures thrive in, so there are benefits all round.

ALUMINUM

Strips of aluminum-coated paper or heavy-duty aluminum foil put down between rows can be used as a mulch. As well as keeping weeds from germinating, they can confuse insect pests and discourage them from landing on your crops.

WOOD CHIPS

These make a long-lasting, weed-suppressing mulch. They're often used for paths and in permanent plantings, such as around your fruit trees and berry bushes. However, rain can wash small pieces away, leading to more work keeping areas near mulched beds clean.

A light-colored mulch such as straw reflects light and keeps soil cool. Dark-colored mulches help to warm the soil.

You will have to amend some types of organic mulch. For example, pine needles and leaves are acidic and should be neutralized with lime. (As a general rule, apply 5 pounds [2.2 kg] of lime per 100 square feet [9.3 sq m] to raise the pH of your soil 1 point. Sandy soils generally need less lime to raise the pH; clay soils need more.) If you use seaweed, rinse away the salt first. If you're uncertain of the nutrient value of a mulching material, have your soil tested annually so you'll know what changes are taking place.

Inorganic Mulches

These mulches include those materials that don't improve soil, such as plastic or gravel. Gravel isn't practical in most vegetable gardens, but black plastic is widely used because it warms the soil early for the fastest crops. Landscaping fabrics are similar to black plastic but have tiny pores to let water and air in. Gardeners might find both black plastic and landscaping fabric expensive, but they can last several seasons if you remove and store them each autumn.

If you decide to use black plastic or similar landscaping fabrics, make sure you purchase the right width and length for your beds or rows. To determine the right width, measure across beds and rows then add at least 6 inches (15 cm) to each side. After you lay it out, anchor the sides with soil, rocks or boards. Cut away holes for planting. At the end of the season, remove and store it until next season, if it's still in good condition.

Part Three

Planting Your Garden

A STEP AHEAD

Punnets of healthy plants save you some time, which may justify their extra expense, especially if your growing season is short.

Choosing Plants and Seeds

Make a list of the plants you want to grow, along with an estimate of the number or amount of seed for each. Refer to your list when at the garden center or ordering from catalogs.

Buying Plants

When buying vegetable seedlings, look for healthy, green plants with lush foliage. Reject tall, leggy seedlings in favor of short, full plants. Upright, annual vegetables, such as bell peppers (capsicums), tomatoes or broccoli, that are planted individually, should be limited to one stem per pot or cell. An extra seedling may look like a bargain, but it's easy to damage both plants if you attempt to separate them, and the vigor

Foolproof Vegetables

There is really no such thing as a "foolproof" vegetable. They all need good soil preparation and regular care. But there are some relatively easy-to-grow crops that are good confidence builders for the novice gardener. Some of the most dependable are listed below, along with some growing hints.

Bean, bush Pick regularly to prolong harvest.
Bean, runner Needs a trellis.
Beet Keep soil evenly moist.
Garlic Plant autumn, harvest summer.
Lettuce Best in cool weather.
Onion Grow from young bulbs.
Radish Sow in spring.
Squash, summer Apply compost.
Tomato, cherry Needs ample water.

Miniature and Baby Vegetables

Experienced gardeners know that the biggest vegetables are not always the tastiest. In some cases, gourmet baby vegetables are full-sized cultivars harvested young. Others are naturally small. Try some of these.

Beans Pick pods when 1/4 inch (6 mm) wide; any cultivar.

Beet Pull when root is about 1 inch (2.5 cm) in diameter; try 'Mini Gourmet', but any cultivar will do.

Bell pepper (capsicum) Pick small peppers as needed; any cultivar.

Carrot Pull when roots are colored; 'Mini Round', 'Tom Thumb'.

Cauliflower Pick when heads are young.

Corn Pick tiny ears 2 days after silks appear, or choose small-fruited cultivars; any sweet corn cultivar will do.

Cucumber Pick when 2–6 inches (5–15 cm) long; any cultivar.

Eggplant (aubergine) Pick up to 4 inches (10 cm) long; any cultivar.

Garlic Pick while young before clove development. Serve as you would baby leeks or roast and squeeze onto bruschetta.

Leek Can be picked while very young and cooked whole.

Lettuce Harvest small, young leaves as needed; sow different cultivars together or choose leaf lettuce such as 'Oak Leaf' and 'Regency'.

Melon Choose small-fruited cultivars; 'Bush Sugar Baby', 'Sugar Baby'.

Onion Pull young for spring onions; pickling onions have small bulbs.

Pea Pick when pods are 2–3 inches (5–7.5 cm) long; any cultivar.

Pumpkin Choose small-fruited cultivars; 'Baby Blue', 'Golden Nugget'.

Squash Pick at 4 inches (10 cm) or longer; 'Patty Pan', 'Green Buttons'.

Tomato Choose small-fruited cultivars; 'Yellow Pear', 'Sweet Red'.

Zucchini (courgette) Pick fruit at any size; 'Lebanese', 'Greenskin'.

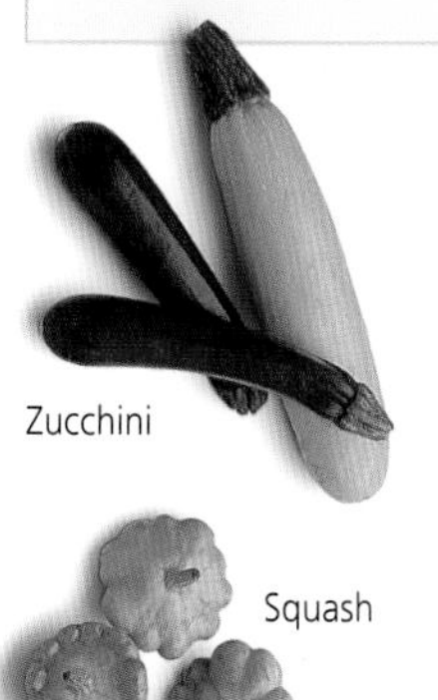
Zucchini

Squash

of both will be reduced if you plant them together. Pots of vegetables such as cucumbers or pumpkins, which are usually planted in hills, should hold only a few small seedlings. Leafy crops, such as arugula (rocket) or leaf lettuce, aren't as fussy about spacing; they can be started, planted and harvested in clumps.

The soil in the seedling pots should be moist but not soggy. Roots should be well developed, but not so much that they've filled the pot. It's normal for a few threads of root to escape the pot, but avoid transplants with solid masses of tightly woven roots. Also check the seedlings for signs of insect pests or disease symptoms. The presence of beneficial insects, such as ladybugs, might indicate a recent pest problem, but it's

Salad Vegetables

Try some unusual plants in salads:
Arugula (rocket) peppery leaves.
Bamboo shoots young shoots.
Celeriac celery-flavored roots.
Celtuce crisp leaves.
Chicory tangy leaves.
Chrysanthemum, garland aromatic leaves.
Corn salad (lamb's lettuce, mâche) nutty/buttery leaves.
Cress spicy leaves and stems.
Dandelion slightly bitter leaves.
Endive and escarole bitter leaves.
Fennel, Florence leaf bases.
Mizuna lacy, mild leaves.
Mustard spicy leaves.
Sorrel tangy, lemony leaves.
Spinach tender, mild leaves.
Sprouts crisp shoots, leaves and roots.
Watercress tangy leaves and stems.

better to take home the beneficials than the residue of pesticides. Look for webs, insect droppings or signs of damage, such as ragged holes or spotty leaves. Don't buy seedlings with discolored or wilted leaves. Look for identification labels, especially if you're unfamiliar with the seedling stages of vegetables. Closely related vegetables, such as broccoli, cauliflower and cabbage, look alike at this stage. If you're interested in a particular cultivar, shop early for the best selection or you might have to settle for unfamiliar cultivars. Most greenhouse

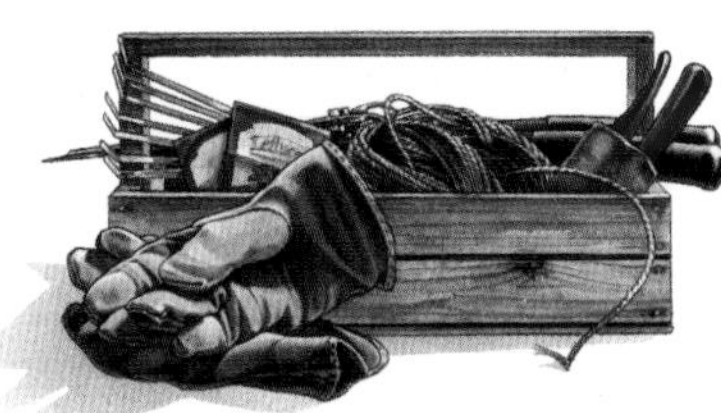

READY FOR ACTION
Keep your gardening kit in a handy carry-all and you won't need to search the house in your muddy boots.

growers have to limit how many cultivars they sow for space reasons. Consult a current seed catalog if you have to choose an unknown cultivar. A good nursery salesperson should be able to recommend the best for your garden.

Ask how the seedlings were grown. If you're strictly organic, look for growers who use starting medium, seeds, fertilizers and pest-control practices that conform to organic standards. If you can't find a source for organically grown seedlings and don't want to raise your own, you may have to settle for non-organic seedlings. At this stage, the

CHOOSE STRONG PLANTS

Seedlings should look dark green and healthy. Avoid spindly plants that have not had enough light and those with discolored leaves. These have been stressed in some way and will not perform as well as they should.

COOK THEM QUICKLY
Steaming, stir-frying and microwaving do the best job of preserving the vitamins in your home-grown vegetables.

amount of synthetic materials imported to your garden is probably negligible. Also ask if the seedlings have been hardened off (gradually acclimatized to outdoor conditions). If they have been in a warm greenhouse or an air-conditioned supermarket, you'll have to introduce them slowly to the outdoors (see page 65).

Once you get your seedlings home, make sure that you keep them watered if you are unable to transplant them to the garden immediately. Place them out of direct sun, keep a close eye on the weather and be ready to bring them indoors if a storm or frost threatens.

Bareroot or Container Plants?

Depending on when and where you buy, your fruiting plants may be bareroot or growing in containers. Bareroot plants are sold when they're dormant (not actively growing), without any soil around the roots. This is the most practical way for mail-order nurseries to ship plants, but one disadvantage is that they are only available at certain times of year (usually late autumn and early spring). Bareroot stock must be planted as soon as possible after arrival.

Local nurseries most often sell their plants growing in containers. The disadvantages of container-grown plants are that they tend to be more expensive

BAREROOT PLANTS
Check that the roots and base of the plant are firm and healthy looking, with no unusual swellings (other than the graft union near the base of the trunk). Look for clean, evenly colored bark, free of suspicious holes.

than bareroot stock, and you'll have a much more limited selection. On the plus side, though, container-grown plants are available throughout the year and can be planted any time the ground isn't frozen. If you can't plant them right away, you can keep them growing in their pots until you're ready to set them in the ground. Container stock is quite easy to plant, and it tends to have a lower failure rate than bareroot stock.

Don't Buy Problem Plants

Buying disease- and pest-resistant plants is important to the future health of your garden. But it's just as important to avoid buying plants that have problems right now. Otherwise, you might introduce serious problems, such as bacterial and viral diseases, that will affect all your crops. To reduce the risk, buy only from nurseries that offer certified disease-free plants. This means that the plants have been checked over and approved by nursery inspectors.

Fast-growers

In areas with a short growing season, fast-maturing crops are often the best chance for a good harvest. In long-season areas, use them for interplanting or succession planting. Here are a few to try: arugula (rocket), beans (bush types), beet, chicory (leafy types), Chinese cabbage, corn salad (lamb's lettuce, mâche), cress, kohl-rabi, lettuce, mizuna, mustard, peas, radish, spinach, Swiss chard (silverbeet).

CHOOSE THE BEST

It may take a few seasons to find the varieties you prefer, but it's well worth the search.

Buying Seeds

The first thing to check when buying seeds is the date on the packet. Buy fresh seeds and buy only enough for the current year, unless you're able to store seeds under the proper conditions of low moisture and low temperature. Seeds are sold by weight or number of seeds. Check how much you're getting in each packet. Shopping around is time-consuming but worthwhile. Naturally, look for a reputable dealer because seeds can differ greatly in quality.

If you can find a source, it's even better to buy "virus-indexed" plants. These come from laboratories that test stock plants and grow only those that are virus-free. These laboratories sell young plants to commercial nurseries, who propagate and grow them under controlled conditions that prevent virus infection. Virus-free stock is available for most fruit trees, as well as for grapes, raspberries, blackberries and strawberries.

Container Vegetables

If space is limited, consider using pots. Fill a suitable container with potting mixture (not garden soil, which will pack down too tightly after watering). Compact or dwarf cultivars are generally the best choice. Try some of these: bean (bush types), borecole, bell pepper (capsicum), carrot (short-rooted cultivars), corn salad (lamb's lettuce, mâche), cucumber (bush cultivars), eggplant (aubergine), lettuce, onion, pea (needs a trellis), radish, summer squash (bush cultivars), Swiss chard (silverbeet), tomato, watercress.

CONTAINER-GROWN PLANTS

Check foliage is a bright, uniform green color. Check underneath leaves and at base of stems for insects or egg clusters hidden there. If you find a problem, send the plant back or don't buy it; you don't want to risk spreading pests or diseases to your other plants.

Starting Seeds Indoors

1. Take a tray with drainage holes and fill with a light, moist growing medium such as sifted compost. Press it firmly into the corners.

2. Level off the surface with a flat piece of wood, so the medium is ½ inch (12 mm) below the rim of the container and won't wash over the edge.

3. Mark furrows 2 inches (5 cm) apart, or sprinkle seeds evenly over surface. Space small seeds ½ inch (12 mm) apart, medium seeds 1 inch (2.5 cm) apart.

4. Firm surface by pressing seeds lightly with a smooth wooden block. Press gently so seeds are in contact with mix, but not so hard as to bury them.

5. Sieve a light layer of growing medium over surface of soil. Do not cover seeds that need light to germinate. Spray with a fine mist of water.

6. Label and cover container with glass or plastic wrap. Check daily for first sprouts. To prevent disease, remove cover when seedlings appear.

STARTING SEEDS

Planting seeds indoors will get your seedlings off to a good start. Because you can control their environment, you can begin the new season earlier than when you plant outdoors.

CONTAINERS

Start seedlings in just about any container that has holes for drainage. Seedlings started in their own pots won't require potting-up later. You can even purchase ready-to-use flats with cells for sowing single seeds. If you use containers such as peat pots or pellets, you can plant the pot along with the plant. These are a good choice for those vegetables that transplant poorly, such as cucumbers.

GROWING MEDIUM

New seedlings need a light, moist medium for a quick start. Fill containers with moistened vermiculite, milled sphagnum moss, perlite or sifted compost Once true leaves have developed, the young plants will require extra nutrients. Water them with a liquid organic fertilizer, such as fish emulsion, at half strength. Gradually increase the dose to full strength. Alternatively, transfer seedlings to a potting blend with extra compost, or prepare a nourishing substitute by adding up to ½ cup (4 fl oz/125 ml) of dry, organic fertilizer to each 5-gallon (22.5 l) batch of homemade potting medium. Remember, the longer seedlings remain in pots, the more nutrients they need.

SPECIAL HANDLING

Seedlings in peat pots need special care. Tear a hole in each side of the pot before you plant it, so that the roots can make their way out. Then, tear away the upper collar of the pot, because exposed peat will act like a wick, drawing the moisture up and away from the roots of the seedling. Plant as you would a normal seedling, but plant pot and all.

Transplanting Seedlings Outdoors

1. Transplant seedlings in early evening or on cool, overcast days to protect them from sun.

2. Gently slide each seedling out of its container, keeping the soil and rootball intact.

3. Holding gently, plant seedling in a hole slightly wider, but the same depth, as container.

4. Replace soil around roots first, fill hole level with bed, gently firm the surface and water.

Hardening Off

At least 2 weeks before transplanting time, begin watering less frequently and withholding fertilizer. A week before you transplant, move the plants outdoors to a spot protected from strong light and wind. This allows young plants to adjust slowly to the extremes of temperature, wind and light. Gradually increase the time they spend outdoors. Within a week, they should be outdoors all the time. They'll need more water at this time, since sun and wind quickly dry the soil. Be prepared to bring them back indoors if a cold snap or storm threatens.

Planting Outdoors

NO WASTE

Plant the seeds of leafy or root vegetables quite thickly and use the thinnings as tender, young additions to salads and stir-fries.

Some plants, such as beans, peas and root crops, do not transplant well. You'll get the best results by sowing these seeds directly into the garden.

Sowing Seed

1. Planting dates vary among species and cultivars, so check your seed packets or a catalog. Ask local gardeners what is the expected date of the last frost for your area.

2. If you're planting in rows, mark them with wooden stakes at both ends before planting. Stretch a length of string down the row and use it as a guide to keep your rows straight while you plant. Transfer it from row to row as you go.

3. If you have raised beds, divide them into sections by plant cultivar, broadcast the seed over the appropriate section and label them, or simply sow your seed in rows across the raised bed.

4. Follow the spacing guidelines on the seed packet. Some packets indicate what length of row the package will sow. Most sowing recommendations are higher than necessary, to account for areas that are less than ideal. If conditions are good for germination, you may have to thin your seedlings later.

5. Cover seeds with soil to a depth two to three times the seed diameter, then firm them by pressing the soil lightly with the flat side of a rake or hoe.

6. The soil should stay moist but not soggy until your seeds begin to sprout. If you plant during a dry season, you may

have to water to ensure germination. If the soil at the planting depth is moist when you sow large seeds, they should have sufficient moisture to germinate. Fine seeds may need extra moisture. You can cover the row with lengths of board to retain moisture. Check the soil under the boards frequently, and remove them as soon as seeds sprout.

7. Once seedlings are growing well, thin them to the final plant spacing. Pull or snip off extras, leaving only the best.

8. Keep records of your plantings, and record the location of each vegetable species on a rough map.

ROOM TO GROW

Once your young plants are well established, they may need to be thinned. Pull them out carefully, disturbing the plants next to them as little as possible, or snip them off at soil level.

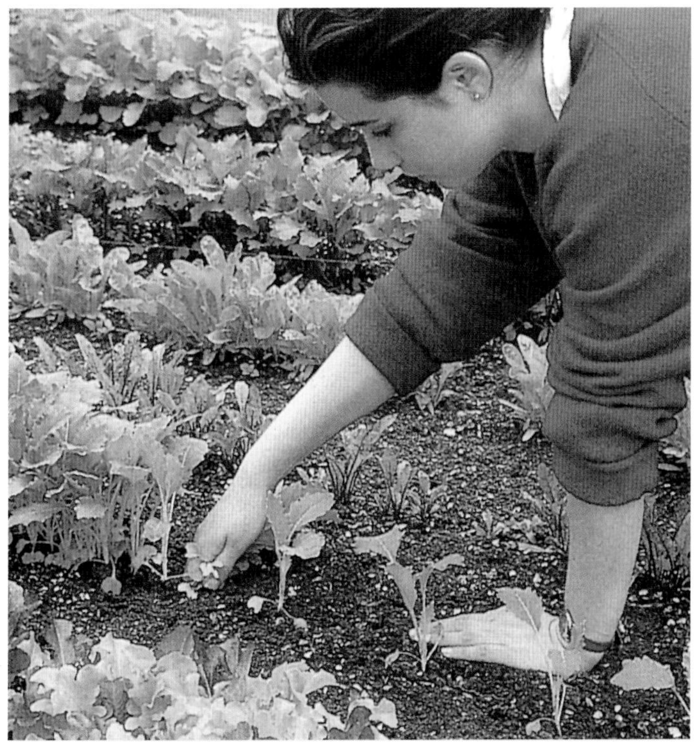

Frost Protection and Extending the Season

Season extension means getting a head start in the spring, and prolonging production in autumn, thus squeezing a little more time into each growing season.

INDIVIDUAL PROTECTION

Covers such as this Wallo Water Protector will keep frost off special plants, but cones made of heavy-duty cardboard also work well.

Cold Frames

If you build your own cold frames, make the back taller than the front so that the glass roof slants at an angle of about 45 degrees, for the best light. A frame measuring about 4 feet (1.2 m) wide by 4 feet (1.2 m) long is a good size. It should be tall enough so your plants can grow in their pots or flats without touching the roof. Attach the roof at the back with hinges and prop it open with a piece of wood to allow for air circulation. Or the roof can simply sit on the frame and you can slide it open when you need to reduce the temperature inside the frame. It's best if the interior is painted white, to reflect light onto your plants.

Keep plants or seedlings in their pots or trays in the frame—you'll find that containers are easier to manage in the small space.

COVER STORY

You can start growing in the garden earlier, and prolong your autumn harvest, if you use row covers to protect the tender plants from frosts.

Row and Plant Covers

These can be made from fabric or transparent plastic, and they provide protection from all but the hardest frosts at night. Lightweight row-cover fabric, made from spun-bonded polyester or

A COLD FRAME THROUGH THE FOUR SEASONS

In spring, harden off your seedlings in the cold frame before transplanting them out in the garden.

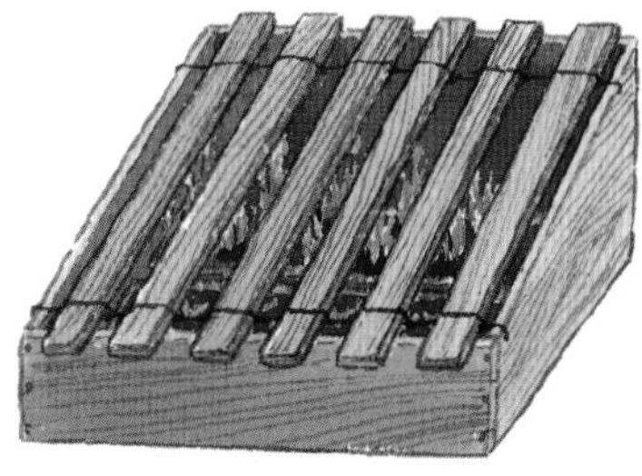

In summer, sow salad crops, such as spinach, for harvesting in autumn. The slats will keep the plants cool, but still let in sunlight.

In autumn, a cold frame will ensure the survival of your late-sown leafy crops, such as lettuce, until well after the first frost.

In winter, use your cold frame to give bulbs, such as golden shallots and garlic, their cold treatment before forcing them on.

INTERPLANTING

The different growth habits and nutrient needs of lettuce and onions make them ideal candidates for interplanting. This way you get twice the yield from the same space.

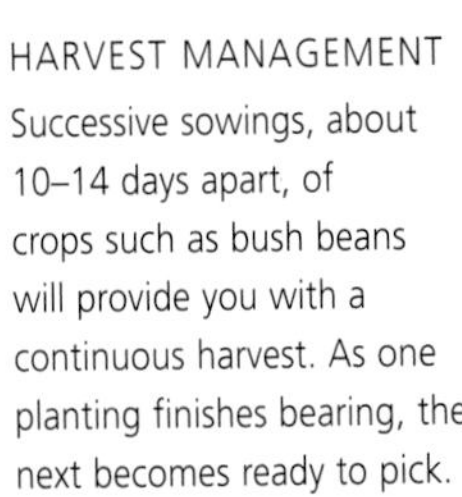

HARVEST MANAGEMENT

Successive sowings, about 10–14 days apart, of crops such as bush beans will provide you with a continuous harvest. As one planting finishes bearing, the next becomes ready to pick.

polypropylene, allows in water, light and air but keeps insects at bay. You can buy shaded or colored covers to reduce sunlight and heat in hot climates.

Plastic row covers will keep plants and soil warmer than fabric. Since heat builds up on sunny days, you'll need to vent plastic covers. Buy slitted plastic covers with built-in ventilation. To use, stretch plastic row covers over wire hoops inserted in the soil on opposite sides of the bed or row. You can buy the supports and covering together.

In a smaller garden, protect individual plants (instead of rows) from frost. Many different types of material are used to make plant covers (also

Succession Planting

Succession planting means harvesting two crops from the same space in one season, by planting the second crop after you've harvested the first. Determine the length of your growing season by counting the days between the average date of the last spring frost and the average date of the first autumn frost. Then select two vegetables whose combined days to maturity fit that limit. Plant seeds or transplants of the first crop in early spring, then harvest them and replant with the second crop in midsummer. Between crops, prepare the soil as needed but avoid tilling. By midsummer, most weed seeds have germinated, and tilling will only bring more seeds to the surface. You can add compost before the second planting, or after planting, as a mulch. Timing is the challenge. Each crop must get off to a quick start and finish. Good choices for quick crops to grow in spring and autumn are: arugula (rocket), beets, carrots, collards, chicory, endive, kohlrabi, mustard greens, radish, shallots, spinach and Swiss chard (silverbeet).

known as cloches). Whatever you use, make sure the covering allows enough light and ventilation. Garden centers offer many choices. Or make your own protectors from plastic milk containers. Cut along three sides of the base so the base forms a flap that can be used to anchor it. Leave the top open during the day. Use until frost danger is past.

GOOD COMPANIONS

Artichokes and plants of the onion family are light feeders, so they will thrive in the same conditions.

Favorite Fruits and Nuts at a Glance

CROP NAME	EXPOSURE	SOIL FERTILITY	HARDINESS	HEIGHT	SPREAD
Almond	Full sun	Average to fertile soil	Zones 6–9	15–30 feet (4.5–9 m)	15–30 feet (4.5–9 m)
Apple	Full sun	Average soil	Zones 3–9	8–30 feet (2.4–9 m)	8–30 feet (2.4–9 m)
Apricot	Full sun	Average to poor soil	Zones 5–9	8–24 feet (2.4–7.2 m)	16–24 feet (4.8–7.2 m)
Blackberry	Full sun	Average to rich soil	Zones 5–9	4–7 feet (1.2–2.1 m)	3–6 feet (0.9–1.8 m)
Blueberry	Full sun	Average to rich soil	Zones 3–9	2–15 feet (0.6–4.5 m)	3–10 feet (0.9–3 m)
Cherry, sour	Full sun	Average to rich soil	Zones 4–8	8–20 feet (2.4–6 m)	8–20 feet (2.4–6 m)
Cherry, sweet	Full sun	Average to poor soil	Zones 4–9	15–30 feet (4.5–9 m)	15–30 feet (4.5–9 m)
Citrus	Full sun to light shade	Average to rich soil	Zones 8–10	10–30 feet (3–9 m)	10–30 feet (3–9 m)
Fig	Full sun	Average soil	Zones 8–10	10–25 feet (3–7.5 m)	10–25 feet (3–7.5 m)
Gooseberry	Full sun to light shade	Average soil	Zones 3–7	3–7 feet (0.9–2.1 m)	3–7 feet (0.9–2.1 m)
Grape	Full sun	Average to rich soil	Zones 4–10	4–6 feet (1.2–1.8 m)	8–15 feet (2.4–4.5 m)
Hazelnut	Full sun to light shade	Average to poor soil	Zones 2–9	6–70 feet + (1.8–21 m) +	20 feet (6 m)
Kiwi	Full sun to light shade	Average to poor soil	Zones 7–9	4–6 feet (1.2–1.8 m)	15 feet (4.5 m)
Mulberry	Full sun	Average soil	Zones 5–8	15–30 feet (4.5–9 m)	10–20 feet (3–6 m)
Peach	Full sun	Average to poor soil	Zones 5–9	8–15 feet (2.4–4.5 m)	10–20 feet (3–6 m)
Pear	Full sun	Average to poor soil	Zones 4–9	8–20 feet (2.4–6 m)	8–20 feet (2.4–6 m)
Pecan	Full sun	Average to rich soil	Zones 6–9	50–150 feet (15–45 m)	35–50 feet (10.5–15 m)
Plum	Full sun	Average to rich soil	Zones 4–10	8–20 feet (2.4–6 m)	8–20 feet (2.4–6 m)
Raspberry	Full sun	Average to poor soil	Zones 3–9	4–6 feet (1.2–1.8 m)	2–4 feet (0.6–1.2 m)
Strawberry	Full sun	Average to rich soil	Zones 3–10	10 inches (25 cm)	1–2 feet (30–60 cm)

A handy reference to 20 of the most popular fruits and nuts for planting in home gardens. Remember that some cultivars may have slightly different needs.

BLOOM TIME	HARVEST TIME	USES AND STORAGE	POLLINATION
Early spring	Midsummer to autumn	Eat fresh; dry for storage	Cross-pollinated
Midspring	Midsummer to autumn	Eat fresh; keep for several weeks in refrigerator; or preserve	Cross-pollinated
Early spring	Early summer	Eat fresh; keep a week or two in refrigerator; dry; or preserve	Cross- and self-pollinated
Midspring	Midsummer	Eat fresh; keep a week or two in refrigerator; or preserve	Self-pollinated
Midspring	Mid- to late summer	Eat fresh; keep a few days in refrigerator; or preserve	Cross- and self-pollinated
Midspring	Early summer	Eat fresh; keep a few days in refrigerator; or preserve	Cross- and self-pollinated
Midspring	Early summer	Eat fresh; keep a few days in refrigerator; or preserve	Cross-pollinated
Varies	Varies	Eat fresh; keep a week or two in refrigerator; make into marmalade	Self-pollinated
Varies	Varies	Eat fresh; keep a few days in refrigerator; dry; or freeze	Self-pollinated
Midspring	Midsummer	Eat fresh; keep a week or two in refrigerator; or preserve	Self-pollinated
Midspring	Midsummer to autumn	Eat fresh; keep a week or two in refrigerator; or preserve	Self-pollinated
Early spring	Late summer to autumn	Eat fresh; keep for weeks in refrigerator; or freeze	Cross-pollinated
Midspring	Autumn	Eat fresh; keep for several weeks in refrigerator; or preserve	Cross-pollinated
Spring	Summer	Eat fresh; freeze; dry; or preserve	Self-pollinated
Early spring	Midsummer	Eat fresh; keep a week or two in refrigerator; or preserve	Self-pollinated
Midspring	Late summer to autumn	Eat fresh; keep for several weeks in refrigerator; or preserve	Cross-pollinated
Early spring	Autumn	Eat fresh; keep for several weeks in refrigerator; or dry	Cross-pollinated
Early spring	Midsummer	Eat fresh; keep a week or two in refrigerator; or preserve	Cross- and self-pollinated
Midspring	Midsummer to autumn	Eat fresh; keep a few days in refrigerator; or preserve	Self-pollinated
Midspring	Early to midsummer	Eat fresh; keep a few days in refrigerator; or preserve	Self-pollinated

Planting Fruits, Nuts, Berries and Vines

It's always exciting when planting day arrives. All the effort you've put into choosing the best cultivars, deciding where to put them and preparing the soil will pay off now as you put in your plants.

Alpine strawberry

Autumn Planting

For those who live in a warm climate (Zones 6–10) autumn is a good time to plant most fruit and nut crops. Dormant, bareroot, mail-order plants will arrive in early to late autumn. Nurseries and garden centers may also offer container-grown plants through autumn.

If you live in Zone 5 or cooler and you have light, well-drained soil and winters that aren't severely cold, you can plant currants, gooseberries and hardy Concord grapes in autumn, but save the rest of your planting for spring.

In warm climates, the planting season extends well into winter. In temperate climates, bareroot apricots go in the ground from mid- to late winter. In warmer regions, blueberries and strawberries are best planted in winter.

Spring Planting

In cool climates (Zone 5 and cooler), early spring is the best time to plant most fruits and nuts. Bareroot mail-order plants will arrive early, so prepare the planting site in autumn so it will be ready when your plants come. You'll want to get the plants in the ground

PLANTING PINEAPPLES

Twist off any sideshoots or cut the crown of leaves off the top of the pineapple and let dry for a few days. Then plant the shoots or crowns about 1 foot (30 cm) apart in a warm, sunny position.

STRAWBERRY BEDS

Set out your strawberries in rows that will allow easy access for cultivation and harvesting. Finish the job by applying a thick layer of organic mulch that will gradually break down and enrich the soil.

as soon as possible, so they will be well established before the heat and drought of summer. If you don't have the time to deal with your bareroot plants when they arrive or if the weather in your area is still dropping well below freezing at night, you may need to hold the plants indoors for a few days.

If you buy your plants locally, they'll most likely be growing in containers. While it's ideal to plant them early, container-grown fruit trees, shrubs or vines are much more forgiving of delays than bareroot plants, as long as you keep them well watered.

Planting Bareroot Plants

If you've never seen a bareroot plant before, you might be surprised when you unpack your box from the nursery. Bareroot plants are just what they sound

SEASONAL INTEREST
Choose dwarf or semi-dwarf fruit trees instead of purely ornamental trees if your space is limited. You will enjoy the display of flowers, followed by a season of harvest.

like—tentacle-like naked roots topped with bare branches or merely a single stem. They can look rather pathetic, but as long as you bought the plants from a reputable nursery and give them proper care, they will grow beautifully. (If you lose plants right after transplanting, which is not all that uncommon, contact the nursery for a refund or replacement.)

USING VERTICAL SPACE
Choose standard forms, such as this gooseberry, if your garden is small.

To get bareroot plants off to a good start:

1. When you're ready to plant, cut off any sickly, damaged or very long roots. Leave healthy roots alone. Give most fruit and nut plants, except blueberries, a preplanting booster by soaking their roots in a bucket of compost tea (see page 34). Soak the roots of strawberries and grapes for 20 minutes; soak bush and tree roots for 2 hours.

2. Dig a hole deep enough to hold the roots without curling them up at the ends. Slice into the walls of the hole with a spade to make them easy for roots to penetrate. Make a tall cone of soil in the center of the hole and firm it well.

3. Remove roots from compost tea, then dip them in a blend of 1 part bonemeal and 1 part powdered kelp. If the bacterial disease crown gall is a problem in your area, apply a preventive treatment of Agrobacterium radiobacter (sold as Galltrol-A and

FOR A SMALLER GARDEN
Dwarf cultivars, like this peach tree, do well in planters that are at least 2 feet (60 cm) wide and 3 feet (90 cm) deep.

PLANTING

Dig a wide, shallow planting hole and slash the sides with the spade so roots can spread easily.

For bareroot plants, spread the roots over a cone of soil in the center of your planting hole.

With ballroot plants, set plant in hole so base of stem is level with the soil surface.

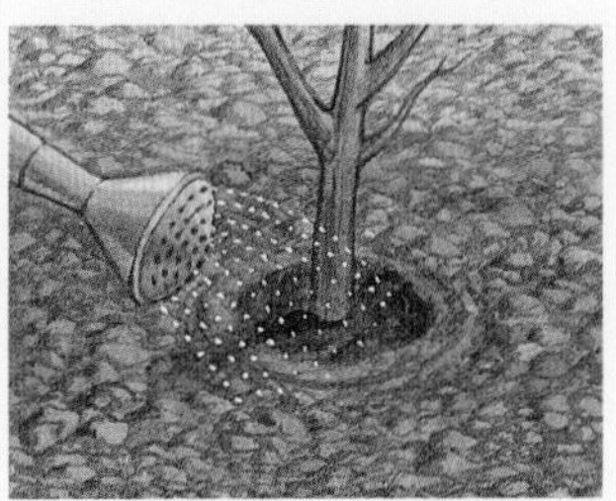

Fill hole, gently firm down soil and water with a fine spray to wet surrounding soil thoroughly.

Norbac 84). Dunk your bareroot fruit plants in it before planting to prevent later crown gall infection.

4. Put crown of plant (where the roots come together and shoots emerge) on top of the soil cone in the planting hole.

5. Check that the crown or graft swelling is level with the surface of the soil. If your soil tends to sink slightly as it settles, you may want to elevate the plant a little to adjust. If your plant sits too high or too low on the soil cone, lift it out, change the height of the cone and try again.

6. When you have the right crown or graft height, spread out the roots evenly over the soil cone. Holding the plant with one hand, fill in around the roots with the soil you removed from the hole. When the hole is half-filled, add some water so the planting site is thoroughly soaked; then finish filling the hole. Firm the soil gently and add a plant label.

QUARTERING

To loosen a tight root ball, use a knife to make four deep cuts through the base of the ball. Spread the quartered root ball over a cone of good soil, fill the planting hole and water.

SPACE-SAVER

This multi-graft citrus tree bears lemons, oranges, mandarins and grapefruit on the one tree, a huge saving in space and in the effort needed to look after four separate trees.

PLANTS IN CONTAINERS

To remove a plant from a pot, squeeze the sides of a plastic pot to loosen, or invert a rigid pot and tap the rim gently, supporting the plant with your hand so that it doesn't fall out and break.

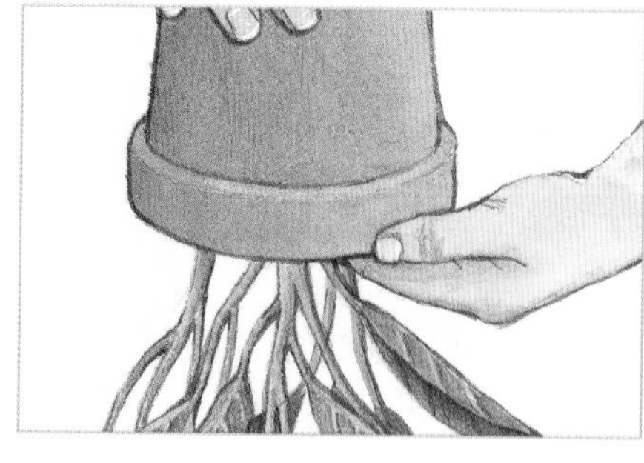

Planting Aftercare

On year-old fruit trees, cut back the main trunk to about 2 feet (60 cm) in height to encourage it to develop new branches for later training. On hickories and walnuts, cut the young tree back by half, leaving several buds on the trunk to form new branches.

On bareroot fruit bushes, cut back up to half of the stems to compensate for the roots lost. Remove all but the base of the old canes from raspberries and blackberries to eliminate any diseases they may carry. And on grapes, remove all but the strongest stem to prepare the vine for future training.

On berries, remove all the flowers the first spring after planting to encourage good growth. Pinch off grape flowers for 2 years after planting.

Planting Plants from Containers

1. Dig a hole the same depth as the pot, leaving the soil in the bottom of the hole undisturbed. If your soil is very heavy (clayey) or light (sandy), dig some composted pine bark or peat moss into the area around the planting hole.

2. Double-check that your plant will sit at the proper level. If you lay a stake across the hole and measure from the stake to the bottom of the hole with a stick, you can judge the right depth without having to lift the heavy plant in and out of the hole.

3. Remove the plant from its pot by putting one hand on the surface of the planting mix to support the top. Then put your other hand under the container, squeezing the sides gently to separate it from the roots. Turn the pot upside-down and slide the plant out.

4. If the plant has been growing in the pot for a long time, the roots will be matted on the outside of the root ball. Use a sharp knife to cut off matted parts. Loosen circling roots with your fingers.

5. Set the plant in the hole, spreading loose roots in different directions so each has its own space. Refill the hole with soil and water thoroughly.

Part Four

Managing Your Garden

Garden Care for Four Seasons

PATIO BOUNTY

Container-grown plants on even a tiny, sunny patio can produce a surprising harvest.

Being organized about your garden tasks reduces the work. Follow this simple guide to doing jobs at the right time and your crops will thrive, rewarding your efforts with abundant produce.

Winter

Winter is as important as any other season. The planning you do on long winter nights will help prevent problems later on. This is the time to decide what you want to grow and how much you are going to plant. As you search through seed catalogs, look for high-yielding cultivars that are insect- or disease-resistant, so you'll have fewer pest problems to cope with. Order seeds and save yourself a trip to the garden center later on. This is also a good time to plan your planting schedule.

Spring

The weather's getting warmer and your garden beds and soil are prepared (see page 28). But before you start digging and planting, take a few minutes to review the plans you made during the winter. Check your planting schedule to see what crops should go in first. Get out the seeds you ordered, or take your shopping list to the garden center and

Keeping Records

Keep track of planting dates, fertilizer rates, pest problems and harvests. Some people make notes in a diary or on a calendar or create tables of garden data. As well as noting your garden's day-to-day progress, your records will also help you plan for greater success next year. For example, you can see how well different cultivars perform in your garden, or when space will be available for replanting. Update your records with each new season.

POTAGER GARDEN

A clump of eschscholzia adds a spot of vivid color to a mixed vegetable and herb garden.

PLANNING PAYS OFF

Think about where the shade will be so that taller plants don't rob smaller ones of precious sunlight. Mulching reduces the need for water and keeps weeds down.

buy the seeds, transplants and other supplies you need. Don't be tempted to buy extra plants or plants that aren't on your list. You'll either end up cramming the extras in with the others or digging new beds to accommodate them.

SUMMER

This season is the time that your winter planning and spring planting pay off. As your vegetables and fruits mature in the warm summer weather, a little extra attention can keep yields high and routine maintenance minimal.

Mulches are the cornerstone of good gardening (see page 50). They help keep critical moisture in the soil and moderate temperature extremes for better root growth. They reduce weeding chores by smothering weed seeds and keep soil from splashing onto plants, which reduces the spread of soilborne diseases and keeps the produce cleaner. And as they break down, organic mulches release a balanced supply of plant nutrients and add organic matter to improve the structure of the soil. Mulches also save water, but not enough that you can forget about watering (see page 94).

AUTUMN

As the lower temperatures arrive, many plants that took a break during the summer heat may make

FRESH FOR THE TABLE
You can pick your vegetables just before the meal.

SUNNY CORNERS
You'll be surprised at what a good supply of fresh vegetables can be produced, with forward planning, in even a tiny space, especially if it is sunny and sheltered.

new growth or set more fruit. Late-summer plantings of crops such as peas and lettuce can yield well into autumn. Once your crops are done for the season, spend a few minutes putting the garden to bed so that it will be ready for spring planting next season. In addition to making it look tidier during the winter, picking up dead plants and dropped vegetable matter eliminates hiding places for insect eggs and disease pathogens.

Check over your garden tools and have any that need sharpening attended to. Wash and dry your tools and apply a light coating of oil before storing them. While you're at it, pull up and clean off any metal or wooden stakes and store them so they don't rust or rot.

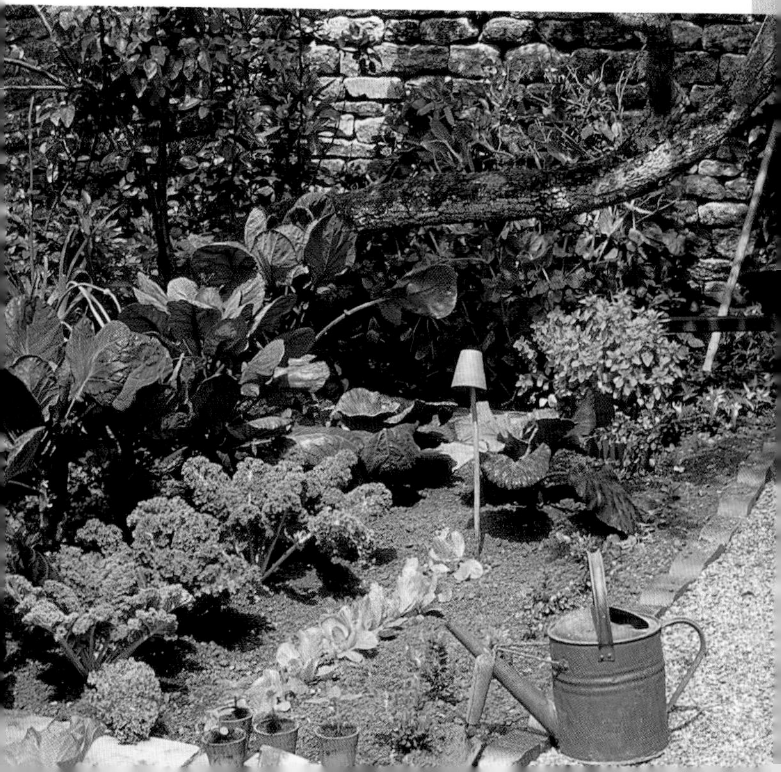

Managing the Vegetable Garden

Carrots and celery

You can plunk a few tomato plants in a corner and get a few fruits. But if you want to get the best harvests you've ever had, it's worth preparing the site and maintaining your plants properly.

Preparing the Soil for Vegetables

In general, vegetables will thrive in normal, healthy garden soil with good drainage. Most grow best in a soil that is slightly acid or neutral (about pH 6.5–7.0). Vegetables that like the nutrient balance in alkaline soil include asparagus, melon, spinach and Swiss chard. If your soil is too acid or alkaline, you may need to adjust the pH by adding lime or sulfur.

Most vegetable crops will thrive in soils with a texture somewhere in the "loam" range: sandy loams, silt loams and even clay loams. Very loose, sandy soils with few rocks are ideal for root crops like carrots, beets and parsnips. Celery and members of the cabbage family, such as cauliflower, cabbage and broccoli,

Special Needs

Some vegetables have more specific nutrient needs than just "more of everything." Cucurbits (cucumbers, melons and squash) require adequate magnesium. Garlic, onions, squash and tomatoes thrive with extra potassium and phosphorus but don't need much nitrogen. In fact, too much nitrogen will keep tomatoes from bearing fruit. To make sure your plants get just what they need, a soil test (see pages 28 and 29) will be invaluable. That way, you'll know if your soil is deficient or if it is adequately supplied with the necessary nutrients.

can handle wetter soils that are more on the clayey side. Of course, working in ample amounts of organic matter can make almost any soil suitable.

HEAD START

There's a small extra cost involved in buying young plants that are ready to be set out, and a more limited selection of cultivars to choose from, but you can save yourself a lot of time.

If you're starting a new site, strip off the existing sod, spread a 1-inch (2.5-cm) layer of compost over the area, and dig or till the top 6–8 inches (15–20 cm). If you've planted an existing garden with a cover crop or green manure, dig or till it in at least 2–3 weeks before planting. Or, if you mulched the soil for winter, rake off the mulch or work it in to let the soil warm up. If you're growing root crops, make sure you dig the soil deeply and

NATURAL CONTROLS

Growing flowers and herbs in your vegetable garden will help to attract beneficial, pest-eating insects. Few pests do enough damage to reduce your harvest noticeably. If you control pest insects without using poisons, you'll encourage beneficial insects that prey on them and keep their populations in check.

remove any rocks or clods that could impede good root development. Before planting, rake the soil to remove surface stones and clods.

Fertilizing

Many gardeners make a science out of fertilizing, but it doesn't have to be so complex. There are two approaches to fertilizing vegetables (well, three, if you count not fertilizing at all, which isn't very practical if you want good yields). The easiest way is to treat all your vegetables the same. Fertilize the vegetable garden each year, before planting, with a balanced material such as compost or a commercially available blend. For a midseason boost, side-dress with a dry fertilizer scratched lightly into the soil near the roots. Or give all of the plants a monthly dose of liquid seaweed or fish emulsion. The

UNFINISHED BUSINESS

If your bell peppers (capsicums) stop producing in midsummer, don't pull them up. They may set more fruit when the slightly cooler autumn weather arrives.

SPACE SAVERS

If space is limited, look for bush or compact cultivars of squash and other favorite crops. You'll get high yields from just a few plants in a small garden.

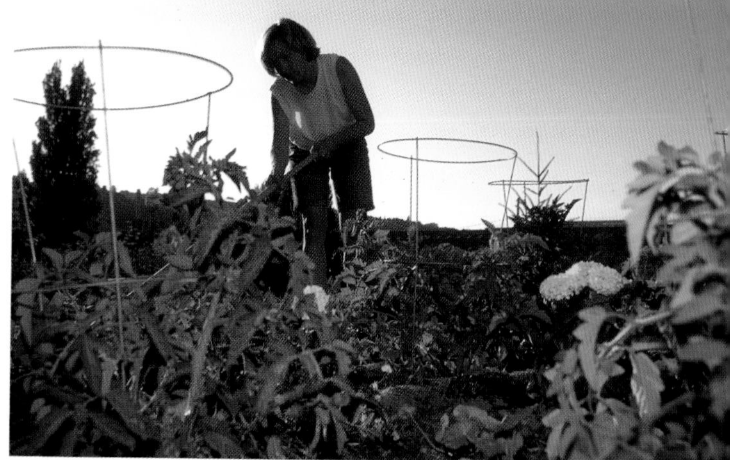

SIMPLIFY THE WORK
Plan your vegetable garden so that plants with similar water and nutrient needs are grouped together.

other approach is to fertilize each plant to meet its needs. This customized fertilizing is worth the trouble if you want to get extra-high yields or if you garden intensively (where closely spaced plants need extra nutrients).

Getting Better Harvests

Beans To get a steady supply of bush beans, plant successive crops at 7- to 10-day intervals. Or try pole beans—they grow tall, so you must set up a tripod of stakes for them to twine around, but they'll produce for a long season from a single planting and they're easy to pick.

Broccoli Look for cultivars like 'Packman' and 'Goliath' that will produce smaller side shoots after you harvest the main head.

Carrots Sow thickly and harvest the thinnings for eating each week.

Corn Plant successive crops every 7–10 days for a more even yield.

Cucumbers If space is limited and you want a high yield of cucumbers, choose bush cultivars to plant.

Lettuce If summer heat stops spring sowings early, try late-summer plantings for harvesting well into autumn.

Peas Like lettuce, peas may stop producing when summer's heat starts. Late-summer plantings will extend the pea season into autumn.

Squash Choose bush cultivars for a high yield from a small space.

Easy-care Fruits and Berries

BERRY DELIGHT

Besides their white spring flowers, blueberries often produce outstanding autumn color, which makes them attractive as ornamentals.

Growing fruit is slightly more complicated than growing vegetables, but the rewards can make it all worthwhile. If you really want low maintenance, stick with the simplest fruit crops.

Backyard Brambles

Brambles, such as raspberries and blackberries, are easily grown, and plants can live as long as 10 years, so prepare the site carefully. They need full sun and should be planted far from wild relatives, which might carry disease. Choose a well-drained site or build a raised bed.

To save space and make harvesting easier, train brambles to a trellis. The double-armed T is an easy system. At either end of the bed, set in two vertical posts as tall as the mature plant will be. On each post, attach two horizontal bars, one in the middle and one at the top. Run a cord from the top corner of one crossbar to the top corner of the other. Repeat for the other side and for the lower crossbars. For easy access, remove the cords when it's time to prune.

Blueberry Basics

Blueberry plants don't bear fruit until they're 3 or 4 years old, but if you're willing to wait, you can enjoy them as ornamentals in the meantime. All species

Alpine Strawberries

Use alpine strawberries *Fragaria vesca* as edgings for flower or vegetable gardens. They bear flavor-packed berries for several years and don't produce runners. Look for plants at your local garden center, or start your own from seed. They have tiny white flowers.

need a moist but loose-textured soil high in organic matter. Most blueberries are not self-fertile, so you'll need to plant at least two, and preferably three, cultivars that can cross-pollinate for good fruit set.

Strawberries Made Simple

Early-summer strawberries produce just the one big crop. Ever-bearing strawberries produce smaller spring and autumn crops. Both types spread by runners from the mother plant, with the

LONG-SEASON HARVESTS

Spread your apple harvests by choosing cultivars that bloom at the same time (to aid pollination), but mature at different times. 'Liberty' and 'Prima', for example, will provide you with apples from late summer until well into autumn.

baby plants putting down roots. A space-saving planting method is the matted row system. Start with the plants in rows 4 feet (1.2 m) apart. Within the rows, space early-summer cultivars every 1½ feet (45 cm) and ever-bearing cultivars every foot (30 cm). For easier harvesting, limit the bed to three rows, leaving enough room at the front, back and sides for runners.

Pinch the flowers off early-summer plants the first year, so they put energy into their roots. For ever-bearing, pinch off flowers only until the start of summer. Throughout the season, let the runners fill in with new plants wherever they take root. In autumn, keep the plants

PEACH AND NECTARINE
Be careful to choose cultivars that suit your climate. While excess cold is harmful, both of these fruit trees need some chilling if they are to flower properly. Don't plant in soil where a similar tree grew recently, as the decaying roots emit a chemical that can kill the new tree roots.

ESPALIER TRAINING
While this takes patience and careful pruning, the result is beautiful, saving precious space in the garden and allowing unequaled access to the crop, be it apples, peaches, pears or whatever.

watered to increase the next year's crop. Mulch with straw to a depth of 2–3 inches (5–7.5 cm) in order to prevent winter damage.

The second summer after planting, rejuvenate the bed right after harvest by setting your lawn mower at 2½ inches (6 cm) and mowing over the whole bed. Rake up the debris, then narrow the width of each row to 1 foot (30 cm) by tilling or turning under the plants on the edges. Spread compost over the bed, and water the plants well to encourage new growth.

FRESH IS BEST

Fig trees are very productive and generally easy to grow. They are seldom troubled by pests, except for birds. You may have to net your tree to keep the birds away.

Depending on how healthy and productive your cultivar is, you can get 3 years or more of harvest. To ensure an ongoing supply, start a new bed in a different spot every 2–3 years. When you are finished with the first bed, dig it under and plant it with another crop until the new bed is exhausted.

Special Needs of Some Fruiting Crops

Apples Spray the leaves with fish emulsion just before the flower buds open. Later, spray leaves every 2 weeks through summer to provide micronutrients.

Blueberries Adjust soil pH levels to fall between 4.5–5.2 for best growth. Blueberries have shallow roots that are easily damaged by cultivation, so mulch deeply instead.

Grapes These are heavy feeders, so add colloidal phosphate to your compost before applying it around the vines. Test for potassium regularly and add as needed. Grapes do best in soil that has a pH of between 5.0–6.0.

Peaches and nectarines These heavy feeders don't have extensive roots, so remove all sod from the root zone and keep the trees well mulched. Mix bonemeal or colloidal phosphate into the planting hole. Add potassium to the compost mulch. Spray the leaves with fish emulsion every 2 weeks through summer to supply micronutrients.

Effective Watering

When rainfall is lacking, you'll need to provide water to keep your plants growing strongly and producing well. There are many different ways you can supply this water to your garden.

DRIP IRRIGATION SYSTEMS

Be careful if you design this type of system yourself—it's easy to make a mistake. You can eliminate errors by having a professional design the system, based on your garden plan. If the emitters wet only one side of a plant, the roots will grow lopsided.

Hand Watering

This is most useful for settling in seedlings and irrigating vegetables in containers or in very small gardens. It's also a handy way to spot-treat wilting plants until you can give a more thorough watering. Hand watering is not ideal for established plants, since it usually can't supply enough water to soak slowly into the soil.

Overhead Watering

While sprinklers are common irrigation tools, they're not efficient. Only a small part of the water reaches the crops that need it. Sprinklers also provide an ideal environment for diseases that are spread on wet leaves.

Soaker Hoses

It's much more effective to provide water at ground level. Run a soaker hose (which leaks droplets or fine sprays of moisture along its length) next to a single-row planting or between a

HOW MUCH WATER?

Water enough to keep your plants growing, but not so much that roots become oxygen starved. For most soils, one good soaking is better than several shallow sprinkles. While hand watering is useful to revive wilting plants, there are better long-term options.

CONSERVING WATER

Group vegetables with low, medium and high water needs and water sections individually.

Use a rain barrel to catch water off your roof and siphon it to your garden with a length of hose.

Cover soil with organic mulch, which holds water like a sponge.

Control weeds that rob your plants of water.

Protect your plants from drying winds.

double-row planting. This will moisten the planting area without benefiting nearby weeds. Weave or loop flexible rubber or plastic soaker hoses in and out among clumps of plants. Canvas and rigid rubber hoses work best when run in straight lines.

DRIP IRRIGATION

These have a customized network of hoses or pipes engineered to carry a specific amount of water to any given place in the garden. They use special emitters that let the water seep out to the rooting area of each plant or plant grouping, soaking the soil deeply.

Pruning Primer for Fruits and Berries

Pruning is probably the most daunting part of fruit-tree care for novices. It takes practice, and you will probably make a few mistakes, but as plants are very forgiving, these are rarely fatal.

PRUNING BASICS
A pruning saw, a very sharp budding knife and hand pruners are the absolute basics. Substantial gloves will save your hands from accidental damage. The narrow blade of the pruning saw gives good access to tight spaces.

Making the Right Pruning Cuts

Each pruning cut you make affects the plant differently and helps you to direct its growth. With just two different kinds of cuts, you can shape practically any fruiting plant as you wish. Once you understand these two cuts, you're well on your way to pruning success.

Thinning cuts open the tree to sunlight. They are especially valuable for rejuvenating older, overgrown fruit trees,

A VERY USEFUL TOOL
Branch loppers have long handles that extend your reach significantly. They can cut branches up to 1 inch (2.5 cm) in diameter.

Removing Large Branches

1. Make a cut halfway through from underneath, about 1 foot (30 cm) from the trunk.

2. Make the next cut from above, about 1 inch (2.5 cm) farther out; the branch will break off.

3. Finish with a clean, straight cut just outside the branch base (the collar).

CLEAN CUTS

Clippers, shears and pruners are handy for cutting back vines and clump-forming weeds. Such plants are effectively weakened by having to use their reserves of nutrients to replace the foliage you have cut off.

where you want to remove a number of smaller branches and suckers and leave the larger branches. To thin a too-long or poorly placed branch, cut it back to the ground, to a side branch or to a shoot that's aimed in an uncrowded or desired direction. If you cut back to the trunk or to another branch, make the cut outside the slanted branch collar that forms a swelling at the base of the branch.

A THINNED TREE

Thinning removes a branch where it arises from another branch, the trunk or the ground. Use thinning cuts to shorten overly long branches, clear out crowded growth, remove a branch that crosses or rubs another, or take out dead and diseased wood.

Heading cuts remove shoot tips, encouraging buds farther back on the stem to sprout. You can choose the best new shoots to become main branches on a young tree or to provide productive new growth on older trees (especially peaches and nectarines). In most cases, it's best to make a heading cut just above a bud to avoid leaving a stub.

Choosing Pruning Tools

A few good tools will make your pruning sessions easier. Here's the basic tool collection you'll need to maintain your fruiting trees, shrubs and vines, along with some tips on how to use them.

The Kindest Cut

If you prune and train your young fruit trees carefully, you can eliminate the need to take out large branches later on. This is a big help, since removing big branches leaves wounds that are easy marks for pests and diseases. But if disease, damage or some other dilemma requires you to remove a large branch, see the three-step approach on page 97, or hire a professional arborist to do the job for you—for your safety and the health of your tree.

Hand pruners (also called pruning shears or secateurs) are used for cutting twigs less than ½ inch (12 mm) in diameter.
Loppers (basically hand pruners with very long handles) are useful for cutting stems up to about 1 inch (2.5 cm) in diameter, depending on the model you buy. The long handles make pruning thorny-stemmed plants much more pleasant, since your hands will be farther away from the thorns.
Pruning saws are perfect for cutting branches larger than 1 inch (2.5 cm) in diameter, especially in tight spaces.
Pole pruners are handy if you need to prune branches farther than your normal reach. They have either shear-type blades or a saw blade (or sometimes both) on a pole 4–6 feet (1.2–1.8 m) long.

HAND PRUNERS

Choose the "bypass" kind, with two curved blades that cut like scissors; they cut more cleanly than the straight-edged blade-and-anvil types. If you are cutting back thorny brambles, blackberries, raspberries or gooseberries, look for cut-and-hold bypass shears that hang onto the trimmings so they're easy to pull out.

Dealing with Pests and Diseases

The best pest controls are specific, safe, easy and effective. If your garden plants are bothered by pests, choose control methods that target the pests and not other organisms.

SAFE CONTROLS

Colorado beetle larvae (top), which attack potato foliage, and aphids (bottom) can be knocked off your plants with a forceful jet of water. Or pick off these and other pest insects by hand early on cool mornings, when they are sluggish.

Proper Identification

This is the first step toward successful pest control. Consult a book on how to identify garden pests, or submit insect or disease samples to a local Cooperative Extension Service. Then select controls that are environmentally safe.

Resistance

One of the easiest ways to avoid problems is to choose cultivars that are designed to resist the pests that plague your vegetables. Plant breeders have developed an array of new cultivars that are able to defend themselves against specific diseases and insect pests. Find out which conditions could be a problem and look for resistant cultivars in catalogs and garden-supply stores.

Weekly Inspection

Check leaves, flowers and stems for signs of insects or pathogens at least once a week. In large stands, examine three to five plants at three different locations. Become familiar with insect life cycles so you'll recognize resting (egg and cocoon) and active (larva and adult) stages.

Common Vegetable Pests and Diseases

PEST	DAMAGE	PREVENTION AND CONTROL
Snails and slugs	Seedlings eaten, irregular holes in leaves.	Place shallow containers of beer in garden, or trap pests under boards.
Aphids	Foliage wilted or curled, deformed buds and flowers.	A short, sharp spray of water from the hose will dislodge them. Spray with insecticidal soap.
Cabbageworms	Leaves eaten.	Use row covers. Spray or dust with BT.
Carrot fly	Carrot roots eaten.	Rotate carrot plantings. Use row covers. Plant crops in late spring to minimize the damage.
Cutworms	Plant stem chewed at soil surface.	Place cardboard or metal cutworm collars around the stem of the plants. Sprinkle moist bran mixed with BTK on the soil surface in the evening. Add parasitic nematodes to the soil at least a week before planting.
Leaf miners	Winding or large, blotchy lines on leaves, especially those of beets, spinach and tomatoes.	Use row covers. Pick off and destroy infected leaves. Control adults with yellow sticky traps or a pyrethrin/rotenone mix.
Squash borer	Holes in base of stem, wilting leaves.	Use row covers until flowers appear.
European corn borer	Tunnels in corn stalks and ears.	Use pheromone lures and sticky traps.
Beetles (flea, Mexican bean, Japanese, cucumber)	Chewed foliage.	Eliminate weeds. Use row covers. Spray with garlic or pyrethrin.
Two-spotted mite	Discoloration and bronzing of the foliage.	Use a garlic or pyrethrin/rotenone spray.

DISEASE	DAMAGE	PREVENTION AND CONTROL
Powdery mildew	Downy patches on foliage.	Provide good air circulation. Control weeds. Spray foliage with compost tea.
Damping-off	Seedlings weaken and collapse because of decay at soil line.	Start seeds in well-drained mix. Avoid overwatering, crowding and poor air circulation. Disinfect reused pots and flats.
Rust	Rust-colored powder on the leaves.	Plant resistant cultivars. Provide good air circulation. Remove infected leaves.
Wilt (Fusarium and Verticillium)	Leaves yellow, plant gradually wilts.	Rotate crops. Plant resistant cultivars. Destroy infected plants.

TIMING IS CRUCIAL
The annual and biennial weeds in this field reproduce by setting abundant seeds. Preventing them from flowering is one key to controlling them.

Dealing with Weeds

A weed is any plant growing where you don't want it. What plant it is doesn't matter, but where it is does. Although any plant can be a weed, some plants are considered weeds more often than others.

Plan a Weed-control Strategy

To control your lawn and garden weeds effectively and efficiently, you need to use the right technique at the right time. This requires an essential piece of knowledge: How long do your particular weeds live?

Annual Weeds Are Spread by Seed

Annual weeds, such as lamb's-quarters *Chenopodium album*, live an entire life within a year; they sprout from seed, grow, flower, set seed and die. Most annuals start this cycle in the spring and finish by autumn. Winter annuals sprout in autumn, grow a few inches tall, then go dormant until early spring. In spring, they resume growing and set seed by early- to midsummer. Winter annuals, such as common chickweed *Stellaria media*, are the first weeds you'll see in the spring.

One part of controlling annuals is never to let them set seed. If the original plants die without making more seed, they won't be back the following year. Unfortunately, seeds from previous years' weeds can survive in the soil for many years, and new weed seeds may drift

Weeds as Hosts

Some weeds harbor harmful insects or diseases. If you control the weeds you reduce the risk of their associated problems. For example, weeds of the nightshade (Solanaceae) family, such as horsenettle and black nightshade, shelter insects that will attack your tomatoes, potatoes and eggplants (aubergines); and bishop's weed *Ammi majus* often shelters carrot rust flies.

LET'S GET PHYSICAL

Pulling up annual weeds is very effective if the soil is damp enough to release the roots. Dispose carefully of any that reroot easily, such as purslane *Portulaca oleracea*, so that you get maximum return from your crop.

in on the wind or be carried in on clothing or fur. For these reasons, the other half of controlling annual weeds involves mulching and other techniques to prevent those seeds from sprouting.

Biennials Take Two Years

For biennial weeds, such as bishop's weed *Ammi majus*, the seed-to-seed cycle spreads over 2 years. These weeds

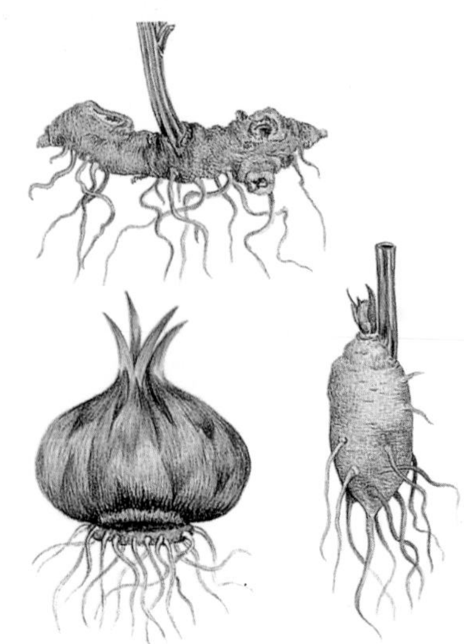

STORAGE SYSTEMS

Plants have many ways to store the products of photosynthesis. Clockwise from top: a rhizome; a tuber; and a bulb.

sprout from seed in the spring or summer, then usually grow into a ground-hugging circle of leaves called a rosette. The leaves produce sugars that move down to the roots and are stored as starch. Next spring, the plant uses the stored food energy to send up a flowering stalk, which may or may not have leaves. The plant flowers, sets seed, then dies.

You have two main options with biennial weeds: Dig out the rosette—root and all—in the first year; or, if the weed isn't too visible or crowding other plants, wait until the second year and cut the plant down to the ground. If you wait until the weed is just about to flower, the plant will have used up most of its stored energy and will be unlikely to return.

Perennials Are Persistent

Wild garlic *Allium vineale*, kudzu vine *Pueraria lobata* and other perennial weeds live for 3 years or more. Like biennials, perennials store carbohydrates

Dig in the Dark

If you're determined to till but also want to keep weeds to a minimum, consider tilling your garden after dark. It sounds crazy, but researchers have had remarkable success with this technique, reducing weed cover by 70 to 80 percent. It seems that exposure to just a few seconds of light is all some weeds need to germinate. If you till only when it's dark, many of the seeds will be reburied without being triggered to sprout. Dig any time between 1 hour after sunset to 1 hour before sunrise.

COLD FRAMES

While generally used to give seedlings a headstart, frames are also effective in keeping weeds from sharing the water and nutrients you have provided for the benefit of your salad greens.

Effective Hoeing

If you have a standard pull or draw hoe, where the neck of the hoe curls back toward you, place your hands with your thumbs pointing up and pull the hoe toward you with a sweeping motion. If you use a push hoe, with the blade pointing away from you, hold the handle with your thumbs pointing down. Push it in front of you as you walk, with the blade just under the soil surface.

to fuel early growth the next spring. That food energy may be stored in a taproot, in spreading underground stems called rhizomes or in spreading aboveground stems called runners or stolons. Or it may be in a tuber (like a potato) or a bulb (like an onion).

Some perennials, such as dandelions *Taraxacum officinale*, reproduce only sexually—by setting seed from fertilized flowers. But some also reproduce non-sexually, by a process called vegetative reproduction. New plants can sprout from rhizomes and stolons. Tubers have "eyes" that produce new plants. And bulbs multiply, giving rise to new bulbs that can each become a plant. You can think of this vegetative reproduction as a type of self-cloning for plants.

Perennial weeds are generally the most difficult to control. Carbohydrates stored in their taproots, rhizomes, tubers or bulbs give them a strong start each

spring, as well as the power to grow again if their leaves are lost or damaged. Just preventing seed formation on perennials is not enough to get rid of them; you must either dig up all of the underground structures or force them to use up their food reserves by repeatedly removing their aboveground growth.

Each time you remove the stems and leaves, the plant must draw on stored carbohydrates to send up new growth. Because the new growth soon starts to photosynthesize more food for the plant, frequent weeding—every 7 to 14 days—is best. If you can't weed that often through the spring and summer, weed before flowering and again later in the season. Perennials build up their food reserves in late summer and autumn to prepare for the next year's early growth. Cut them down until they are too weak to survive winter.

SUSTAINED ATTACK
Mowing an area repeatedly until the new sprouts stop shooting can help control both biennial and perennial weeds. The roots may be too depleted to survive winter.

INVASIVE PLANTS
Weeds can be a big problem at the edges of the vegetable garden, where grasses and a variety of weeds may creep in. A mowing strip will help, but the best way to deal with these weeds is by hand, giving them regular attention before they can take over.

Controlling Weeds in the Vegetable Garden

While prevention can go a long way toward reducing weeds, a few are sure to pop up during the season. When they do sneak past your defenses, you have several ways to get rid of them.

COMPETITION

A smother crop is a plant that grows well when crowded. By growing close together, smother crops choke out weeds. If you have a really bad weed infestation, you may have to take the vegetable garden out of production for a year to let the smother crop do its job.

Hand-pulling and Hoeing

When it comes to killing weeds among your crops, the tried-and-true methods are pulling them out by hand or hacking them down with some type of blade (usually a hoe). You can also try flaming them, if you take care not to damage the vegetable plants nearby, but don't be fooled into thinking that one weeding will get you through the season.

The secret to control is persistence. Take a little time each week and pull up weeds as they emerge. Weaken perennial weeds by forcing them to use up food stores to regrow. And no weed should ever get the chance to set seed. Best of all, you'll use less time and energy weeding a little each week than you would if you waited until the weeds were a tall, menacing, seed-filled mess.

Smothering Weeds

Weeds like the same things as your vegetables: light, water and nutrients. If you're willing to leave part of the garden unplanted for a season, you can deprive

HAND-WEEDING

There's nothing so discouraging to weeds as a constant personal attack.

RAISED BEDS

Weeds are easier to control when the bed is raised, as lawn grasses are less invasive. Also, hand-weeding in a raised bed is easier because it places much less strain on your back.

the weeds of all three with a smother crop. Such a crop must do its work before or after the vegetable season.

A smother crop of a winter annual grass such as winter wheat *Triticum aestivum* covers the soil in the autumn as well as in early spring, but you can turn it under early enough for it to break down (2–4 weeks before you plan to plant). Other effective smother crops include grasses, such as annual rye *Lolium multiflorum* and winter rye *Secale cereale*, as well as some broad-leaved plants, such as buckwheat *Fagopyrum esculentum*. Plant buckwheat in spring, turn it under before it goes to seed, then follow it with another buckwheat crop in summer and winter wheat in autumn.

If your vegetable garden backs onto a fence, don't plant right against the fence. Use a mulch along the fence or create a barrier with black plastic or cardboard and check regularly for invasive weeds.

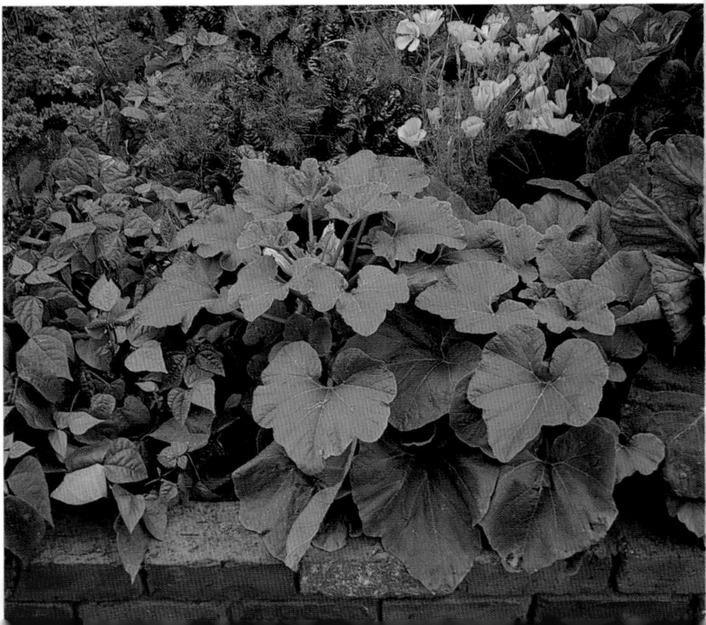

CONTROLLING WEEDS IN THE FRUIT GARDEN

Unlike a vegetable garden, which you replant each year, fruit plantings are relatively permanent, so make sure the area is as free of weeds and weed seeds as possible before you start planting.

AUTUMN SWEETNESS
Mulch under grape vines to control weeds. Once the vines are well established, reduce the water supply and keep the soil dryish.

STRAWBERRIES

Strawberries send out runners to produce new plants, so any mulch you use must be sparse enough to let the runners reach the soil. Straw is a popular choice, as are pine needles. Spread the mulch about 1 inch (2.5 cm) thick. Pull out any weeds as they emerge through the mulch. Add another 1–2 inches (2.5–5 cm) of mulch in the autumn to protect the plants during the winter.

BERRY BUSHES AND BRAMBLES

A hoe and about 4 inches (10 cm) of mulch are your best tools for keeping down weeds around berry bushes and brambles (such as raspberries and blackberries). You'll especially appreciate the long handle on your hoe if you grow bramble cultivars with thorns. Training brambles to a post-and-wire trellis will make weed control easier.

FRUIT TREES

Your fruit trees are probably already surrounded by one of the best weed-control materials: grass. Even commercial orchards have returned to growing grass between the rows of trees because it

EASIER WEEDING

If berry vines are supported on wires, it is much easier to keep the weeds down among them. Once the area around the plants is cleared, apply a layer of mulch to discourage regrowth and to conserve moisture.

stops the soil from washing or blowing away and competes well against weeds. Remove the grass in a 2-foot (60-cm) ring around the base of each tree to make mowing simpler and reduce the chance of damaging the trunk with the mower. Mulch the bare area with a good layer of straw, compost, pine needles or some other organic mulch. Keep it away from the trunk and rake it away in autumn to keep rodents from nesting in it.

CLEAN FRUIT

Besides keeping the weeds down, a good layer of mulch around your strawberries will keep the fruit from coming in contact with the soil.

Part Five

Plant Directory

Vegetables

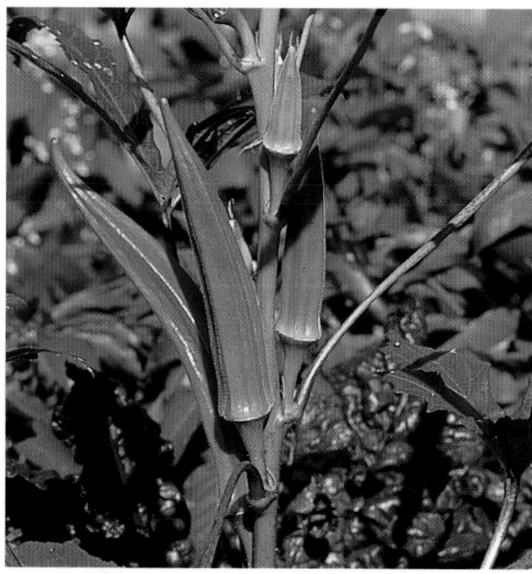

HARDINESS
Zones 5 and warmer.

DAYS TO MATURITY
50–60 frost-free days.

COMMENTS
Cultivars include 'Annie Oakley', 'Clemson Spineless' and 'Emerald'.

OKRA (GUMBO)

THE ESSENTIAL INGREDIENT IN GUMBO, OKRA IS ALSO ADMIRED FOR ITS LOVELY, HOLLYHOCK-LIKE FLOWERS. IT THRIVES IN HOT WEATHER.

Position Plant in full sun in fertile and well-drained soil; pH 6.5–7.5.

Cultivation Sow seed when frost danger is past and the soil is warm. Prewarming the soil with black plastic mulch will speed up germination. In cooler areas, start seed indoors in individual pots 2–4 weeks before the last frost and set out when the weather is settled. Set out or thin to stand 12–15 inches (30–37.5 cm) apart. Grows quickly in warm weather and needs both food and water; irrigate in dry spells and give it compost tea or fish emulsion once a month.

Pests and diseases Little troubled by pests, but aphids are a sign of water stress. In cool areas, okra will not bear as prolifically as in warm climates. Red-podded cultivars, such as 'Burgundy', are often the most prolific producers.

Harvesting and storage Clip or pinch off young pods when they are 1–4 inches (2.5–10 cm) long and still soft. Larger pods will be woody. Harvest daily in warm weather. Okra freezes well.

Special tips Blossoms are edible.

HARDINESS
All Zones for green (spring) onions; Zones 3 and warmer for bulb onions, but choose cultivars to suit the day length.

DAYS TO MATURITY
60–115 days from transplanting. Green (spring) onions from sets can be harvested in as few as 35 days.

COMMENTS
More mature plants can withstand severe frost.

ONION

A STAPLE FOR MANY CENTURIES, THE BULB OF THE VERSATILE ONION PROVIDES PLENTY OF GOOD EATING IN LITTLE GARDEN SPACE.

Position Plant in full sun in well-drained soil that is rich in humus; pH 6.0–7.5.

Cultivation For summer harvest, sow indoors 3–4 months before last spring frost and set out 3–4 inches (7.5–10 cm) apart a month before last frost. For onions to store, sow thickly a month before the last frost and thin to 3–4 inches (7.5–10 cm) apart. For quicker crops or in colder areas, grow onions from small bulbs called "sets," available at garden centers or by mail. Plant sets 1 inch (2.5 cm) deep and 2 inches (5 cm) apart, pulling every second one when ready for use as green (spring) onions. Grow onions in beds or small patches to maximize yield in small spaces. Keep well weeded because they are easily shaded out. Irrigate and fertilize with fish emulsion or compost tea to encourage good early growth, which will determine eventual bulb size.

Pests and diseases Garden-grown onions have few pest or disease problems. Where onion maggots are troublesome, use row covers supported by hoops to prevent egg-laying by the onion maggot fly. Rotate onions and their relatives with other crops. Cold weather may

Bulbing onion cultivars can be pulled before the bulbs have begun to form and used as green (spring) onions.

prevent bulb formation, but failure to form bulbs more often indicates use of an unsuitable onion cultivar. Bulb formation is triggered by day length. Long-day cultivars are best in areas farther from the equator; short-day types in areas closer.

Harvesting and storage Pull green (spring) onions and onions for fresh use as needed. For storage onions, wait until most tops have fallen over, then knock over any upright stalks with a rake. Pull the onions 1–2 days later and let them dry on the ground. (In wet weather, dry them on open mesh or shallow trays in a well-ventilated place.) Use onions with thick, green stems immediately; they will not store. When onions are thoroughly dry, braid the tops and hang in a cool, dry place or clip off the tops and store bulbs in mesh bags or slat-sided boxes.

Special tips For space-saving green onions, sow several seeds in one pot and transplant later as a clump.

Related plants

Potato onion *A. cepa*, Aggregatum Group Also called multiplier onion. Forms a cluster of underground bulbs. Usually harvested the second year after planting. Eat the larger bulbs and replant the smaller ones.

Pickling onion *A. cepa* Also called pearl onion. Cultivars produce small

Red onions are also called Italian or Spanish onions. These red-skinned cultivars are often sweeter than types with white or yellow skins.

bulbs that are cooked or pickled whole. Try 'Snow Baby' and 'Early Aviv'.

Red (Italian or Spanish) onion *A. cepa* Cultivars include 'Bennie's Red', 'Rossa di Milano' and 'Red Florence' (elongated shape).

Slicing onion *A. cepa* Refers to mild-flavored onions grown for fresh use. Most store poorly. Grow Vidalia types (such as 'Texas Grano') in warmer areas, and Walla Walla types (such as 'Walla Walla Sweet') in colder ones.

Spanish onion *A. cepa* Large bulbs with mild flavor, usually with yellow or white skin. In favorable climates, bulbs can weigh up to 5 pounds (2.5 kg).

Egyptian onion *A. cepa*, Proliferum Group Also called tree onion, top onion or catawissa onion. Edible, but strongly flavored. Instead of flowers, it produces a curious-looking head of small onion bulbs, some of which can be planted in spring or autumn to produce the next year's crop.

Welsh onion *A. fistulosum* Also called ciboule, Japanese bunching onion or green (spring) onion. Does not form a bulb, but rather a slender, white stalk.

HARDINESS
All Zones; can be planted in autumn in Zones 6 and warmer.

DAYS TO MATURITY
120–150 days; or pull earlier to eat as green (spring) onions.

COMMENTS
Will withstand moderate frost. Named cultivars are not generally available; most suppliers offer generic French (or golden) shallots.

SHALLOT

A RELATIVE OF THE ONION, THE SHALLOT PRODUCES SMALL, FIRM BULBS THAT KEEP LIKE GARLIC BUT ARE MUCH SWEETER AND MILDER IN FLAVOR.

Position Plant in full sun in well-drained soil that is rich in humus. Shallots will tolerate all but the most acid soil.

Cultivation Shallots do not grow from seed but from bulblets or "sets." Plant 2–4 weeks before the last spring frost, 1 inch (2.5 cm) deep and 4–6 inches (10–15 cm) apart. Keep cultivated or mulch and water regularly to encourage strong early growth. Each set will divide and produce eight to 10 shallots. Where climate permits, autumn planting will produce larger shallots the following summer.

Pests and diseases To avoid root maggots, do not plant where shallots or their relatives, such as onions or leeks, have grown the previous year. Dry conditions or poor soil produces scrawny shallots. Work in plenty of compost or well-rotted manure and water regularly.

Harvesting and storage When the tops are nearly dry, pull out the plants and dry the bulbs in a well-ventilated, sunny area. Store by hanging in a cool, dry place, or clip off the stems and store the bulbs in mesh bags.

HARDINESS
Zones 3 and warmer; grow as a winter vegetable in mild areas.

DAYS TO MATURITY
70–105 days in the garden.

COMMENTS
'King Richard' and 'Titan' are early leeks; 'Carina' and 'Alaska' are good for overwintering. "Baby" leeks can be harvested earlier.

LEEK

THIS ONION RELATIVE IS GROWN FOR ITS STOUT, FLAVORFUL STEM. IT HOLDS WELL IN THE GROUND FOR LATE HARVESTING.

Position Plant in full sun in loose, very rich, well-drained soil; pH 6.0–7.5.

Cultivation Start seed indoors up to 12 weeks before last spring frost. Transplant from seed flats to small, individual pots when large enough to handle. This produces larger transplants and better leeks. Set out after frost, 6 inches (15 cm) apart, in a trench 6 inches (15 cm) deep or in holes made with a hoe handle or dibble, covering all but 1 inch (2.5 cm) or so of the leaves. Keep well weeded. As leeks grow, fill in the trench gradually or, if planted on level soil, "hill" them by drawing soil up around the stems. This produces a longer white stem, which is the edible part. You can also use a deep mulch to blanch the stems. Keep the soil moist, especially early in the season.

Pests and diseases To avoid damage by root maggots, do not plant leeks where other members of the onion family have grown the previous year. Short, tough stems indicate either a lack of moisture or soil fertility or inadequate hilling.

Harvesting and storage Dig up or pull out leeks when they are large enough for use. Before a hard

Feed your leeks regularly to ensure that their growth is unchecked and that they will have plump, tender stems.

freeze, mulch the bed heavily to keep it diggable through winter. Harvest overwintered leeks before spring growth begins. Pack leeks in damp sand or peat moss and store in a cool place. Harvested leeks stored in this way will keep for 6–8 weeks.

Special tips Young plants will tolerate light frost; mature ones, severe frost. Cultivars include 'Carina' (large, thick stem, matures in late autumn, very cold-tolerant); 'Splendid' (long, thin, tender stem, produces high yields); 'Titan' (long, thick stem, grows quickly).

Related plants

Asian leek *A. tuberosum* Also called Chinese leek, Chinese chives or garlic chives. A hardy perennial grown for its mildly garlic-flavored leaves, which are used in stir-fries and soups. The spring flowers are also edible. Named cultivars are not generally available.

Chives *A. schoenoprasum* A popular herb that can be grown in a pot or as an edging for the vegetable garden. The long, cylindrical leaves are usually cut and used as a flavoring or garnish. The mauve flowers are also edible and make a pretty garnish.

HARDINESS
Zones 3 and warmer; must be prechilled before planting to form bulbs in warmer climates.

DAYS TO MATURITY
120–150 days for spring plantings; autumn plantings are harvested the following summer.

COMMENTS
Crush and soak garlic to make an effective garden spray for insects.

GARLIC

GARLIC IS AN EASY-TO-GROW AND REWARDING CROP. PLANT IT IN AUTUMN TO HARVEST THE FOLLOWING SUMMER.

Position Plant in full sun or partial shade, but bulbs will be smaller in partial shade. Likes well-drained, fertile soil that is rich in humus; pH 6.0–7.0.

Cultivation Best planted in autumn, 2–4 weeks before first frost. Plant individual cloves, pointed end up, 1–2 inches (2.5–5 cm) deep and 4–6 inches (10–15 cm) apart. Deeper planting is best where frequent freezing and thawing may cause heaving (when the soil lifts due to temperature changes and plants are dislodged from their roots). Apply fish emulsion or compost tea in spring to encourage vigorous growth. Keep the bed cultivated or mulched. Irrigate until tops begin to brown, then withhold water to let the plant dry naturally.

Pests and diseases Little troubled by pests, but reduce threat of root maggots by not planting where garlic or its relatives, such as onions and shallots, have been planted the previous year. Humid conditions at harvest may induce neck rot. Use these heads immediately or freeze, as they do not keep well.

Harvesting and storage Use spring shoots and flower stems chopped in salads and dips, as you would

Garlic continued

The soft drying stems of garlic plants are easy to braid in the traditional way. The braided bunches are then hung up to finish drying out.

chives. Pull mature garlic plants when about 75 percent of the foliage is brown; tie in bundles and dry in a dark, well-ventilated place. Braid for storage or clip stems and store in mesh bags in a dry, cool area. Freeze peeled cloves; thaw slowly before using.

Special tips Pot garlic heads or cloves and grow indoors for wintertime use as greens.

Related plants

Elephant garlic *A. ampeloprasum* Elephant garlic is milder and has larger heads (up to a pound [500 g]) than other types of garlic. Plant deeper than garlic, up to 4 inches (10 cm) deep.

Hard-neck garlic *A. sativum*, var. *ophioscorodon* Also called serpent garlic, top-setting garlic or rocambole. Prized in oriental cuisine, it produces a coiled flower stem. Remove the stem to direct growth to the roots. Cloves are large and form in a single ring around a central, woody stem. Cultivars include 'Russian Red' and 'Chet's'.

Soft-neck garlic *A. sativum* The standard commercial type, also called artichoke garlic. Cloves form in an overlapping pattern, like the scales of an artichoke. More productive than hard-neck types, but the cloves are smaller. Cultivars include 'French Silverskin' and 'California Early'.

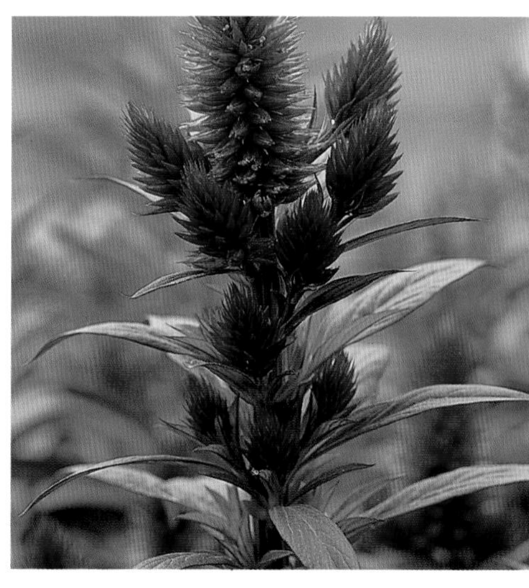

HARDINESS
Zones 4 and warmer, but needs some protection in colder areas.

DAYS TO MATURITY
Requires 40–55 frost-free days, although thinnings can be harvested earlier.

COMMENTS
Other common names include Chinese spinach, Joseph's-coat, leaf amaranth, tampala and vegetable amaranth.

AMARANTH

GROW AMARANTH FOR ITS NUTRITIOUS LEAVES, WHICH CAN BE EATEN BOTH RAW IN SALADS AND COOKED AS GREENS.

Position Prefers heat and full sun. Not fussy, but prefers soil rich in humus; pH 6.0–7.0.

Cultivation Sow seed after frost, when soil has warmed. Barely cover and keep moist until germinated. In short-season areas, start amaranth indoors 4 weeks before last frost date. Water freely and thin to 18 inches (45 cm) apart.

Pests and diseases Protect plants from flea and cucumber beetles with row covers, or spray with a garlic infusion. Rotate plantings to avoid stem rot from soilborne diseases. In cooler climates, it may require soil-warming plastic mulch.

Harvesting and storage Harvest whole plants as thinnings; pick the young, tender leaves from mature plants. Harvest frequently to encourage new growth. Can be frozen in the same way as spinach.

Special tips Plant away from cabbage-family plants or cucumbers to reduce pest damage; or plant adjacent to those crops to serve as a "trap crop." There are no named cultivars, but oriental seed companies often carry natural variants with light green, dark green or red-striped leaves.

CELERY

IT ISN'T EASY TO GROW, BUT WITH A LITTLE ATTENTION TO ITS NEEDS, CELERY DOES BEAUTIFULLY IN THE BACKYARD.

Position Plant in full sun in moisture-retentive, rich soil, with adequate calcium and plenty of well-rotted manure or compost worked in; pH 5.5–7.5.

Cultivation Start seed indoors 4–6 weeks before the last spring frost. Germination and seedling growth are slow. Keep seedlings watered and do not expose to temperatures below 55°F (13°C), which can cause plants to bolt to seed. Set plants out when the weather is well settled (about a month after the last frost), 10–12 inches (25–30 cm) apart. Because the roots are relatively shallow, do not allow the soil to dry out; feed the plants with compost tea or fish emulsion at least once a month. If desired, you can blanch celery before harvest by slipping a bottomless paper bag over the plant and tying it in place, or by putting wide boards on edge on both sides of the celery row and holding the boards in place with stakes. The idea is to keep the sun off the stems. This whitens them and keeps them from becoming tough, although self-blanching cultivars are available. Excessive heat, lack of moisture or low soil fertility will also result in tough, stringy celery.

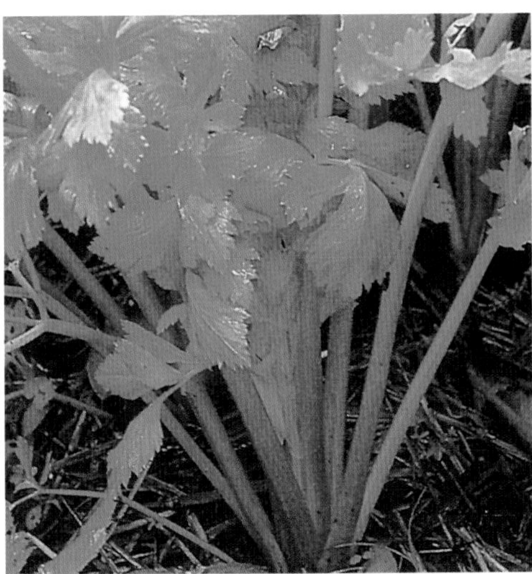

HARDINESS
Zones 5 and warmer, except where temperatures in early summer drop below 55°F (13°C). Autumn and winter crop in mild areas.

DAYS TO MATURITY
80–105 days.

COMMENTS
Young plants cannot tolerate frequent falls in temperature below 55°F (13°C); mature plants withstand severe frost.

Single stems of 'Improved Utah' can be picked as needed to give a continuous harvest of small quantities of celery for 2–3 months.

Pests and diseases Rotate plantings with other crops to avoid blight problems. Handpick off parsleyworms or celeryworms (green caterpillars with yellow and black bands).

Harvesting and storage Cut celery for immediate use just below soil level. In cooler areas, harvesting can be extended if plants are protected by an insulating mulch of straw and covered with opaque white polythene. However, before a hard freeze, pull up the entire plant and roots, and store, packed in dry leaves or straw, in a cool cellar or garage.

Special tips Plant celery in well-manured beds, three or four plants abreast and 10–12 inches (25–30 cm) apart. Dense growth will shade out weeds and automatically blanch the celery. Cultivars include 'Improved Utah' and 'Tendercrisp', both green cultivars, while 'Stokes Golden Plume' is a yellow celery. 'Giant Red' has stalks tinged with red, while 'Lathom Self-Blanching' has been bred to resist bolting to seed.

HARDINESS
Zones 5 and warmer. Use as an autumn and winter crop in mild areas.

DAYS TO MATURITY
110–120 days; can withstand increasingly severe frost for the last 30–45 days.

COMMENTS
Cultivars include 'Large Smooth Prague', which is widely available.

CELERIAC

IN SALADS, SOUPS AND STEWS OR AS A COOKED VEGETABLE, THE ROOT OF CELERIAC HAS ALL THE FLAVOR OF CELERY.

Position Plant in full sun in rich, moisture-retentive soil, with adequate calcium and plenty of well-rotted manure or compost worked in; pH 5.5–7.5.

Cultivation Start seed indoors 6–8 weeks before last spring frost and set out, 10–12 inches (25–30 cm) apart, when the threat of frost is past. Celeriac can be direct-seeded, but it germinates slowly and can be overtaken by weeds. Keep bed well weeded and watered. Apply compost tea or fish emulsion at least once a month.

Pests and diseases Rotate plantings of celeriac and celery with other crops to avoid the blights to which they are both vulnerable. Handpick off celeryworms or parsleyworms (green caterpillars with yellow and black bands). Inadequate moisture will yield small, tough, fibrous roots.

Harvesting and storage Harvest the turnip-like root when large enough for your needs. Harvest all plants before the ground freezes; cut stems close to the roots and store like turnips (see page 155) in damp sawdust or sand in a cool place.

Special tips Other common names include celery root, German celery, knob celery, turnip celery.

Arachis hypogaea FABACEAE

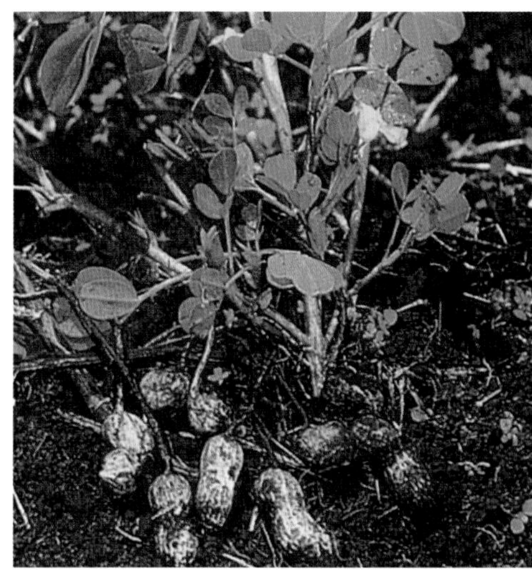

HARDINESS
Zones 7 and warmer, but may produce light crops in Zones 5–6.

DAYS TO MATURITY
110–120 frost-free days.

COMMENTS
Other common names include goober, groundnut and pindar. Cultivars include 'Jumbo Virginia', 'Spanish' and 'Tennessee Red'.

PEANUT

NOT A NUT BUT A PROTEIN-RICH MEMBER OF THE LEGUME FAMILY, THE PEANUT CAN BE ROASTED, BOILED OR MADE INTO A SAUCE.

Position Plant in full sun in loose, well-drained soil rich in humus and with adequate calcium; pH 5.8–6.2.

Cultivation In warmer climates, sow seed 1 inch (2.5 cm) deep and 3 inches (7.5 cm) apart after last spring frost when soil is warm, and thin to 1 foot (30 cm) apart. In cooler areas, start in individual pots 4–6 weeks before last frost and set out, 1 foot (30 cm) apart, in soil that has been prewarmed with black plastic mulch. Plant whole shells, or remove shell first, taking care not to damage the papery skin. Keep weeded. Do not mulch; if plastic mulch is used to warm soil, it must be removed when the peanuts flower. Stems bearing fertilized flowers dive into soil around the plant, and a peanut forms at the end of each stem.

Pests and diseases Little troubled.

Harvesting and storage Dig up plants when frost has killed the foliage. Hang by the roots in a well-ventilated place until the pods have completely dried. Roast shelled nuts, or roast them in the shell by soaking clean pods in salted water for several hours, then heating in a 300°F (150°C) oven until completely dry and crisp (about 1 hour).

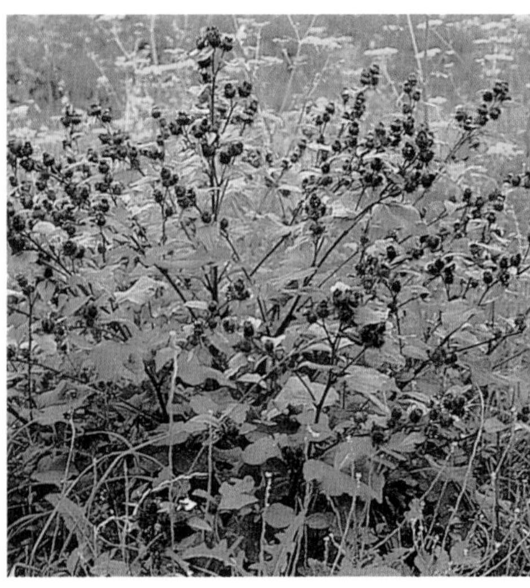

HARDINESS
All Zones, although the eventual length of the root will depend on the length of the growing season.

DAYS TO MATURITY
120 days or more.

COMMENTS
Other common names include gobo and nagau pong.

BURDOCK

MILDLY BITTER AND AN EXCELLENT ADDITION TO SOUPS AND STEWS, BURDOCK IS A NUTRITIOUS ROOT VEGETABLE.

Position Plant in full sun. Requires deep, well-prepared soil, as the roots can grow to 2 feet (60 cm) or more in length; pH 6.0–7.3.

Cultivation Sow seed in spring for an autumn harvest, or in late summer for overwintering. Thin the plants to 2–3 feet (60–90 cm) apart. Cultivated burdock looks much like its relative, the common burdock *A. minus,* with large, heart-shaped leaves, but it can grow to 8 feet (2.4 m) tall. Cultivate shallowly until the plant is large enough to shade out weeds.

Pests and diseases Burdock is rarely troubled by pests. In rocky or heavy soil, roots may fork or become deformed, making harvesting difficult. Planting in raised beds will help to avoid this problem.

Harvesting and storage Harvest after autumn frosts, or leave roots in the ground for spring harvest. Burdock stores well in a cool cellar if you treat it in the same way as you would turnips or carrots (see pages 155 and 180 respectively).

HARDINESS
All Zones, but best in Zones 5 and warmer.

DAYS TO MATURITY
150–180 days in first year where the season permits; otherwise, first harvest is in the second year.

COMMENTS
Severe frost will kill horseradish leaves but will not damage the roots. Young leaves of horseradish can be added to salads.

HORSERADISH

HORSERADISH IS A HARDY PERENNIAL GROWN FOR ITS ROOTS, WHICH ARE GRATED FOR USE AS A TANGY CONDIMENT.

Position Plant in full sun in well-drained, deep and preferably light soil; pH 6.0–7.0.

Cultivation Plant this invasive vegetable in a bottomless bucket sunk into the soil. Plant root divisions in spring, 2 inches (5 cm) deep and 12–18 inches (30–45 cm) apart. Weed or mulch after the leaves appear above the ground. Even soil moisture encourages rapid growth and large roots.

Pests and diseases Flea beetles sometimes attack but rarely do more than cosmetic damage. Avoid growing in heavy, shallow or stony soil. May be difficult to eradicate or move once established—new plants grow from root bits left in the soil.

Harvesting and storage Dig up roots when 12–15 inches (30–37.5 cm) long, up to 2 inches (5 cm) thick and fairly smooth. Dig up as needed until the ground freezes. Store whole roots in sand or sawdust in a cool place.

Special tips Pack smaller roots in sawdust and save for planting next year. Cut tops flat and bottoms at an angle, so you put them in the ground right-side up, so producing straighter and more uniform roots.

Asparagus

THIS CLASSIC SPRING VEGETABLE REQUIRES WELL-PREPARED SOIL WITH HIGH FERTILITY. A WELL-MAINTAINED PATCH CAN YIELD ABUNDANTLY FOR DECADES.

Position Avoid low-lying areas subject to heavy dew and morning fogs, to reduce the possibility of rust. Prefers full sun, but will tolerate some shade. Likes fertile, well-drained soil; will tolerate slightly alkaline pH (6.5–6.8) and saline soils.

Cultivation Grow from seed started indoors or in an outdoor seedbed; or hasten the first harvest by using year-old crowns. Dig a trench 8 inches (20 cm) deep in well-composted and well-limed soil. Place the crowns in the trench 15 inches (37.5 cm) apart, fanning the roots in all directions. Cover with soil to half the depth of the trench. When foliage peeks above ground level, finish filling the trench with soil. Mulch or cultivate shallowly and irrigate during dry spells. Keeping the foliage healthy and lush after harvest is critical to the next year's crop. Each autumn, cut back the dead ferny foliage and mulch heavily with compost or straw-rich manure. Early each spring, rake off all but 1–2 inches (2.5–5 cm) of mulch to let the spears emerge.

Pests and diseases Asparagus rust can be a serious problem in damp

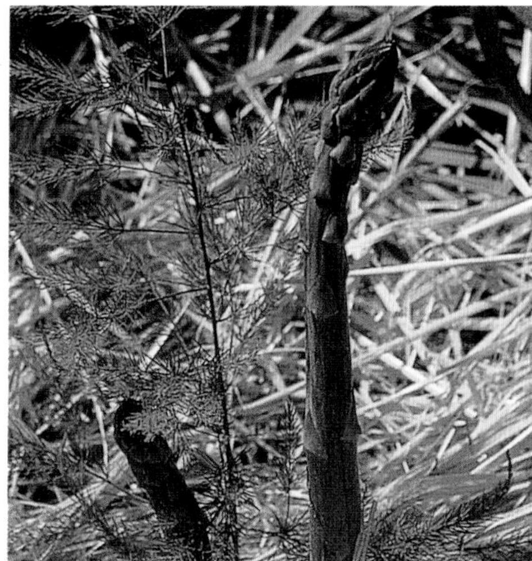

HARDINESS
Zones 3 and warmer; asparagus grows best in areas where the soil freezes in winter.

DAYS TO MATURITY
Gardeners used to wait until the third year to take a first small harvest of asparagus; newer hybrid cultivars can be picked sparingly for 1–2 weeks in the second year. A mature patch can be harvested for as long as 10 weeks.

A dense stand of ferny fronds (left) grows up after you stop harvesting the emerging spears. The foliage helps the plants to build up the nutrients needed for the next crop.

locations; use rust-resistant cultivars. Reduce damage from asparagus beetles, which overwinter in garden debris and emerge in spring to feed on the young spears, by burning or hot-composting the old asparagus foliage and cultivating the asparagus patch shallowly before applying the autumn mulch. Perennial weeds and grasses can be troublesome in the asparagus patch. Be sure the area is free of perennial weeds before planting, and mulch or cultivate to stay ahead of them.

Harvesting and storage Carefully cut the spears at ground level or simply snap them off, leaving any woody stem behind. Harvest while the tips of the spears are still tightly closed; in warm spring spells, this may mean daily harvesting. Bottle or freeze excess spears. A mature patch, say 5 years old, can yield 1 pound (500 g) or more of asparagus per foot (30 cm) of row.

Special tips In heavy soils, plant in raised beds to improve drainage. Lay crowns at ground level, rather than in trenches, and mound the soil over them. Cultivars include 'Jersey Centennial', a high-yielding hybrid; 'Martha Washington' and 'Mary Washington', rust-resistant old favorites; and 'Viking KB3', which is recommended for extremely hot or cold climates.

HARDINESS
All Zones.

DAYS TO MATURITY
40–50 days; thinnings can be harvested sooner. Will withstand moderate frost.

COMMENTS
Other common names include French spinach, mountain spinach and sea purslane.

ORACH

THE VIVID FOLIAGE OF RED ORACH MAKES IT AN ATTRACTIVE ADDITION TO BOTH ORNAMENTAL AND VEGETABLE GARDENS.

Position Plant in full sun. Not fussy, but prefers fertile, well-drained soil; pH 7.3–8.0.

Cultivation Sow seed 4–6 weeks before the last spring frost; thin to stand 8 inches (20 cm) apart, using the thinnings in salads. Like spinach, orach bolts to seed quickly in hot weather; unlike spinach, it will germinate and grow in warm weather. For an extended harvest, keep the flower heads pinched out. Frequent small plantings will assure plenty of young, tender leaves in spring, summer and autumn.

Pests and diseases Little troubled by pests. Pull bolting plants, as they can grow to 6 feet (1.8 m) or taller when in flower and may self-sow, becoming a weed problem.

Harvesting and storage Pick the succulent, young leaves as needed.

Special tips Red orach *A. hortensis* var. *rubra* (shown above) holds its color during cooking and is striking in salads and as a garnish. Named cultivars are not generally available, but seed companies offer variants based on leaf color, usually dark green, light green or red.

HARDINESS
Zones 7 and warmer.

DAYS TO MATURITY
120–150 frost-free days, but some leaves can be harvested earlier.

COMMENTS
Cultivars include 'Rubra', which has red-veined leaves and red stems. Other common names include Ceylon spinach and Indian spinach.

SPINACH, MALABAR

A VINING PLANT NATIVE TO TROPICAL AFRICA AND ASIA, MALABAR SPINACH HAS GLOSSY LEAVES THAT ARE USED IN THE SAME WAYS AS SPINACH.

Position Plant in full sun, near a fence or trellis, in moist soil that is rich in humus; pH 6.0–7.5.

Cultivation Start seed indoors up to 8 weeks before the last frost and set out after frost danger is well past. In warmer areas, seed can be planted *in situ*. Alternatively, grow from stem cuttings. Likes heat and grows slowly if at all until the temperature is to its liking. Set out plants 3 feet (90 cm) apart and provide a fence or trellis to support them. Water well in dry weather.

Pests and diseases Little troubled by pests. In warm climates, Malabar spinach can spread to 30 feet (9 m) in a season, overrunning small gardens, but a spread of 6–10 feet (1.8–3 m) is more common.

Harvesting and storage Pick the fresh leaves as needed; in ideal weather it regrows rapidly.

Special tips Malabar spinach grows quickly and can be treated as an annual climber in cooler areas. Try growing it as an ornamental cover over a trellis, arch or pergola, using the leaves as required.

Beta vulgaris subsp. *cicla* CHENOPODIACEAE

HARDINESS
Zones 3 and warmer; grow as a winter vegetable in mild areas.

DAYS TO MATURITY
50–60 days; thinnings can be harvested sooner.

COMMENTS
Other common names include leaf beet, silverbeet. Cultivars include 'White King', 'Fordhook Giant', 'Rhubarb Chard' (a red-stemmed cultivar).

SWISS CHARD

VIGOROUS AND EASY TO GROW, A SINGLE PLANTING OF SWISS CHARD CAN PROVIDE A FULL SEASON OF FRESH LEAVES. USE IT AS YOU WOULD SPINACH, OR PLANT IT IN THE FLOWER GARDEN FOR ITS VIVID COLOR.

Position Plant in full sun or, in warm areas, partial shade. Not fussy, but prefers rich, well-drained soil; pH 6.0–6.8.

Cultivation Sow 1–2 weeks before last spring frost. Plant ½ inch (12 mm) deep and firm the soil with the back of a hoe. Thin to stand 8–12 inches (20–30 cm) apart, using the thinnings in salads or transplanting them to new beds. Cultivate, and water regularly to keep your plants growing strongly.

Pests and diseases Little troubled by pests. Row covers will deter flea beetles. Swiss chard is fairly drought tolerant, but water stress results in tough stems.

Harvesting and storage Pick the large outer leaves by pulling stems from the base with a slight twist. Leave the center to sprout new leaves. Leaves are usually cooked separately from the wide inner rib, which is often steamed and eaten like asparagus. You can freeze the leaves as you would spinach.

Special tips Swiss chard is attractive and has a neat growing habit. Interplant it with flowers for an ornamental and edible border.

HARDINESS
Beets thrive in almost any climate, but where summers are hot (Zones 8 and warmer), grow them as an autumn, late winter and early spring crop.

DAYS TO MATURITY
55–70 days in the garden, or sooner if you grow quick-maturing cultivars such as 'Little Egypt' after starting seedlings indoors.

BEET

DON'T WASTE BEET LEAVES—THEY ARE DELICIOUS. STEAM OR LIGHTLY FRY IN OIL AS YOU WOULD SPINACH, OR USE THE YOUNG LEAVES RAW IN SALADS.

Position Plant in full sun in well-drained, rich, neutral soil, free of stones. If soil is heavy or shallow, grow only round cultivars; long-rooted ones may be deformed or tough at maturity; pH 6.0–7.5.

Cultivation Beet seeds are compound—each "seed" actually contains as many as a half-dozen seeds. For this reason, many gardeners sow beets sparingly to reduce thinning tasks. But because beets are known for spotty germination, other gardeners sow them heavily to assure a full stand. The middle course is a moderately heavy seeding after first soaking the seeds in tepid water for several hours to encourage germination. Plant 1 inch (2.5 cm) deep and 2–4 inches (5–10 cm) apart, about 1 month before the last spring frost. Firm the seedbed well with your feet or the back of a hoe. Thin the young plants when they are 2–3 inches (5–7.5 cm) tall. Beets are among the few root vegetables that can be transplanted, so you can move any excess seedlings to another spot, taking care not to double over the taproot when transplanting. The thinnings can also be used as salad greens. Beets tend to

Beet continued

All types of beet can be served raw or cooked. Start harvesting when the beets are about 1 inch (2.5 cm) in diameter.

become woody and tasteless when left in the ground too long; small monthly sowings will give you a continuous supply of tender, sweet beets for the table. The exceptions are cultivars bred for the root cellar, such as 'Lutz Winter Keeper'. Plant these in midsummer, at least 2 months before the first autumn frost (or in the spring if your growing season is short), and leave in the ground until a hard frost threatens. Beets need regular watering to keep them tender and to prevent interior discoloring that results from uneven soil moisture.

Pests and diseases Row covers will thwart flea beetles and leafminers. Discourage the disease leafspot by not growing beets where they or their relatives, such as spinach and chard, have been grown in the previous year. Beets do poorly in hot weather and dry soil; if your summers are scorchers, grow beets in the cool seasons, including winter in mild-climate areas.

Harvesting and storage Harvest greens as soon as they are large enough for use. Harvest beets as "babies" when they are 1 inch (2.5 cm) or more in diameter; check by gently probing the soil at the plant's base. When removing the tops, leave 1 inch (2.5 cm) of stem attached to the roots to prevent

'Golden Beet', with its golden orange flesh, adds a gourmet touch to salads. Grate or julienne the flesh, which, like that of all beets, is rich in folic acid and vitamin C.

bleeding. Cook with stems attached and cut away the stems before serving. Pull beets for storage before a hard frost, cut tops close to the roots, and store in sand or sawdust in a cool place. Beets can also be bottled or pickled.

Special tips Grow small-rooted cultivars, such as those bred as specialty "baby beets," in a cluster without thinning. Plant two or three seeds together, each cluster 6 inches (15 cm) apart, and harvest when the beets reach eating size.

Related plants

Cylindrical beet *B. vulgaris* subsp. *vulgaris* Tapered roots, up to 7 inches (17.5 cm) long and 2 inches (5 cm) in diameter. Hill the crowns to keep the topmost part of the root from being exposed and toughened. 'Cylindra' and 'Formanova' are popular cultivars. They are easy to peel and slice into uniform pieces for pickling or bottling.

Golden beet *B. vulgaris* subsp. *vulgaris* Sweet and tender-fleshed, but golden orange in color. Prized for its unusual color, which does not "bleed" when cooked as red beets do. Plant golden beets more thickly than other types because they tend to germinate poorly. Cultivars include 'Golden' and 'Burpee's Golden'.

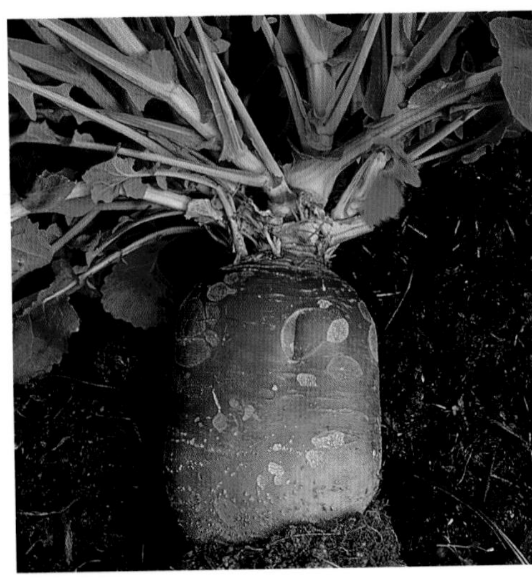

HARDINESS
Zones 3 and warmer; grow as a winter vegetable in mild areas.

DAYS TO MATURITY
90–110 days. Will withstand severe frost.

COMMENTS
Other common names include swede, swede turnip and yellow turnip.

RUTABAGA

A FAVORITE IN SCANDINAVIAN COUNTRIES, RUTABAGA IS A RUGGED GARDEN VEGETABLE THAT SHRUGS OFF THE COLD AND OTHER ADVERSE CONDITIONS.

Position Plant seed in full sun in fertile, well-drained soil. Will tolerate heavy soil better than most other root vegetables; pH 5.5–6.8.

Cultivation Sow 12–14 weeks before first autumn frost and thin to stand 4–6 inches (10–15 cm) apart. Cultivate early; the large leaves will quickly grow to shade out weeds.

Pests and diseases Rotate rutabaga and other root crops to avoid root maggots. Protect young plants from flea beetles with row covers; larger plants may suffer cosmetic damage, but that will not affect the yield.

Harvesting and storage Pull rutabagas when they are large enough for use. The greens are also edible. Harvest all roots before a hard freeze and store in damp sand or sawdust in a cool place. Rutabagas can be waxed to prevent wrinkling during storage. Trim the root and crown and dip them briefly in a pot of water with a layer of melted paraffin on top.

Special tips Cultivars include 'Altasweet' and 'Laurentian'. Rutabagas that reach maturity in hot weather can be tough.

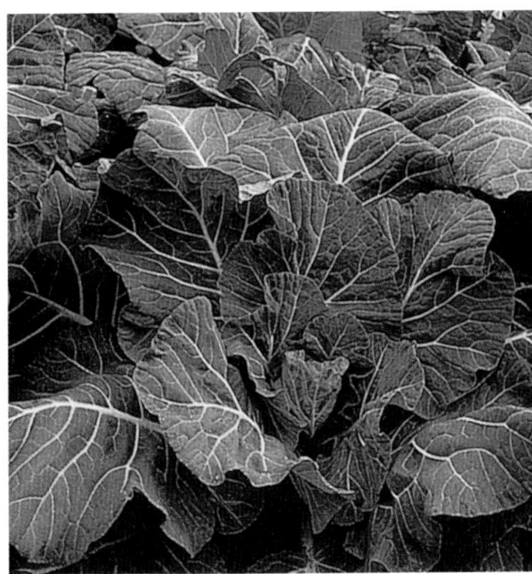

HARDINESS
Zones 3 and warmer; use as a winter vegetable in mild areas.

DAYS TO MATURITY
65–80 days, but thinnings can be harvested earlier and used as table greens. Young plants withstand light frost; mature ones, severe frost.

COMMENTS
Cultivars include 'Champion', 'Georgia Blue Stem' and 'Vates'.

COLLARD

A CABBAGE RELATIVE, COLLARD IS AMONG THE MOST NUTRITIOUS OF GARDEN GREENS.

Position Plant in full sun in fertile, moist soil with adequate calcium; pH 6.5–6.8.

Cultivation Sow seed in early spring and thin to 1½ feet (45 cm), or transplant as you would cabbage. Spring-planted collards, if well cared for, will keep producing past the first frost, but you can also plant in midsummer for an autumn crop only. Tolerates summer heat, but prefers cool weather, so mulch to keep the soil cool. Keep moist and apply fish emulsion or compost tea once a month for lush growth.

Pests and diseases Protect young plants from flea beetles and cabbageworms with row covers. Rotate collard and other cabbage-family members to avoid soilborne diseases. Direct-seeding too thickly may result in crowded and spindly plants. Thin gradually, first to 6 inches (15 cm), then 1 foot (30 cm), then 1½ feet (45 cm).

Harvesting and storage Harvest leaves as needed from bottom of plant, leaving the crown to sprout new leaves. Harvest crown before hard freeze for tender "baby collards." Freeze for winter use.

Special tips It can tolerate heat but is tastier after frost.

Brassica oleracea Acephala Group BRASSICACEAE

HARDINESS
All Zones; may overwinter in areas as cool as Zone 6.

DAYS TO MATURITY
55–65 days, but thinnings can be harvested sooner.

COMMENTS
Cultivars include 'Red Russian', a noncurly cultivar with purplish stems and leaves, 'Dwarf Blue Curled Vates' and 'Winterbor'. Common names include borecole and colewort.

KALE, CURLY

HARDY AND NUTRITIOUS, CURLY KALE PROVIDES TASTY GREENS LATE IN THE SEASON, EVEN UNDER A BLANKET OF SNOW.

Position Plant in full sun in fertile and well-drained soil, with adequate calcium; pH 6.5–6.8.

Cultivation Direct-seed 4–6 weeks before the last spring frost, about ½ inch (12 mm) deep. Thin to 1–1¼ feet (30–37.5 cm) apart; use the thinnings in salads. Cultivate shallowly or mulch to control weeds. Tolerates heat but prefers cool soil. Plant autumn crop 6–8 weeks before first frost, or later to overwinter. Give fish emulsion or compost tea liberally once a month to encourage lush leaf growth. Leaves toughen with age. Keep plant well picked; plant an autumn crop for a second harvest of tender leaves. Kale is sweeter after frost.

Pests and diseases Use row covers to protect young plants from flea beetles and cabbageworms, or use BT, a microbial insecticide, to control cabbageworms. Rotate kale and other cabbage-family plants to avoid soilborne diseases.

Harvesting and storage Pick leaves as needed from base of the plant; new ones will sprout from top.

Special tips Young plants will take a light frost; mature ones, severe frost.

HARDINESS
Zones 3 and warmer. Use as spring and autumn crops in cool-spring areas, and as a winter crop in mild climates.

DAYS TO MATURITY
50–120 days.

COMMENTS
Cultivars include the attractive 'Purple Head Improved' (left). The color fades during cooking.

CAULIFLOWER

CAULIFLOWERS ARE HEAVY FEEDERS THAT REQUIRE PLENTY OF WATER. THE HEADS OF WHITE VARIETIES MUST BE PROTECTED FROM THE SUN (BLANCHED) TO KEEP THEM WHITE.

Position Plant in full sun in rich, well-drained soil with plenty of calcium, and ample amounts of well-rotted manure or compost worked in; pH 6.0–7.0. A light dressing with lime will be necessary if the soil is too acidic. This will also reduce the likelihood of club root infection.

Cultivation Start spring crops indoors and do not set out too early; severe frost can cause the plant to form a "button" instead of a full-sized head. Space plants 1½–3 feet (45–90 cm) apart, and mulch to keep the soil cool. Start autumn crops 90–120 days before the autumn frost; set out when seedlings are 4–5 weeks old. Keep cauliflower growing steadily with plenty of water and one or more applications of fish emulsion or compost tea. When heads appear, use a clothespin to clip several large leaves together over the head to shade it and keep it white, or remove a large lower leaf and lay it over the developing head. "Self-blanching" cultivars grow their own "shading" leaves, but may still need help from you if high heat wilts the protective leaves. Cauliflower cultivars have also been bred

Cauliflower continued

Try planting aromatic herbs, such as pennyroyal, peppermint, sage and thyme, near your cauliflowers. It may help to deter insect pests.

to cater for various climates. For instance, where long, hot summers are the norm, choose early-maturing types to prevent the occurrence of problems, such as leaves forming among the curds, or the curds forming loose heads.

Pests and diseases Control cabbageworms with row covers, or a dose of BT, a microbial insecticide. Do this early, as it is difficult to control worms when they have become established inside the developing head. Row covers will also deter flea beetles on young plants; older, vigorous plants can withstand flea beetle attack. Rotate cabbage-family plantings to avoid soilborne diseases. In humid areas, heads may discolor during blanching due to excess moisture. Clip or tie the leaves together loosely to keep sunlight off the head, but do not cut off the circulation of air.

Harvesting and storage Cut heads before the curds begin to coarsen and separate. Cool weather may slow head development. When harvesting, leave a few leaves around the head to avoid breaking it. Cauliflower keeps, refrigerated, for up to 2 weeks. It can also be broken up into segments before being plunged into boiling water, refreshed in cold water and then frozen or used for making pickles.

As an interesting change, try growing some of the cauliflowers with colorful, more open heads that do not need to go through the blanching process.

Special tips Young plants will withstand a light frost; mature ones, moderate frost. 'Snow Crown' and 'Rushmore' are early cultivars; longer-season cultivars include 'Snowball Elite' and 'Andes'.

Related plants

Green cauliflower *B. oleracea*, Botrytis Group A specialty cauliflower with yellow-green, rather than white, curds. Green cauliflower, like purple cauliflower, is easier to grow than the white cultivars, since it does not require blanching. Popular cultivars include 'Alverda'.

Mini cauliflower *B. oleracea*, Botrytis Group Grow minis if space is limited, or if family needs dictate. They have smaller curds, measuring 4 inches (10 cm) across. Up to five can be grown in the space taken by one cauliflower of the usual size.

Purple cauliflower *B. oleracea*, Botrytis Group Like a cauliflower in habit, but it has looser flower heads, like broccoli. Purple cauliflower is milder and more tender than broccoli. The head has a deep purple cast, which disappears during cooking. No blanching is required. Cultivars include 'Purple Head Improved', 'Violet Queen' and 'Burgundy Queen'. The attractive purple flower heads can be used as a garnish or to add color to salads.

Cabbage

VALUED FOR THOUSANDS OF YEARS BECAUSE OF ITS HARDINESS AND STORAGE LIFE, CABBAGE CAN BE GROWN ALMOST ANYWHERE, ALTHOUGH IT IS SUBJECT TO ATTACK BY PESTS.

Position Plant in full sun. Any soil texture, provided it is well drained and fertile; pH 6.0–6.8.

Cultivation Grow as a spring and autumn crop in most areas, or as a winter crop where temperatures rarely drop below freezing. Avoid plantings that will mature in hot, dry weather. Start spring crops in a cool place indoors 6–8 weeks before the last spring frost and set out 4 weeks before the last frost. Give seedlings plenty of light and withhold fertilizer to discourage spindly growth. Set plants 1–1½ feet (30–45 cm) apart, depending on expected head size. In cool-summer areas, you can plant successive crops every month, ending with a storage-type cabbage about 2 months before autumn frost. Summer plantings may fail in warmer climates. Heavy mulch will help to retain moisture and keep the soil cool. Cabbage prefers rich soil; add compost or rotted manure before planting and apply fish emulsion or compost tea a month after planting.

Pests and diseases Use row covers or BT, a microbial insecticide, to control cabbageworms. Aphids are

HARDINESS
Zones 3 and warmer, with soil-cooling mulch in hotter climates. Use as a winter vegetable in mild areas.

DAYS TO MATURITY
60–110 days. Young cabbage plants will withstand light frost; mature ones more severe frost.

COMMENTS
Cabbage is an excellent source of calcium in the diet.

Standard cabbage types (above) form a tighter head than the Savoy cabbage (left), which has puckered or crinkled leaves. Savoy cabbage is also milder and sweeter.

a sign of heat or water stress; hose them off with a strong water spray or spray the plants thoroughly with insecticidal soap. Rotate cabbage-family plantings to avoid soilborne diseases. To avoid head splitting, use a shovel to sever roots on one side of the plant when the head is fully formed. This slows maturity and helps the cabbage to "hold" without splitting.

Harvesting and storage Harvest early cultivars as needed, as they do not store well. Harvest storage-type cabbage before a hard freeze and store, roots and all, in dry leaves in a cold cellar or garage. Can be pickled or made into sauerkraut.

Special tips Cut early and midseason cabbage high on the plant, leaving as many loose lower leaves as possible. As many as six small cabbages, called "cabbage sprouts," will form on the stem, providing a delicious second harvest. Grow cabbages with plants that won't compete for calcium.

Related plants

Flowering cabbage *B. oleracea*, Acephala Group This is actually a kale, rather than a cabbage. The flowering cabbage forms a loose head or rosette of colorful green and red, white or magenta leaves. It differs from flowering kale in that the leaves are smooth-edged rather

Cabbage continued

Red cabbage makes excellent coleslaw and soup, and is pretty enough to grow in the flower garden. Marigolds and aromatic herbs planted nearby may help to deter pests.

than frilly or ruffled. Both types are edible but are grown chiefly as ornamentals for autumn color (cool temperatures are needed for the striking colors to develop fully). Good cultivars are 'Osaka' hybrids (flowering cabbage) and 'Nagoya' hybrids (flowering kale).

Pointed head cabbage *B. oleracea*, Capitata Group Forms a cone-shaped head. It is quick-maturing, and has been popular for centuries. Cultivars include 'Early Jersey Wakefield', 'Greyhound' and 'Trumpet F1 Hybrid'.

Red cabbage *B. oleracea*, Capitata Group Attractive blue-purple leaves and red-purple heads with white veining. Cultivars include 'Ruby Perfection Hybrid', 'Red Acre' and 'Red Rookie'.

Round head cabbage *B. oleracea*, Capitata Group Globe-shaped or flattened round heads. Early cultivars include 'Darkri', 'Polar Green' and 'Emerald Acre'. Midseason cultivars include 'Stonehead' and 'Copenhagen Market'. Late or storage cultivars include 'Late Flat Dutch' and 'Danish Ballhead'.

Savoy cabbage *B. oleracea*, Capitata Group Puckered, crinkly, light green or blue-green leaves. Heads are often less tight than smooth-leaved cabbage, but the flavor is superior. Cultivars include 'Savoy King' and 'Savoy Ace'.

HARDINESS
Zones 3 and warmer; grow as a winter crop in mild areas. Where springs are cool, grow as a spring and autumn crop; otherwise, does best in autumn.

DAYS TO MATURITY
70–95 days.

COMMENTS
Calabrese broccoli (left) is perfect for small gardens. It produces new sprouts over a long period.

BROCCOLI

VIRTUALLY UNKNOWN IN HOME GARDENS 50 YEARS AGO, BROCCOLI IS NOW A COOL-WEATHER FAVORITE.

Position Full sun. Well-drained soil with plenty of calcium; pH 6.7–7.2.

Cultivation Start spring seedlings indoors, about 2 months before the last spring frost. Set out hardened-off transplants in the garden a month before the last frost. Space plants 1–2 feet (30–60 cm) apart; wider spacing will yield larger heads. Cultivate or mulch and keep the soil evenly moist. Lack of water will stress the plant, which may fail to head or may become vulnerable to insect pests. Sow autumn crops directly about 90 days before the first autumn frost, or transplant about 60 days before frost.

Pests and diseases Use cardboard or metal "collars" to deter cutworms. Row covers will thwart flea beetles, cabbageworms and root maggots. Spray or dust with BT, a microbial insecticide, if cabbageworms are a problem. To avoid soilborne diseases, don't plant broccoli and other cabbage-family plants in the same spot more than once every 3 years. In some areas, spring broccoli bolts to seed prematurely at the onset of hot weather. Choose quick-maturing cultivars and expect spring-grown broccoli heads to be smaller than those grown in autumn.

Broccoli continued

A cool-weather favorite, broccoli is now known to be a valuable addition to the diet, and is thought to provide protection against a number of ills, including some cancers.

Harvesting and storage Harvest broccoli heads when they have reached maximum size but before the tight, green flower buds begin to loosen and show yellow. Spring crops are best harvested once, with as much of the edible stem as possible. Cut autumn broccoli heads with less stem attached, leaving as much of the plant intact as possible so that it will produce smaller sideshoots or "florets," which you can harvest until there is a hard freeze. After picking, broccoli freezes well.

Special tips A small planting of Chinese cabbage nearby will draw flea beetles away from broccoli.

Related plants

Chinese broccoli *B. oleracea*, Alboglabra Group Also called Chinese kale, kaai laan or gai lan. Similar to calabrese broccoli, but the buds and leaves are lighter green and sweeter. The stems and young leaves are also eaten steamed or stir-fried. More heat-tolerant than standard broccoli.

Purple broccoli *B. oleracea*, Cymosa Group Identical to green broccoli except that the head has a distinct purplish cast, which disappears during cooking.

Romanesco broccoli *B. oleracea*, Cymosa Group Unusual conical heads of pale green, peaked florets that resemble little rocket ships.

This variety of purple broccoli is striking even in the flower garden but, unfortunately, the color fades during cooking.

The crunchy texture is more like cauliflower than broccoli. Requires wider spacing—up to 3 feet (90 cm)—and a longer growing season than most standard broccoli. In most areas it is planted in late spring for autumn harvest.

Calabrese broccoli *B. oleracea*, Italica Group Also called Italian broccoli, asparagus broccoli, or sprouting broccoli. Does not form a large central head but a profusion of smaller, looser heads or "sprouts." Cut when about 4 inches (10 cm) long, with surrounding small leaves, and use like regular broccoli. The plant will produce new sprouts over a long period.

Broccoli raab *B. rapa*, Ruvo Group Also called rapini or rapine; this vegetable is prized in Italy. It is usually blanched, then chopped and fried in olive oil with garlic. The glossy, dark green leaves are harvested along with the flower buds and stems. Spring crops may bolt to seed quickly; autumn plantings usually produce three or more harvests of flower shoots and leaves.

Brassica oleracea Gemmifera Group

BRASSICACEAE

HARDINESS
Zones 4–7, and Zone 8 as a winter vegetable. Generally unsuited to warmer climates.

DAYS TO MATURITY
90–120 days. Mature plants withstand heavy frost but grow only slowly.

COMMENTS
Harvested sprouts are a late-season treat, when a light frost has sweetened their flavor. They freeze well.

BRUSSELS SPROUTS

INDIVIDUAL BRUSSELS SPROUTS LOOK LIKE TIGHTLY WRAPPED MINIATURE CABBAGES.

Position Plant in full sun in well-drained and fertile soil, with adequate calcium levels; pH 6.0–6.8.

Cultivation Require a long growing season and are best when matured in cool weather. Short-season vegetable gardeners can set out transplants when they sow other spring crops; in other areas, wait until late spring. Space plants about 2 feet (60 cm) apart and keep weeded or mulched. Pinch off top leaves to encourage side growth.

Pests and diseases Rotate with non-cabbage-family crops to avoid soilborne fungal and viral diseases. Use row covers to deter cabbageworms, flea beetles and root maggots, or BT, a microbial insecticide, for cabbageworms. Water well and grow in fertile soil to reduce vulnerability to aphids.

Harvesting and storage Harvest the lower sprouts by breaking off the leaf below and snapping off the sprout. Sprouts higher up will continue to grow. Entire stalks can also be harvested. Harvest anytime until early winter to complete harvest before the ground freezes.

Special tips Sprouts keep for several weeks on the stalk if you pull up the whole plant and keep it cold.

Brassica oleracea Gongylodes Group BRASSICACEAE

HARDINESS
Zones 3 and warmer. Grow in mild areas as a winter vegetable, and in most areas to harvest in spring and autumn.

DAYS TO MATURITY
38–55 days.

COMMENTS
Cultivars include 'Early Purple Vienna' (purple-skinned cultivar), 'Early White Vienna' and 'Grand Duke Hybrid'.

KOHLRABI

BOTH THE SWOLLEN, TURNIP-LIKE STEM AND THE LEAVES OF KOHLRABI ARE EDIBLE, AND THEY ARE OFTEN COOKED TOGETHER.

Position Plant in full sun in fertile and well-drained soil with adequate calcium; pH 6.0–7.0.

Cultivation Direct-seed 2–4 weeks before the last spring frost or start indoors 6–8 weeks before last frost and set out 6 inches (15 cm) apart. Use thinnings of direct-seeded crops as salad greens. Mulch or cultivate to control weeds. Set out autumn crops from transplants, or direct-seed 2 months before autumn frost.

Pests and diseases Use row covers to protect the young plants from flea beetles and cabbageworms, or control cabbageworms with BT, an insecticide. Rotate kohlrabi and other cabbage-family plants to avoid soilborne diseases. Keep watered or mulched and avoid plantings that will mature in hot weather, which produces tough, woody kohlrabi.

Harvesting and storage Harvest the entire plant when swollen stem is about 2 inches (5 cm) in diameter. Overgrown kohlrabi can be woody. Best eaten fresh, but will keep for 2 weeks in the refrigerator.

Special tips Will withstand a light frost. Thin raw slices are a good low-calorie nibble, with a crunch like stir-fried water chestnuts.

Cabbage, Chinese

NUTRITIOUS AND FAST-GROWING, CHINESE CABBAGE CAN BE ADDED TO STIR-FRIES, OR EVEN EATEN FRESH IN SALADS. IT IS A GOOD SOURCE OF DIETARY CALCIUM.

Position Likes to be planted in full sun in well-drained soil that is rich in humus; pH 6.0–6.8.

Cultivation Head-forming types of Chinese cabbage quickly go to seed in warm weather or if seedlings are exposed to severe frost, so plant quick-maturing cultivars for early crops. Transplants poorly in spring, but can be moved successfully in peat pots. Direct-seed after the last frost; thin to stand 1 foot (30 cm) apart. Set autumn crops from transplants or direct-seed 2–3 months before the first frost, and give wider spacing, up to 2 feet (60 cm) apart. Transplant or direct-seed leafy types from spring through late summer, thinning to 6–12 inches (15–30 cm) apart, depending on the cultivar.

Pests and diseases Use row covers to protect from flea beetles.

Harvesting and storage Harvest spring crops before warm weather. Harvest autumn cabbages before a hard freeze; will keep in a cool cellar for several weeks if trimmed and wrapped in newspaper.

Special tips Plant Chinese cabbages at the base of your pea trellises,

HARDINESS
Zones 2 and warmer. Plant leafy types in summer or early spring in the coldest climates. Plant head-forming types in spring and autumn in cool climates, autumn only in warmer ones; use as a winter vegetable in the warmest climates.

DAYS TO MATURITY
43–80 days. Mature plants will tolerate moderate frost.

Cook fast-growing choy sum (facing page) and bok choy (above) only briefly so you can fully enjoy their delicate flavor.

where they will get some shade and be sheltered from the wind.

Related plants

Bok choy *B. rapa*, Chinensis Group Also called pak choi, Ching-Chiang cabbage or Chinese chard. A leafy Chinese cabbage with spoon-shaped, light green to blue-green leaves and thick, crisp stems, favored for stir-fries. Popular cultivars include 'Mei Qing Choi' and 'Joi Choi'.

Michihli cabbage *B. rapa*, Pekinensis Group Head-forming cabbage. Tall-growing, cylindrical in shape. Cultivars include 'Jade Pagoda' and 'Michihli'.

Napa cabbage *B. rapa*, Pekinensis Group Head-forming, barrel-shaped, and larger than Michihli types, this type grows up to about 10 pounds (4.5 kg). Early cultivars include 'Springtime' and 'Blues', and late ones include 'China Pride' and 'Wintertime'. 'Lettucy Type' is a Napa cultivar with a loose, open top, like romaine (Cos) lettuce.

Choy sum *B. parachinensis* Similar to bok choy, but the leaves are thick, glossy and dark green. Named cultivars are not generally available, but seed suppliers may offer variants.

HARDINESS
All Zones; grow as a winter vegetable in mild climates.

DAYS TO MATURITY
40 days; the thinnings can be harvested earlier. Will withstand a moderate frost.

COMMENTS
Cultivars include 'Tokyo Beau', 'Tokyo Belle'. Other common names include Japanese mustard and kyona.

MIZUNA

MILDER THAN MOST MUSTARDS AND EASY TO GROW, MIZUNA ADDS DASH TO SALADS AND STIR-FRIES, OR IT CAN BE COOKED IN THE SAME WAY AS OTHER GREENS.

Position Plant in full sun. Not fussy, but best in light, well-drained soil; pH 5.8–6.2.

Cultivation Sow 2–4 weeks before last spring frost, or 6–8 weeks before first autumn frost as an autumn crop. Thin to stand 4–6 inches (10–15 cm) apart, using thinnings in salad. Irrigate to promote rapid growth.

Pests and diseases Row covers will protect young plants, especially spring crops, from flea beetles. Mizuna can become strong-flavored in hot weather. Avoid plantings that will mature during hot spells, or use as cooked greens then, rather than in salads.

Harvesting and storage Leaves will grow to 12–14 inches (30–35 cm); cut when 4–6 inches (10–15 cm) long for best salad greens. Harvest as needed with scissors about 1 inch (2.5 cm) above the crown; the plant will sprout new leaves. Four or five harvests are possible. Or harvest whole plants for cooking.

Special tips Seeds packaged as "cutting mix" contain mizuna along with other lettuce and spicy salad greens. Eat as mixed baby leaves.

HARDINESS
All Zones; grow as a winter vegetable in mild climates.

DAYS TO MATURITY
35–60 days. Turnips can withstand light frost.

COMMENTS
Cultivars include 'Tokyo Cross Hybrid', 'Purple-Top White Globe', 'Seven Top' (grown for greens) and 'Golden Ball' (with yellow flesh).

TURNIP

GROWN BOTH FOR ITS TENDER LEAVES AND FOR ITS CRISP ROOT, TURNIP HAS THE BEST FLAVOR AND TEXTURE IN COOL WEATHER.

Position Plant in full sun in loose, deep soil that is rich in humus; pH 5.5–6.8.

Cultivation Sow ½ inch (12 mm) deep 4–6 weeks before last spring frost. Thin to stand 3 inches (7.5 cm) apart; use thinnings as fresh or cooked greens. Sow your autumn crop 8–10 weeks before first autumn frost. Water regularly for fast growth in spring, because turnips bolt to seed in hot weather.

Pests and diseases Use row covers to protect from flea beetles. Reduce root maggot damage, especially in spring crops, by not planting where other root crops have grown the preceding year. Turnips that mature in hot weather may be fibrous or strong-flavored. For spring crops, choose quick-maturing cultivars.

Harvesting and storage Pull turnips as needed, as 1-inch (2.5-cm) wide "babies" up to 3–4-inch (8–10-cm) roots. Larger turnips can be woody. Turnips are more tender than other root vegetables and are damaged by hard frost. Store roots in damp sand or sawdust in a cool place; freeze leaves as you would spinach.

Special tips Avoid overhead watering to prevent mildew.

HARDINESS
All Zones; grow as a winter vegetable in mild areas. Can survive low temperatures.

DAYS TO MATURITY
90 days.

COMMENTS
Named cultivars are not generally available. Tyfon's other common names include Holland greens.

TYFON

A MILD-FLAVORED CROSS BETWEEN TURNIP AND CABBAGE, TYFON IS A FROST-HARDY, QUICK-GROWING GREEN THAT IS COOKED IN THE SAME WAY AS SPINACH.

Position Plant in full sun or partial shade. Not fussy, but prefers rich, well-limed soil; pH 6.0–7.0.

Cultivation Sow ½ inch (12 mm) deep 4–6 weeks before last spring frost, 8–10 weeks before first autumn frost, or later as a winter vegetable in mild areas. Thin to stand 4–6 inches (10–15 cm) apart; use thinnings as salad or cooking greens. Or grow unthinned if you plan to harvest leaves by shearing. Water regularly to encourage abundant leafy growth.

Pests and diseases Use row covers to protect plants, especially spring crops, from flea beetles. Avoid plantings that will mature in hot, dry weather. Like its cabbage-family relatives, tyfon bolts quickly in heat.

Harvesting and storage Pick fresh leaves as needed, or harvest by cutting with garden shears or scissors, leaving 1 inch (2.5 cm) above the crown to resprout. In cool weather, a planting should provide several cuttings, about a month apart. Freeze leaves as you would kale or spinach.

Special tips In most climates, a light row cover will extend your harvest well into the winter.

HARDINESS
All Zones; grow as a winter vegetable in mild areas.

DAYS TO MATURITY
40–50 days; thinnings can be harvested earlier. Will withstand moderate frost.

COMMENTS
As the weather gets hotter, so do the leaves of mustard plants.

MUSTARD

MUSTARD IS GROWN MAINLY FOR ITS SPICY SEEDS, WHICH ARE GROUND OR LEFT WHOLE TO PRODUCE A POPULAR CONDIMENT. THE LEAVES OF SOME VARIETIES ADD A DELICIOUS ZING TO SALADS.

Position Plant in full sun. Not fussy, but prefers light, well-drained soil; pH 5.8–6.2.

Cultivation Sow 2–4 weeks before the last spring frost or 6–8 weeks before the first autumn frost. Thin to stand 4–6 inches (10–15 cm) apart, adding the thinnings to salads or soups. Irrigate, especially during dry spells, to promote rapid growth.

Pests and diseases Rarely troubled by pests. Good air circulation prevents mildew. Bolts to seed quickly in hot weather. Avoid plantings that will mature in hot, dry weather; grow as an autumn crop in warm-spring areas.

Harvesting and storage Pick leaves as needed from the outside of the plant, allowing new leaves to sprout from the center. Tender leaves do not store well in the refrigerator.

Special tips Cut off the flower stalk as soon as it makes its appearance in the center of the plant. This will prolong your harvest of leaves, which can be mixed with cress in the traditional "mustard and cress" combination salad. However, if you are growing this crop for its black

Mustard continued

The striking purple-red leaves of red mustard *B. juncea* var. *foliosa* add color to salads, but use sparingly, as the bite can be startling to diners unfamiliar with mustard leaves.

seeds, leave the flowers undisturbed until the seeds are set and ripened. Always harvest your seed crops in dry weather.

Related plants

Black mustard *B. nigra* Has edible leaves, but is grown chiefly for its seed, which is used to produce a traditional spicy condiment.

Brown mustard *B. juncea* 'Crispifolia' Large, curly or frilled green leaves, usually grown for greens. Other cultivars include 'Green Wave' and 'Southern Curled'.

Rape *B. napus* Grown mainly as an oilseed crop. Rape is also grown by organically minded gardeners, who make use of the way its strong tap roots break up heavy clay soils; they also grow it to dig in as a green manure crop to help in the control of nematodes.

Red mustard *B. juncea* var. *foliosa* Broad, flat leaves with red or purple coloring, very spicy. Cultivars include 'Osaka Purple' and 'Red Giant'.

White mustard *B. hirta* The seeds are ground for a condiment; less pungent than black mustard.

HARDINESS
Zones 4 and warmer.

DAYS TO MATURITY
55–80 days from transplanting for green peppers; 15–20 days more for mature, fully colored peppers.

COMMENTS
Scientific studies show that planting marigolds nearby reduces the number of aphids on bell peppers.

BELL PEPPER (CAPSICUM)

BELL PEPPERS ARE CRISP AND JUICY WHEN GREEN, BUT SWEETER WHEN ALLOWED TO RIPEN TO RED, YELLOW OR ORANGE.

Position Plant in full sun in light, well-drained soil, not overly rich; pH 6.0–7.0.

Cultivation Start seeds indoors 6–8 weeks before last spring frost. Do not overwater pepper seedlings, as they are vulnerable to root rot. Set out 10–15 inches (25–37.5 cm) apart when frost danger is well past and the soil has warmed. In colder areas, prewarm the soil with black plastic mulch. Young bell peppers will tolerate cool spells but will not thrive until warmer weather arrives. Cultivate shallowly; do not mulch until the soil is thoroughly warm. Too much nitrogen will produce lush foliage and few peppers, but an application of fish emulsion or compost tea when the plants are in flower can help to increase the yield. Magnesium is critical; in magnesium-poor soils, scatter 1 teaspoon of Epsom salts around the base of each plant. Irrigate in dry spells. Bell peppers, particularly thick-fleshed sweet peppers, are prone to blossom-end rot if they become drought-stressed.

Pests and diseases Do not plant where pepper or other nightshade family members, such as tomatoes and eggplants (aubergines) have

Essential to many Asian and Mexican dishes, hot peppers come in many sizes, shapes and degrees of "heat." Wear gloves when cutting up and avoid contact with eyes.

been grown in the preceding 2 years. Protect young plants from cutworms with cardboard or foil collars. Keep bell peppers away from corn plantings to reduce earworm damage to the fruit. Sunscald can cause dry, sunken patches on the fruit. Plant more closely, keep watered and grow cultivars with good leaf canopies to avoid fruit damage.

Harvesting and storage Pick immature or green peppers when they are large enough for use. Leave some fruit on the plant to mature. Fully ripe peppers will be yellow, orange or red, depending on the cultivar. Pick mature peppers when 50–75 percent colored; they will finish ripening in 1–2 days at room temperature. When frost threatens, harvest all the remaining fruit. Fresh peppers will keep for 2 weeks or more if stored at around 55°F (13°C) (a refrigerator is too cold), or freeze them for winter cooking. Freeze or pickle thick-fleshed hot peppers, such as jalapeño and hot cherry; dry thin-fleshed ones, such as cayenne.

Special tips Hot peppers and sweet peppers may cross-pollinate. Plant them well away from each other, especially if you intend to save the seed. Bell peppers are attractive plants of bushy habit that can be

Less juicy than bell peppers, frying peppers retain their shape and flavor well during cooking. They may drop their flowers in the heat, so provide shade during hot spells.

interplanted in the flower garden. They can also be successfully grown in containers. Handle hot peppers with care—the capsaicin they contain will burn sensitive tissues, such as the eyes and mouth.

Related plants

Hot peppers *C. annuum*, Longum Group Also called chili peppers. Hot peppers come in a wide variety of shapes, sizes and degrees of "heat." The milder cultivars include 'Ancho' or 'Poblano', a large, mildly hot pepper that is often served stuffed. Medium-hot peppers include jalapeño and 'Hungarian Wax'. Fiery peppers include cayenne and Thai peppers. Hot weather intensifies the flavor and heat.

Pickling peppers *C. annuum*, Conoides Group Usually small, thin-fleshed peppers with a cone shape, borne upright on the plant. 'Sweet Pickle' is ornamental, with red, orange, yellow and purple fruits on the same plant. The long and thin 'Pepperoncini' is an Italian favorite, usually picked when green but turning red at maturity.

Sweet peppers (bell) *C. annuum*, Grossum Group Blocky in shape and thick-fleshed, these peppers are most often used fresh in salads and relish trays or for stuffing. Most cultivars turn red or yellow when

These small pickling peppers, which ripen to red, yellow and orange, also provide a lovely contrast in color in the salad bowl.

fully ripe; purple and "chocolate" peppers are colored at their immature stage and turn red when fully ripe. Popular cultivars include 'Ace' (red at maturity), 'Orobelle' (yellow), 'Jupiter' (red), and 'Oriole' (orange).

Sweet peppers (other) *C. annuum*, Grossum Group Frying peppers, also called Italian, ramshorn, Cubanelle or banana peppers, have elongated fruit up to 1 foot (30 cm) long. They are generally thinner-fleshed than bell peppers and hold their shape and flavor better in cooked dishes. Cultivars range from dark green to light yellow when immature and ripen to red, orange or yellow; they include 'Biscayne' (pale green, ripens red), 'Sweet Banana' (yellow, ripens red), 'Bullhorn' (yellow, ripens orange) and 'Gypsy' (yellow, ripens red). Pimento peppers, also called cheese peppers, are thick-fleshed and flattened in shape. Excellent when fresh and the best pepper for roasting. Popular cultivars of pimento include 'Super Red Pimento' and 'Yellow Cheese'.

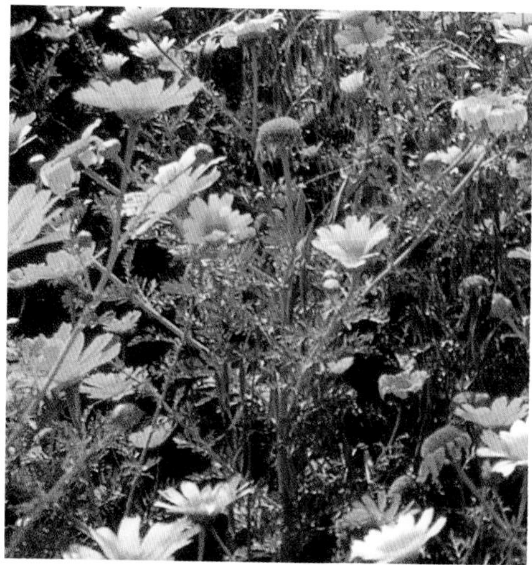

HARDINESS
Zones 2 and warmer; use as a winter vegetable in mild areas.

DAYS TO MATURITY
45 days, but thinnings can be harvested earlier. Tolerates light to moderate frost.

COMMENTS
There are no named cultivars, but some seed companies offer variants based on leaf size and shape.

CHRYSANTHEMUM, GARLAND

THE AROMATIC, EDIBLE LEAVES OF THE GARLAND CHRYSANTHEMUM ARE POPULAR IN ORIENTAL CUISINES, EITHER STIR-FRIED OR DROPPED INTO SOME OF THE CLASSIC SOUPS.

Position Avoid hot, dry areas. Not fussy, but prefers fertile, moist soil; pH 6.0–6.7.

Cultivation Direct-seed about ½ inch (12 mm) deep in early spring or autumn and thin to 4–6 inches (10–15 cm). Use the thinnings in stir-fries, soups or salads.

Pests and diseases Little troubled by pests, but to avoid leaf diseases, don't plant where flower garden chrysanthemums (now more correctly called dendranthemas) have been grown. Hot weather and inadequate moisture can cause premature bolting to seed. The flowers, however, are attractive.

Harvesting and storage Harvest whole plants or side leaves as needed, but avoid planting in hot weather, as the leaves become disagreeably bitter. Garland chrysanthemum "cooks down" in the pot, so several plants may be needed for a soup.

Special tips Remove flower buds to prolong the harvest of leaves. Other common names include crown daisy, edible chrysanthemum, shungiku and tong ho choi.

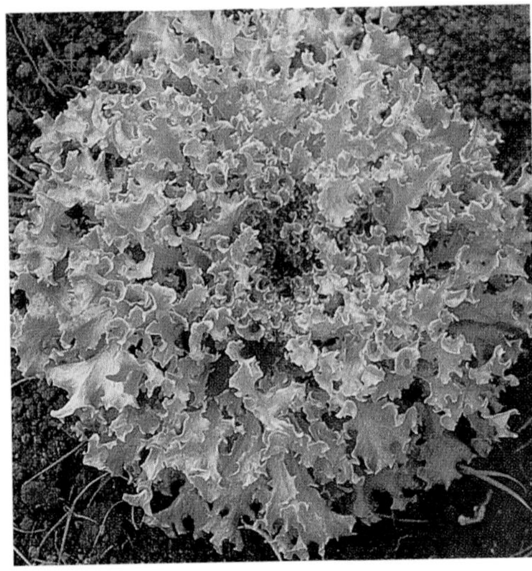

HARDINESS
Zones 4 and warmer; grow as a winter vegetable in mild areas.

DAYS TO MATURITY
80–100 days.

COMMENTS
Escarole (left) cultivars such as 'Full Heart Batavian' are easy to find. Curly- or fringed-leaved cultivars of endive, also called frisée, include 'Salad King', 'Giant Fringed Oyster' and 'Traviata'.

ENDIVE AND ESCAROLE

IN WARM AREAS GROW ENDIVE AND ESCAROLE BETWEEN TOMATOES, WHERE THEY WILL APPRECIATE THE SHADE.

Position Full sun or partial shade in warm areas. Prefers fertile, well-limed, well-drained soil; pH 5.5–7.0.

Cultivation In cool-spring areas, start indoors 8 weeks before last frost and set out a month before last frost, 10–12 inches (25–30 cm) apart. Cover plants if a hard frost threatens. In warmer areas, they're best as autumn crops, started in midsummer and set out 2 months before first autumn frost, or even later in mildest areas. They can be blanched by inverting a pot or box over the plant, or by tying the outer leaves together at the top. In humid areas, blanching by tying may cause the inside leaves to rot.

Pests and diseases Provide good air circulation to avoid molds. Control slugs with shallow pans of beer set in the soil. Water well and provide shade in hot spells to prevent brown, crisp ends on endive leaves.

Harvesting and storage Cut entire head at base in the morning while dew is still on plant. Rinse; wrap in paper towels, then in a plastic bag. Keeps up to 2 weeks refrigerated.

Special tips Broadleaf endive is known as escarole. See "Forcing chicory" page 166 for Belgian endive.

HARDINESS
Zones 3 and warmer; only leafy types grow in the coldest areas; they also grow as a winter crop in mild areas. Some cultivars can be planted in autumn for spring harvest in areas as cool as Zone 5.

DAYS TO MATURITY
40–130 days, depending on type. Leafy types, such as cutting chicory (left), grow fast.

CHICORY

THE LEAVES OF CUTTING CHICORY IMPART A TANGY FLAVOR TO GREEN SALADS. CUT THE LEAVES FROM THE PLANT AS NEEDED.

Position Full sun. Well-drained, moderately fertile soil; pH 6.0–6.5.

Cultivation Direct-sow after frost or set out as transplants, 8–12 inches (20–30 cm) apart. Sow or transplant the autumn crop 2 months before first frost. Avoid plantings that will mature during hot weather. Keep well watered to avoid bolting to seed. Modern cultivars of head-forming chicories do not require cutting back to form heads.

Pests and diseases Chicory is little troubled by pests. Keep the soil moist to avoid interior browning of head-forming types. Head-forming types are inconsistent; many plants will produce only leaves or loose rosettes, despite the best conditions.

Harvesting and storage Harvest leaves of leafy types as needed. Cut head-forming types as needed when the heads are firm (plants will hold in the garden for several weeks). Harvest chicories grown for their roots before a hard frost.

Related plants

Cutting chicory *C. intybus* Also called catalogna, leaf chicory or Italian dandelion. It is grown for its leaves, which vary in shape from dandelion-like to smooth or

Chicory continued

Heading chicory, which is popular in Europe broiled, roasted or served in salads, grows faster than loose-leafed types, but more slowly than endive.

rosette-like, and in color from light to dark green and also red-tinged. Some can be cut and left to resprout for continued harvest. Cultivars include 'Rouge di Verone', 'Catalogna', 'Elodie' and 'Bionda'.

Forcing chicory *C. intybus* Also called witloof and Belgian endive. Cut initial head in autumn, then dig up roots, trim to 8 inches (20 cm), and bury upright in moist sand or peat. Kept in complete darkness at 50–60°F (10–15°C), the roots will produce small pale sprouts or "chicons" in about 3 weeks. Cultivars include 'Witloof Improved'.

Heading chicory *C. intybus* Also called radicchio or Italian chicory. Red-tinged leaves surround a small, red head with white veining, resembling red cabbage. Older cultivars, such as 'Rossa di Treviso', may require cutting back to 1 inch (2.5 cm) in midsummer to form heads in autumn. Modern cultivars form heads without cutting back. Cultivars include 'Adria', 'Giulio' and 'Rossa di Verona'. 'Pan di Zucchero', or sugarloaf, makes large heads similar to romaine (Cos) lettuce.

Root chicory *C. intybus* Also called coffee chicory or Sicilian chicory. Has edible leaves, but is usually grown for its large roots, which you can dig up in autumn, dry, and grind. This is infused to make a coffee-like beverage. Cultivars include 'Magdeburgh'.

HARDINESS
Zones 4 and warmer.

DAYS TO MATURITY
Grown from seed, sea kale will not provide a harvest until the third year. After that, harvest annually in spring.

COMMENTS
Tolerates salty environments very well.

KALE, SEA

GROW SEA KALE FOR THE TENDER SHOOTS THAT EMERGE IN SPRING. YOU CAN BLANCH AND EAT THESE LIKE ASPARAGUS.

Position Plant in full sun or partial shade in rich, well-drained, slightly alkaline soil; pH 6.0–7.0.

Cultivation Best started from divisions, but specialty suppliers usually stock only seeds. Plant about six seeds in mounds 2–3 feet (60–90 cm) apart, 2–4 weeks before last spring frost. Thin to three or four plants per hill. In colder areas, mulch over winter.

Pests and diseases Rarely troubled by pests. Sea kale roots tend to rise to the surface. Cover exposed roots with soil each autumn to prevent winter-kill and to increase shoot production the following year.

Harvesting and storage In late winter, before the first shoots appear, invert a large clay pot or basket over the mound. To speed shoot emergence, mulch around the pot with straw or dry leaves. Check periodically for shoots, and cut them with a knife below the soil surface when they are 6–8 inches (15–20 cm) long. Cut third-year plants for 1–2 weeks; harvest older plants for 3–4 weeks. Remove the pot when the harvest is finished.

Special tips Top-dress with compost or well-rotted manure each spring.

CUCUMBER

THESE HEAT-LOVING PLANTS CAN BE GROWN ON A TRELLIS OR FENCE TO SAVE GARDEN SPACE. THEY ARE COOL AND REFRESHING IN SALADS, BUT THEY CAN ALSO BE PICKLED.

Position Plant in full sun, in a site with good air circulation, in light soil with well-rotted manure or compost worked in; pH 6.0–7.0.

Cultivation Cucumbers dislike cold soil, so wait for 3–4 weeks after the last frost to direct-seed or transplant them into the garden. Indoors, sow seed in peat pots 2–3 weeks before you plan to set them out, or presprout in a moist paper towel and plant into soil that has been warmed by covering with a sheet of black plastic mulch. Thin plants to stand 1–1¼ feet (30–37.5 cm) apart in rows, or plant in "hills" (each with four or five plants) about 4 feet (1.2 m) apart. Mulch, or keep cultivated until plants begin to vine. Cucumbers need ample food and water; irrigate during dry spells and give them fish emulsion or compost tea once a month. Where the growing season permits, plant successive crops 6 weeks apart. Support on a trellis or fence.

Pests and diseases Use row covers to protect young plants from cucumber beetles, but remove the covers when the plants bloom. Trellising will improve air circulation and reduce the risk

HARDINESS
Zones 4 and warmer.

DAYS TO MATURITY
48–70 frost-free days, slightly less for gherkins or baby pickles.

COMMENTS
Spiny amaranth *Amaranthus spinosus* plants standing among cucumbers may attract and trap black cutworms away from your cucumbers.

Keep picking your cucumbers to encourage the vines to keep producing fruit. Try finely chopping the flesh, draining, and combining with Greek yogurt, garlic and mint.

of mildew. Do not grow cucumbers or their relatives, such as squash and melons, in the same spot more often than once every 3 years. Sudden collapse of cucumber plants indicates wilt disease, which is spread by cucumber beetles. Straw mulch may help to deter beetle attack, and some cultivars are less vulnerable to the beetles. Successive plantings will extend the harvest even where these beetles are troublesome.

Harvesting and storage Cucumbers are best picked small, at 3–4 inches (7.5–10 cm) for pickling types and 6–8 inches (15–20 cm) for slicers. A yellowish tinge at the blossom end indicates overmaturity. Pick often, especially during hot spells, to encourage continued fruiting. Pickle your excess cucumbers.

Related plants

'Burpless' cucumber *C. sativus* Also called Lebanese cucumber or oriental cucumber. Cultivars include 'Sweet Slice', 'Burpless Hybrid' and 'Japanese Long Pickling'.

Gynoecious cucumber *C. sativus*
This cultivar was bred to produce only female flowers, which greatly increases the yield per plant. Gynoecious cucumbers require another cucumber cultivar to pollinate them (seeds of a pollinator are included with packets of

If you choose high-yielding bush cultivars, you will need only a small space to put in a few cucumber plants in order to maintain a good supply for the table.

gynoecious cucumbers). They also need higher soil fertility to support the higher yields. Cultivars include 'Saladin Hybrid' and 'Early Pride'.

Pickling cucumber *C. sativus* The fruits are also called gherkins or cornichons. Although all cucumbers can be pickled, some cultivars were selected for this purpose because of their small size, crispness or small seed cavity. They are often lighter green than slicing cultivars, with soft "spines" on the fruit. Suitable cultivars include 'Picklebush', 'Vert de Massy' and 'Bush Baby'.

Serpent cucumber *Trichosanthes cucumerina* var. *anguina* Also called snake gourd or club gourd. A popular vegetable in Asian countries. The long, thin fruits will curve and coil on the ground, but grow straight if the vine is trellised.

Slicing cucumber *C. sativus* These cultivars are generally grown for fresh or salad use, rather than pickling, and are usually longer, smoother and darker green than the pickling types. Cultivars include 'Straight Eight', 'Spacemaster' and 'Marketmore'.

Hardiness
Zones 3 and warmer.

Days to maturity
42–65 frost-free days.

Comments
Colorful 'Golden Crookneck' squash (left) thrives in warm weather. All types of summer squash need ample moisture to keep the fruit coming.

Squash, summer

SUMMER SQUASH GROW QUICKLY, SO PICK THE FRUITS EVERY FEW DAYS, WHILE THEY ARE YOUNG AND TENDER.

Position Plant in full sun in well-drained soil rich in humus; pH 6.0–6.5. Needs good circulation.

Cultivation Sow when all danger of frost is past, or start indoors in individual pots 2–3 weeks before last frost and transplant carefully to avoid breaking roots. Space bush types 1½–2 feet (45–60 cm) apart; vining types need wider spacing, up to 4 feet (1.2 m), and should be planted in hills, with three or four seeds to a hill. Cultivate or mulch. Squash benefits from plenty of compost or rotted manure.

Pests and diseases Use row covers to protect young squash plants from cucumber beetles and squash borers; remove covers when the plants bloom. Radishes or basil interplanted with squash helps repel beetles and squash bugs. Do not plant where squash or its relatives, such as melon and cucumber, have grown the preceding year. Good air circulation helps prevent mildew. However, if plants are attacked by mildew, spray foliage thoroughly with a mild baking soda solution (1 teaspoon to 1 quart [1 l] of water). You can reduce the chance of many squash diseases by planting resistant cultivars. A straw mulch will help to deter insects and keep

'Gold Rush', an attractive yellow-skinned zucchini (courgette). The fruit forms behind the flower, which gradually collapses as the fruit swells and grows.

the soil moist, which is essential for healthy fruit. Dust foliage with wood ashes to deter insect pests. Fruit that is not pollinated turns black and rots before reaching picking size. This often happens early in the season, before male blooms appear, or in cool spells, when pollinating insects are less active.

Harvesting and storage Pick summer squash small for best flavor. Harvest every few days to encourage more fruiting. Cut squash off with a sharp knife and handle carefully, as the skin bruises easily. Freeze or pickle excess fruit. For stuffing, pick blossoms in early morning, before they have been pollinated.

Special tips Successive plantings of just a few plants, sown a month apart, will extend the picking season in areas where squash often succumb to insects and disease. Vining types of summer squash can be grown up a trellis to save space.

Related plants

Pattypan squash *C. pepo* var. *melopepo* 'Early White Bush', 'Peter Pan Bush Scallop'.

Yellow squash *C. pepo* var. *melopepo* 'Seneca Prolific' and 'Butterstick' (straightnecks), or 'Golden Crookneck' and 'Pic-n-Pic Hybrid'.

Zucchini *C. pepo* var. *melopepo* 'Aristocrat' (dark green), 'Gold Rush' (yellow), 'Cocozelle' (striped).

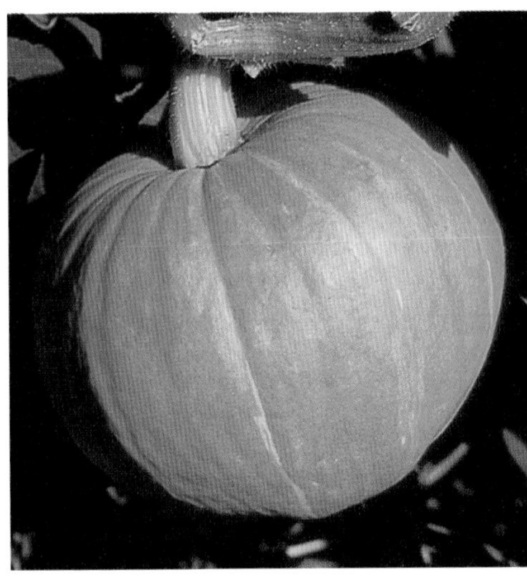

HARDINESS
Zones 4 and warmer.

DAYS TO MATURITY
100–115 frost-free days. For use as homegrown jack-o'-lanterns in short-season areas, grow a cultivar such as 'Autumn Gold', which is orange even when immature.

COMMENTS
Pumpkin vines like to sprawl, but can be gently pushed back into place.

PUMPKIN

AS FAMILIAR AS FALLING LEAVES IN AUTUMN, THE HANDSOME PUMPKIN MAKES FINE PIES AND BAKED DISHES, AS WELL AS JACK-O'-LANTERNS FOR HALLOWE'EN.

Position Plant in full sun. Not fussy about soil texture, but likes a fertile soil; pH 6.0–7.0.

Cultivation Sow in hills 4–5 feet (1.2–1.5 m) apart, two or three seeds to a hill, after the last spring frost. In short-season areas, start your pumpkins indoors in individual pots 2–3 weeks before the last frost. Set out carefully to avoid disturbing the roots. A good shovelful of compost or well-rotted manure in each hill will boost growth. Mulch or cultivate until the plants begin to vine. The pumpkin plant's broad leaves will shade out most weeds. If garden space is limited, try growing some of the space-saving extra small, bush-type pumpkins.

Pests and diseases Row covers will help to deter cucumber beetles and squash borers, but remove them when the plants bloom to allow pollination. Straw mulch also helps to deter cucumber beetles. Prevent mildew by providing good air circulation. Plants that collapse before setting fruit are probably the victims of the squash borer. Those that collapse before the fruit ripens may be infected with a wilt disease

Pumpkins come in a huge variety of sizes and colors. The flowers, like those of other kinds of squash, can be stuffed, lightly fried and eaten.

spread by cucumber beetles. Cover the plants until they bloom to reduce the risk of crop loss.

Harvesting and storage Harvest pumpkins when they are fully colored and their shells are hard, or after light frost has killed the vines. Store in a cool, dry area. Pumpkins keep for several months but lose flavor in long storage. The cooked flesh freezes well, however. Cultivars meant for cooking, such as 'Small Sugar', taste better than large field pumpkins.

Special tips If you want to win the big-pumpkin contest, cultivate plants such as borage and lemon balm near your pumpkin patch to attract bees. Research shows that pumpkins pollinated by numerous bees form larger fruits. A crop of beans, peas or clover in the pumpkin patch will enrich the soil for next year's crop.

Related plants

Japanese pumpkin *C. mixta* Also called Hokkaido squash or Chinese pumpkin. This variety has a green skin and dark orange, moist, sweet flesh. While not suitable for carving, it has a superb flavor.

Hardiness
Zones 4 and warmer.

Days to maturity
85–110 frost-free days.

Comments
The flesh of the fast-growing 'Gold Nugget' (left) is rich in flavor.

Squash, Winter

AROMATIC PLANTS, SUCH AS NASTURTIUM OR MINT, MAY HELP REPEL PESTS FROM SQUASH.

Position Plant in full sun, in an area with good air circulation. Prefers rich, well-composted, well-drained soil; pH 6.0–6.5.

Cultivation Sow 1–2 weeks after the last spring frost, 1½–2 feet (45–60 cm) apart in rows or in hills 4–5 feet (1.2–1.5 m) apart with three or four plants in each hill. In short-season areas, start indoors in individual pots 2–3 weeks before planting and set out in soil that has been prewarmed with black plastic mulch. Transplant carefully to avoid damaging the roots. Mulch to hold in the soil moisture.

Pests and diseases Use row covers to protect young plants from cucumber beetles and squash borers, but remove when plants are in bloom. Straw mulch will help to deter insects, as will interplantings of radishes or basil. Provide good air circulation to avoid mildew. Do not plant where squash or its relatives, such as cucumbers and melons, have been grown in the preceding year. Mildew can be a serious problem, especially in late-summer damp spells. Plants may be killed, or weakened too much to ripen fruit. At the first sign of mildew, spray foliage thoroughly with a mild baking soda solution (1 teaspoon to 1 quart [1 l] water).

'Sweet Dumpling' is a small and attractive squash that requires no curing before storage. Squash flowers can be stuffed, fried lightly and served as an entrée.

Harvesting and storage Harvest when the shell is hard enough that it cannot be dented with a fingernail. Harvest all fruit as soon as light frost has killed the vines; any more than a light frost will shorten storage life. Leave on the ground to "cure" in the sun for 10–14 days, but cover the fruit if frost threatens. This curing sweetens the flesh and toughens the skin for storage. Wipe the skin with a cloth dipped in a weak bleach solution to prevent rot. Store in a cool, well-ventilated place.

Related plants

Acorn squash *C. pepo* var. *pepo* Also called pepper squash. Acorn-shaped, usually dark green to near black. Sweet, moist, orange flesh. High-yielding, usually five to seven fruits per plant. Try 'Ebony Acorn', 'Table Queen', 'Swan White' and 'Cream of the Crop' (white-skinned with off-white flesh).

Delicata squash *C. pepo* Also called sweet potato squash. Oblong fruits striped green and ivory, 8 inches (20 cm) long and 3 inches (7.5 cm) in diameter. Orange flesh. Doesn't need curing. Cultivars include 'Delicata' and 'Sugarloaf'.

Spaghetti squash *C. pepo* Also called vegetable spaghetti. Oval-shaped, with buff or light yellow skin and pale orange-yellow flesh. Bake, then scrape out the flesh with a fork (it separates into pasta-like

The vegetable marrow squash, also called Lebanese zucchini, is commonly eaten while small and immature, but can be left on the vine to attain its full size.

strands). Serve topped with tomato sauce. Cultivars include 'Vegetable Spaghetti' and 'Orangetti Hybrid'.

'Sweet Dumpling' squash *C. pepo* Flattened, round fruit, 3–4 inches (7.5–10 cm) in diameter, with pale orange flesh and striped skin.

Vegetable marrow squash *C. pepo* var. *pepo* There are bush forms, but most cultivars are trailing vines that can be trellised. Pick at 8–12 inches (20–30 cm) and use like summer squash or eggplant (aubergine). Cultivars include 'Cousa'.

Buttercup squash *C. maxima* Dark green and blocky, with a "button" or small turban at the blossom end. Orange-fleshed fruits that keep well. The Japanese kabocha squashes are similar. Cultivars include 'Sweet Mama' and 'Honey Delight'.

'Gold Nugget' squash *C. maxima* A quick-maturing winter squash with round, orange fruits. A bush-type plant good for small gardens.

Hubbard squash *C. maxima* Also called blue hubbard. Large, warty fruits, usually one or two to a vine, with hard rind. An excellent keeper. Nonstringy flesh can be cooked, puréed and frozen. Cultivars include 'New England Blue Hubbard' and 'Hubbard Improved Green'.

Butternut squash *C. moschata* Small seed cavity with a thick neck of solid, orange flesh. An excellent keeper. Cultivars include 'Waltham Butternut' and 'Ponca'.

Cynara cardunculus ASTERACEAE

HARDINESS
Zones 5 and warmer. Perennial in most climates.

DAYS TO MATURITY
120–150 days for first harvest; in areas where cardoon is perennial, spring shoots can be blanched and eaten like mature stalks.

COMMENTS
Cultivars include 'Italian Dwarf' and 'Plein Blanc Inorme'.

CARDOON

THIS THISTLE-LIKE PLANT, A RELATIVE OF THE GLOBE ARTICHOKE, IS GROWN CHIEFLY FOR ITS STALKS, WHICH ARE BLANCHED AND USED MUCH LIKE CELERY.

Position Plant in full sun in well-drained, fertile soil with ample moisture; pH 6.0–7.0.

Cultivation Start seedlings indoors if season is short; otherwise, direct-seed 1–2 weeks before the last frost. Thin to 2 feet (60 cm) apart. A month before autumn frost, or earlier if the plant is large enough, tie the leaf stalks together and wrap the plant with burlap or heavy paper to exclude sunlight and whiten the stalks. Stalks will be fully blanched in 3–4 weeks.

Pests and diseases Few pests trouble this formidable-looking plant. Provide good drainage to prevent crown rot.

Harvesting and storage Harvest blanched stalks as needed until a hard freeze threatens, then bank the plant with earth or straw to prolong your harvest into winter. You can also dig up and eat the main roots.

Special tips Where growing seasons are short, cardoon plants may not reach their full height but will still supply usable stalks. Will withstand light frost.

HARDINESS
Zones 8–9, mild coastal climates; in Zones 5–7 with special winter care.

DAYS TO MATURITY
May produce edible buds in the first year but the first harvest is more likely to be in the second year. In warm climates, buds appear in late spring; where cooler, in summer.

COMMENTS
'Green Globe' is widely available.

ARTICHOKE, GLOBE

THIS PLANT IS GROWN CHIEFLY FOR ITS LARGE, EDIBLE FLOWER HEADS, BUT THE YOUNG SUCKERS CAN ALSO BE BLANCHED OR STEAMED AND EATEN LIKE ASPARAGUS.

Position Plant in full sun with protected exposure. Prefers rich, well-drained soil; near-neutral pH.

Cultivation Start seed indoors in late winter and transplant in late spring, when soil has warmed thoroughly. Can reach 5 feet (1.5 m) or more in height; space seedlings 2 feet (60 cm) apart in the row and allow 3 feet (90 cm) or more between rows. Be generous with compost or manure. Water deeply and mulch between the rows.

Pests and diseases Little troubled by insect pests but is susceptible to crown rot. Well-drained soil is essential. Do not allow mulch to smother the crown. In Zones 7 and colder, winter-kill is the chief problem. Cut the plant back in late autumn and protect over winter by inverting a basket or box over the crown and mulching deeply.

Harvesting and storage Cut the buds before the scales have begun to open, with 1 inch (2.5 cm) of stem still attached.

Special tips Side-dress with blood meal or other high-nitrogen fertilizer in early spring.

CARROT

THE NUTRITIOUS CARROT IS A POTENT ALLY IN YOUR BODY'S FIGHT AGAINST ILLNESS.

Position Plant in full sun in deep, light soil without stones or other obstructions. In heavier or shallow soil, plant round or half-long cultivars. Improve clay soil with organic matter; pH 5.5–6.8.

Cultivation Sow the first crop in early spring, after threat of severe frost is past. Seed is very small; mix half-and-half with fine sand to help avoid overseeding. Plant a scant ½ inch (12 mm) deep and firm the seedbed gently with the back of a hoe. Mark the row well; carrots are slow germinators and may not appear for 3–4 weeks. Or drop a radish seed every 2 inches (5 cm) into the row with your carrot seeds to help mark it. Radishes germinate quickly and will also help break up any soil-crusting that could smother the more delicate carrot seedlings, which look like fine blades of grass. Keep the soil evenly moist until the carrots are up. Thin to 2–3 inches (5–7.5 cm) apart. Plant successive crops every few weeks until 3 months before autumn frost. Weed carrots carefully during their growing period. Do not overwater as continually wet soil causes rot.

Pests and diseases Use row covers to deter carrot rust flies, which lay eggs at the base of carrot plants.

HARDINESS
Zones 3 and warmer. Plant early-maturing types in cold areas.

DAYS TO MATURITY
50–70 days. Will tolerate light frosts.

COMMENTS
Early-maturing 'Parmex' and 'Planet' suit heavy soils. 'Minicor' and 'Scarlet Nantes' do well in moderately deep soils. Long 'Imperator' and 'Gold Pak' suit deep, light soils.

Short carrot cultivars, such as 'Early Horn' (above), do well in containers. The longer Nantes or Amsterdam-type cultivars (facing page) are grown in deeper soils.

The larvae feed on the roots. Crops planted after late spring and harvested before late summer often escape damage without protection. Rotate carrot plantings to avoid bacterial diseases. Twisted roots point to inadequate thinning. Forked roots often mean that the seedbed was not fine enough. Hairy roots indicate excessive fertility. Do not use fresh manure or high-nitrogen fertilizer on carrot beds. Splitting occurs when heavy rain follows a dry period.

Harvesting and storage Carrots are ready to eat when fully colored. Pull when the ground is moist to avoid breaking roots, or dig with a garden fork. Harvest autumn crops before the ground freezes, or earlier if shoulders (root tops) appear above the ground. Dry in the sun and store, packed in dry leaves or straw, in a cool, moist place. To spread the harvest, carrots can be harvested while they are still young.

Special tips Cover newly seeded carrot rows with boards or black plastic for 3 weeks, then remove. This preserves soil moisture and prevents sprouting of weeds ahead of the slower-germinating carrots. Never step on the carrot seedbed. If space is limited, grow carrots in the ornamental garden. Their brilliant feathery tops are pretty in a border.

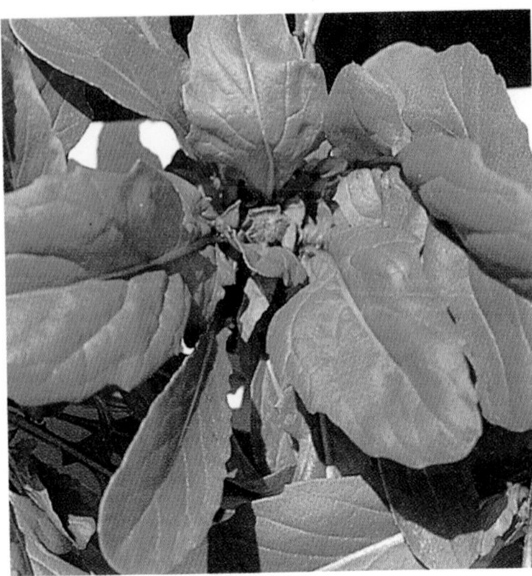

HARDINESS
All Zones.

DAYS TO MATURITY
40 days, although thinnings can be harvested earlier.

COMMENTS
Other common names include roquette, rucola and rugula.

ARUGULA (ROCKET)

THE TENDER LEAVES OF THIS EUROPEAN GARDEN FAVORITE ADD A NUTTY, PEPPERY BITE TO SALADS AND SANDWICHES.

Position Plant in full sun as well as half-day sun or partial shade. Avoid hot, dry positions. In mild climates, grow as a winter vegetable. Not fussy, but prefers fertile, moist soil; pH 6.0–7.0.

Cultivation Direct-seed as early as possible in spring. Light frost will not harm the seedlings. Thin to 8 inches (20 cm) apart, using thinnings in salads.

Pests and diseases Cover with row cover to deter flea beetles. Sown too late, spring-planted arugula will bolt to seed in warm weather before reaching a harvestable size. In cold climates, sow seed indoors and set out as soon as the ground can be worked. An autumn crop, direct-seeded or set out as seedlings 1–2 months before the first frost, will stand longer without bolting. Try making successive plantings a week apart.

Harvesting and storage Pick large leaves from the bottom of the plant. New leaves will sprout from the center crown. Weekly picking should yield eight to 12 large leaves per plant. Use fresh; do not freeze.

Special tips Add the flowers of bolting plants to salads.

HARDINESS
Zones 4 and warmer; grow as a winter vegetable in mild areas.

DAYS TO MATURITY
65–90 days.

COMMENTS
Tolerates light frost. Cultivars include 'Zefa Fino' and 'Romy'. Other common names include finocchio.

FENNEL, FLORENCE

FLORENCE FENNEL IS GROWN CHIEFLY FOR ITS ENLARGED LEAF BASES, WHICH HAVE AN INTRIGUING FLAVOR OF LICORICE.

Position Plant in full sun in fertile, well-drained soil; pH 6.5–7.0.

Cultivation In cool-spring areas, direct-seed spring crop 2–4 weeks before last frost and thin to stand 8–10 inches (20–25 cm) apart. Transplants poorly. Since it bolts to seed quickly in hot weather, start seedlings in warmer areas in peat pots or individual pots a month before last frost; do not let roots outgrow the pots before setting out. Sow small, successive crops where the season permits; avoid plantings that will mature in hot, dry weather. Autumn crops are easier to transplant; set out 2 months before first frost. Keep weeded and mulched; water during dry spells.

Pests and diseases Handpick off celery- or parsleyworms, which are green caterpillars with black and yellow stripes. Florence fennel becomes woody when overmature. Plant small, successive crops to prolong your harvest.

Harvesting and storage Cut the entire plant below the base of the bulb. Use fronds as seasoning for fish. Fennel does not freeze well.

Special tips Use the ripe seed of bolted plants in salads.

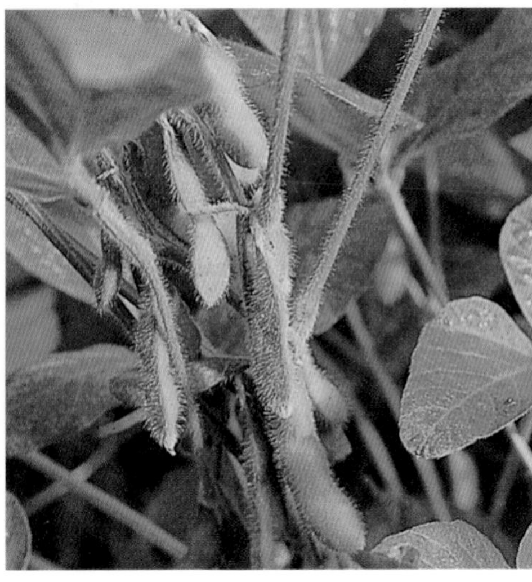

HARDINESS
Zones 5 and warmer.

DAYS TO MATURITY
65–120 frost-free days.

COMMENTS
Seed companies sometimes offer variants by seed color, usually yellow, green or black.

SOYBEAN

ONE OF THE OLDEST FOOD CROPS, THE NUTRITIOUS SOYBEAN IS WIDELY USED IN ORIENTAL CUISINES, EITHER FRESH OR PREPARED AS TOFU, SOY SAUCE OR MISO.

Position Plant in full sun in light, well-drained soil; pH 6.0–7.0.

Cultivation Sow after frost danger is past, 1 inch (2.5 cm) deep and 2 inches (5 cm) apart. Keep cultivated until plants grow large enough to shade out weeds. Water is critical when plants are in flower.

Pests and diseases Less troubled by pests than other beans. Rotate plantings of soybean and its legume relatives, such as beans and peas. May not mature for use as a dried bean in short-season areas, but some cultivars can be grown for use as fresh beans.

Harvesting and storage Harvest for fresh use when beans are plump and tender. Bottle or freeze fresh beans. For dry soybeans, pull the plants when most of the foliage has died and hang them to finish drying in a well-ventilated place. Shell and store as you would any dried bean.

Special tips 'Envy' and 'Hakucho Early' are short-season cultivars, primarily for using fresh. 'Panther' and 'Black Jet' need a longer season and are grown primarily for use as dried beans.

Helianthus tuberosus

ASTERACEAE

HARDINESS
All Zones.

DAYS TO MATURITY
110–150 days for a spring-planted, first-year crop. Autumn-planted crops are ready the next autumn.

COMMENTS
'Fuseau' is a smooth-skinned yam type; 'French Mammoth White' is a traditional knobby tuber; 'Sugarball' is a round tuber.

JERUSALEM ARTICHOKE

THE JERUSALEM ARTICHOKE IS A HARDY PERENNIAL VEGETABLE. IT PRODUCES TASTY POTATO-LIKE TUBERS.

Position Plant in full sun or partial shade. Plant away from other garden beds, as most cultivars are perennial in all Zones and many are invasive. Not fussy, but prefers loose, fertile soil; pH 6.0–6.5.

Cultivation Plant pieces of tuber 6–8 weeks before the last spring frost or in autumn. Plant in the same way as potatoes, each piece with one or more "eyes," 3 inches (7.5 cm) deep and 1–1½ feet (30–45 cm) apart in rows or beds. Mulch or weed early; plants will grow quickly and shade out weeds.

Pests and diseases Rarely troubled by pests and diseases. Difficult to eradicate once it is established, but diligent harvesting each year will keep the bed under control.

Harvesting and storage Mulch the bed to keep the ground diggable after a hard freeze. Jerusalem artichokes do not store well, so dig as needed. Cook them as you would potatoes.

Special tips Plants can withstand moderate frost; freezing does not damage tubers. Other common names include sunchoke.

HARDINESS
Zones 7 and warmer.

DAYS TO MATURITY
100–120 days. It grows poorly in cool seasons and will not withstand frost.

COMMENTS
Named cultivars are not generally available. Oriental seed suppliers may offer variants based on growth habit or leaf size.

SPINACH, WATER

A MEMBER OF THE MORNING GLORY FAMILY, WATER SPINACH IS A PERENNIAL WHEN GROWN IN ITS NATIVE SUBTROPICS.

Position Plant in full sun or partial shade in rich, constantly moist soil; pH 5.5–6.5.

Cultivation Start the seed indoors and set out after frost danger is well past. Allow plenty of space as this plant sends out runners and roots at the leaf nodes, quickly growing into a clump. Keep the soil quite moist, as water spinach is really a semi-aquatic plant.

Pests and diseases Not generally troubled by pests. Water spinach needs day temperatures higher than 72°F (22°C) to grow quickly. Do not plant too early.

Harvesting and storage Pick young leaves and shoots for use in salads, stir-fries or cooked dishes.

Special tips You can eat both the young leaves and the shoots. Other common names include swamp cabbage and kankon.

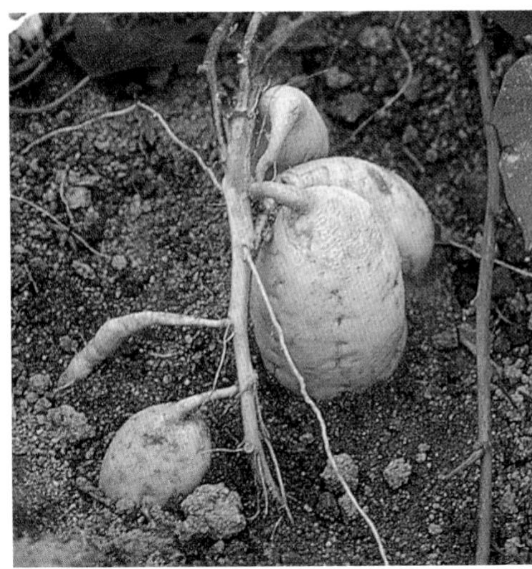

HARDINESS
Zones 5 and warmer.

DAYS TO MATURITY
90–120 frost-free days.

COMMENTS
Wait until the soil is thoroughly warm before mulching heat-loving plants, such as sweet potato, otherwise you are keeping the underlayer of soil cold.

SWEET POTATO

SWEET POTATOES ARE A WARM-WEATHER CROP THAT PRODUCE TASTY AND NUTRITIOUS TUBEROUS ROOTS. THEY CAN BE COOKED IN THE SAME WAY AS POTATOES.

Position Plant in full sun in loose, well-drained soil that is not too rich; pH 5.5–6.5.

Cultivation Plant from growing shoots or "slips," which are available by mail order or at many garden centers. Plant after frost danger is well past. With a rake, make a ridge of soil 6–10 inches (15–25 cm) high and 6–8 inches (15–20 cm) wide. Plant the slips into the ridge about 12 inches (30 cm) apart. Mound the soil onto the ridge at least once before the vining plants make further cultivation impossible. Keep the newly set slips watered until they begin to grow. After that, irrigate sweet potatoes only during extended dry spells. Although sweet potato is a perennial, it is usually grown as an annual in cooler climates. The stems sprawl across the garden bed and tend to grow roots at leaf nodes, many producing more tubers, so don't be tempted to trellis your plants or keep the stems off the ground. Allow plenty of space for a bountiful crop.

Pests and diseases Use certified disease-free slips. Rotate plantings and keep soil organic matter high

The leaves of sweet potato look very similar to those of its close relative, morning glory *Ipomoea purpurea*.

to reduce nematode damage. Deer love the tender leaves and shoots; if they are a problem in your area, you may need to fence off your sweet potatoes.

Harvesting and storage Dig up sweet potatoes before frost or as soon as the vines have been killed by a light frost. Left in the ground, they will spoil. The tuberous roots are very tender, so dig and handle them carefully. Cure them for 10–14 days in a warm, fairly humid area, and store where the temperature does not fall below 55°F (13°C). With proper storage, they will keep for 6 months or more. You can also cook the roots and freeze the pulp.

Special tips Sweet potatoes are divided into dry-flesh and moist-flesh types. The latter are often called "yams," although they are not botanically related to yams. The cultivars 'Georgia Jet', 'Vardeman' and 'Centennial' are moist-flesh sweet potatoes. Dry-flesh cultivars, which keep better, include 'Orlis' and 'Yellow Jersey'.

HARDINESS
All Zones; grow as a winter vegetable in mild areas.

DAYS TO MATURITY
40–90 days. The young leaves and thinnings can be harvested earlier. Leaf lettuces mature most quickly, followed by bibb and romaine (Cos).

COMMENTS
The iceberg lettuce (left) forms a crisp, cabbage-like head.

LETTUCE

HEAD LETTUCES REQUIRE A LONGER SEASON THAN SOME OTHERS. THE YOUNG PLANTS WILL WITHSTAND LIGHT FROST OR MODERATE FROST WITH PROTECTION.

Position Plant in full sun in cool weather, partial shade in warm weather. Prefers fertile, well-drained soil; pH 6.0–6.8.

Cultivation Sow the seed of leafy types directly in the ground a month before the last frost. Barely cover the seeds and firm the soil with the back of a hoe. Start head-forming types indoors 6–8 weeks before the last frost and set out, 8–10 inches (20–25 cm) apart, 1–2 weeks before last frost. Leave leaf lettuces unthinned for "baby" salad greens and pick at about 21 days, or thin to encourage large-leaved plants. Sow or transplant successive crops until a month before the first frost, ending with a cold-tolerant cultivar such as 'Winter Density'. Grow summer-maturing crops in partial shade, or cover with a lath frame to shield them from the midday sun. Cultivate shallowly or mulch; water frequently, especially during hot spells, as the stress of a water shortage can cause them to bolt, running to seed prematurely. Water at ground level, rather than spraying with the garden hose, because damp foliage encourages various rots. For best results when growing these quick-to-mature

Lettuce continued

The cultivar 'Little Gem' forms a neat little heart. These and other similar attractive varieties can be planted as an edible border around your flower beds.

vegetables, provide a regular, light application of a nitrogen fertilizer, compost tea or fish emulsion to ensure that growth is not checked in any way.

Pests and diseases Quick-growing lettuce seldom has pest problems, but rotate crops to avoid soilborne diseases. Control slugs by trapping them in shallow pans of beer set flush with the soil surface. Bitter leaves suggest heat and water stress, or simply overmature lettuce. Plant small crops at frequent intervals, 7–10 days apart, for a continuous supply.

Harvesting and storage Harvest as needed for fresh use. Cut unthinned leaf lettuce with scissors 1 inch (2.5 cm) above roots, leaving the plants to resprout for a second harvest. Cut larger whole plants at soil level. Harvest lettuce in the morning, when it is juicy and crisp.

Special tips Many of the varieties that can be cut leaf by leaf for the salad bowl make attractive additions to the flower or vegetable garden border and are decorative enough to grow in containers on a sunny terrace or apartment balcony. If your family is small or your needs are limited, look for packets of seeds that contain a mixture of varieties. These are often sold under the name of "Mesclun lettuce mix."

Many of the crinkly, red-leafed cultivars of lettuce make a welcome addition of both color and texture to a bowl of mixed salad greens.

Lettuce germinates poorly at temperatures above 80°F (27°C). Prechill seed before sowing, or start summer crops in a cool place.

Related plants

Bibb lettuce *L. sativa* Also called Boston, butterhead or cabbage lettuce. Forms loose heads of soft, folded leaves. Cultivars include 'Buttercrunch', 'Dark Green Boston', 'Sangria' (red-tinged leaves) and 'Tom Thumb' (miniature bibb).

Iceberg lettuce *L. sativa* Also called crisphead or cabbage lettuce. Forms a tight head of crisp-textured leaves. Prefers a long, cool growing season. Cultivars include 'Great Lakes' and 'Ithaca'.

Leaf lettuce *L. sativa* This is the quickest and easiest-to-grow member of the lettuce clan. It can double as an ornamental garden edging. It is also called cutting lettuce. Instead of heads, it forms loose leaves that can be harvested while quite small. Cultivars include 'Black Seeded Simpson', 'Red Sails', 'Salad Bowl' and 'Oak Leaf'.

Romaine lettuce *L. sativa* Also called Cos lettuce. Forms an upright, elongated head of crisp, ribbed leaves. Has a better heat tolerance than does iceberg. Cultivars include 'Parris Island', 'Valmaine' and 'Rosalita' (a red-leafed cultivar). This variety is the one preferred for the famous Caesar salad.

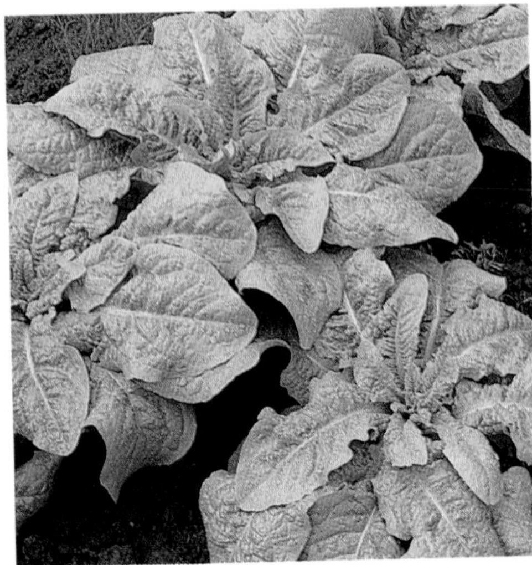

HARDINESS
Zones 3 and warmer. In colder areas, harvest the leaves only if the stalk takes too long to develop.

DAYS TO MATURITY
45 days for leaves (thinnings can be harvested earlier); 90 days for stalks. Tolerates light frost.

COMMENTS
Named cultivars are not generally available.

CELTUCE

CELTUCE HAS LETTUCE-LIKE LEAVES AND CELERY-LIKE STALKS. WHEN COOKED, IT TASTES LIKE A CROSS BETWEEN SUMMER SQUASH AND ARTICHOKE.

Position Plant in full sun in well-drained soil; pH 6.0–6.7. Otherwise not fussy.

Cultivation Sow in early spring and again in midsummer. Best if matured in cool weather. Seeds are small; sow thinly and cover lightly. Thin to 1 foot (30 cm) apart, using the thinnings with other salad greens.

Pests and diseases Usually free from pests and diseases. Water frequently to delay the leaves becoming bitter and to help keep the central stalk tender. Warm weather induces the plants to bolt to seed, which also toughens the stalk.

Harvesting and storage Pick the leaves as needed. Use young leaves in salads and cook older ones. Cut the stalk at its base and peel for use as a raw or boiled vegetable, or in stir-fries and soups.

Special tips Other common names include asparagus lettuce.

HARDINESS
Zones 5 and warmer.

DAYS TO MATURITY
90 frost-free days for mature gourds; a shorter period for immature, edible-sized fruits.

COMMENTS
Other common names are cucuzzi, po gua and yugao. Other types of *L. siceraria* include calabash, dipper gourd and sugar trough.

GOURD, BOTTLE

ALTHOUGH EDIBLE, BOTTLE GOURDS ARE COMMONLY GROWN AS ORNAMENTALS.

Position Plant in full sun in well-drained, rich soil; pH 6.0–6.5. Provide good air circulation.

Cultivation Plant after frost danger is past. Sow two or three seeds to a hill and site hills 6 feet (1.8 m) apart, or sow more closely if you can train the vine to a trellis or fence. Mulch or keep weeded. If allowed to sprawl, the vining plant will eventually shade out weeds. It is drought-tolerant, but irrigate for larger and more numerous fruits.

Pests and diseases Use a trellis to improve air circulation and lessen mildew problems. Rotate plantings of gourds and their relatives, such as squash and melons. In short-season areas, pinch off flowers after the plant has set several fruits, to ensure maturity before frost.

Harvesting and storage Pick young fruits and cook as you would summer squash. For use as a birdhouse, dry the mature gourd until the seeds inside rattle. Wax the gourd to preserve it.

Special tips Hang up dried gourds for birdhouses. Cut an entrance for the birds by drilling many small holes close together, then scrape out the center and dry out the gourd.

Lens culinaris FABACEAE

HARDINESS
Zones 5 and warmer.

DAYS TO MATURITY
120–150 days.

COMMENTS
Named cultivars not generally available.

LENTIL

A STAPLE IN MEDITERRANEAN CUISINES, THE PROTEIN-RICH RED LENTIL IS A RELATIVE OF THE PEA AND IS NEARLY AS EASY TO GROW.

Position Plant in full sun in light, well-drained soil; pH 5.8–6.2.

Cultivation Sow 1–2 weeks before last spring frost, about 1 inch (2.5 cm) deep and 3–4 inches (7.5–10 cm) apart. Plants have tendrils, like peas, but grow only about 1⅓ feet (40 cm) tall and do not need a trellis. Weed or mulch and irrigate during dry spells until the pods begin to dry, then withhold water to hasten drying.

Pests and diseases Avoid mildew by providing good air circulation. If weevils are a problem, do not grow where beans or peas have grown in the preceding year. Rainy or humid weather may cause mature seeds to sprout or rot in their pods. Pull plants when most of the foliage has died and hang up by the roots in a well-ventilated place to finish the drying process.

Harvesting and storage Harvest as you would dried bean varieties, but do not remove from pods until you are ready to use. Freeze well-dried pods for several hours to avoid potential weevil problems, and store in airtight cans or jars.

Special tips Lentils keep better if they are left in their pods.

Lepidium sativum

BRASSICACEAE

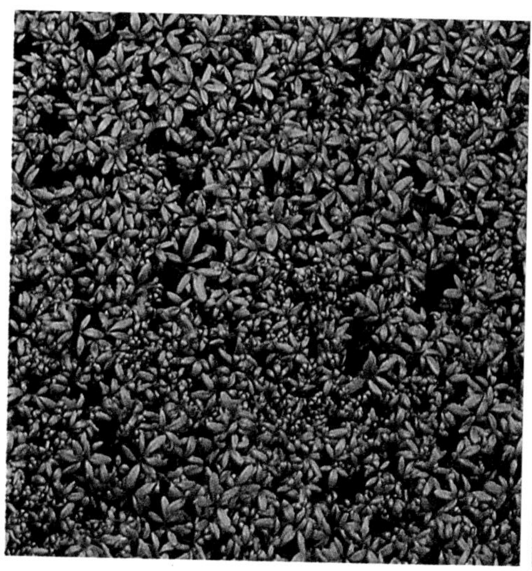

HARDINESS
Zones 2 and warmer; grow as a winter vegetable in mild areas.

DAYS TO MATURITY
21–35 days. Will withstand severe frost.

COMMENTS
Other common names are curly cress and peppergrass. Named cultivars are not generally available.

CRESS

QUICK AND EASY TO GROW, CRESS ADDS A SPARK TO SALADS OR IS A PRETTY GARNISH.

Position Plant in full sun or partial shade in soil that is moist and rich in humus; pH 6.0–7.0.

Cultivation Sow thickly in rows in early spring, 4–6 weeks before the last frost. Barely cover and firm the soil with the back of a hoe. Sow successive small plantings every 7 days until 2 weeks after last frost. Later plantings may bolt to seed in summer heat. Sow autumn crop 2–4 weeks before the first frost.

Pests and diseases Do not grow where members of the cabbage family have been grown in the preceding year. Row covers will help to deter flea beetles. Hot weather and inadequate supplies of water will cause cress to bolt to seed prematurely.

Harvesting and storage Cut with shears just above the crown and let the plants resprout for two or three more cuttings.

Special tips Upland cress *Barbarea verna* is also called American cress, scurvy grass or cressy greens. It has a spicy flavor like watercress (see page 202). It forms a small rosette of dark green, rounded leaves, which can be harvested whole or leaf by leaf. Sow as above and thin to 6 inches (15 cm).

HARDINESS
Zones 5 and warmer.

DAYS TO MATURITY
80 days for immature, edible fruits. Up to 150 days for fully mature fruits.

COMMENTS
Common names include Chinese okra, dish cloth vine, loofah and vegetable sponge.

LUFFA

LUFFA PRODUCES SQUASHLIKE FRUITS THAT ARE EDIBLE WHEN YOUNG. ITS MATURE FRUITS ARE DRIED AND USED AS SPONGES.

Position Plant in full sun, near a fence or trellis, in rich, well-drained soil; pH 6.0–6.5.

Cultivation In warm areas, plant after last frost, two to three seeds in hills about 6 feet (1.8 m) apart, or closer. In colder areas, start seeds indoors 2–3 weeks before last frost. Set out when frost danger is past. Train to a fence or trellis; luffa vines grow to 15 feet (4.5 m) or more.

Pests and diseases Little troubled by pests and disease, but provide good air circulation. In cooler areas, pinch off flowers after several large fruits have set, to ensure maturity before the first frost.

Harvesting and storage Pick fruits when 4–6 inches (10–15 cm) long and cook them as you would summer squash. For sponges, leave fruits on until they turn yellow, then hang up and dry in an airy place. Soak to loosen the skin from the fibrous interior, remove skin, and let dry again. Shake out the seeds.

Special tips Named cultivars are not generally available. *L. acutangula* produces 1¼-foot (37.5 cm), dark green, smooth-skinned fruit; *L. cylindrica* produces 1¾-foot (52.5 cm), light green, ridged fruit.

Lycopersicon esculentum

SOLANACEAE

HARDINESS
Zones 3 and warmer.

DAYS TO MATURITY
52–90 frost-free days from transplanting. Small-fruited cultivars mature fastest.

COMMENTS
Low-acid tomatoes, such as 'Orange Boy' (left), are milder and sweeter than some other cultivars.

TOMATO

PURCHASED TOMATOES CAN'T COMPARE WITH AN OLD-FASHIONED TOMATO GROWN IN YOUR OWN GARDEN. TRY TO FIND SOME OF THE "HEIRLOOM" CULTIVARS FOR FLAVOR YOU WON'T BELIEVE.

Position Plant in full sun in fertile, deep, well-drained soil; pH 6.0–7.0.

Cultivation In long-season areas, tomatoes can be direct-seeded, but they are usually started indoors 5–6 weeks before the last spring frost. Set out 2–3 feet (60–90 cm) apart if plants are to be allowed to sprawl, or as close as 1¼ feet (37.5 cm) if they are to be staked or caged. Use black plastic mulch to prewarm the soil in short-season areas. Plant tomatoes by burying the stem horizontally, right up to the topmost leaves. New roots will emerge from the buried stem, making a sturdier plant. If the tomato is staked, tie the vine to the stake with soft cloth strips, not wire or string, to avoid damaging the plant. Some gardeners prune tomatoes by pinching out leafy shoots that emerge from leaf axils, but this type of pruning is not necessary. Water tomatoes regularly but do not fertilize until the plant is well established and in full blossom. Then give weak compost tea or fish emulsion. Too much nitrogen will result in lots of foliage but few fruits. Mulch will help retain soil moisture but will also cool the soil,

Tomato continued

Cherry tomatoes produce generous quantities of fruit in a variety of colors. They are perfect for salads and lunch boxes.

so do not mulch tomatoes until the soil is well warmed.

Pests and diseases Protect young plants from cutworms with cardboard or metal collars. Handpick off tomato hornworms or control them with BT, a microbial insecticide. Folklore states that planting basil with tomatoes helps repel hornworms. To avoid soilborne diseases, do not plant where tomatoes or their relatives, such as eggplants (aubergines) and potatoes, have been grown in the preceding 2 years. If that is not possible, grow disease-resistant cultivars if you suspect your soil harbors diseases such as Fusarium or Verticillium wilt. Blossom-end rot indicates that the plant is not taking up enough calcium from the soil. If soil calcium levels are adequate, the problem is probably a lack of soil moisture. Keep the soil moist but not soggy. Dark brown, circular spots on tomato leaves suggest fungal disease or blight, which can be a serious problem in prolonged humid weather. Provide good air circulation and do not disturb plants when they are wet.

Harvesting and storage Pick the fruit when it is evenly colored but still firm. Bottle, freeze or dry excess tomatoes. Cover tomato plants to protect them through a light, early

Paste tomatoes have fewer seeds and less juice than slicing tomatoes, which makes them the right choice for soups and sauces.

frost, but harvest all fruit when more severe frost threatens. Completely green tomatoes will not ripen; pickle them or make into chutney. Blemish-free fruit that has begun to whiten or change color will continue to ripen. Wrap each tomato in tissue or newspaper and keep in a spot that stays above 55°F (13°C); check often and discard any fruit that develops bad spots.

Special tips Tomato cultivars are usually described as "indeterminate" or "determinate." Indeterminates continue to grow and set fruit all season, and usually require a sturdy cage or stake. Determinates stop growing and flowering when they reach a certain height. They are often earlier to mature and may not require caging, but they produce fruit for shorter periods than indeterminates. The letters often given after a cultivar's name indicate resistance to the following diseases or pests: V—Verticillium wilt, F—Fusarium wilt, N—nematodes, T—tobacco mosaic virus. Where space is limited, plant tall-growing tomatoes at the back of the flower garden or tie them to a wire fence.

Related plants

Beefsteak tomato *L. esculentum*
Large, fleshy fruit, up to 2 pounds (1 kg) and more, with meaty flesh and often a thick central core. Most

The tiny fruits of currant tomatoes are produced in abundance. They look most attractive left in sprays in salads, and as garnishes.

are indeterminate. Cultivars include 'Burpee's Supersteak Hybrid', 'Beefmaster' and many "heirloom" cultivars such as 'Giant Belgium' and 'Pink Ponderosa'.

Cherry tomato *L. esculentum* var. *cerasiforme* Prolific bearers of fruit that is usually about 1 inch (2.5 cm) in diameter, often borne in grape-like clusters. Cultivars include 'Sweet 100' (red, indeterminate), 'Gold Nugget' (yellow-orange, determinate) and 'Green Grape' (green-yellow, determinate).

Low-acid tomato *L. esculentum* Reduced acidity usually means milder flavor, with sweet undertones. Yellow-skinned cultivars are often, but not always, low in acid. Try 'Pink Girl' (pink skin, indeterminate), 'Lemon Boy' (yellow skin, indeterminate), 'Jetstar' (red skin, determinate) and 'Orange Boy' (orange skin, indeterminate).

Paste tomato *L. esculentum* Meatier than other tomatoes, with fewer seeds and less juice. Most cultivars are determinate, and many have concentrated fruit-set, with up to 90 percent of the fruit ripening at once. Cultivars include 'Roma' (small, pear-shaped), 'Milano' (early maturity, plum-shaped) and 'Royal Chico' (large, flat-sided, plum-shaped).

Patio tomato *L. esculentum* Determinate cultivars bred for growing in containers, but also

The large, meaty beefsteak tomato is the classic, old-fashioned garden tomato. Because the fruits are so heavy, most cultivars need sturdy stakes or cages for support.

good for small gardens. Cultivars include 'Patio' and 'Better Bush'.

Pear tomato *L. esculentum* var. *pyriforme* The fruits look like tiny pears. Red and yellow variants are available. The vigorous, indeterminate vines will need staking or caging.

Slicing tomato *L. esculentum* Grown primarily for fresh use. Scores of cultivars are available in a wide range of colors, growth habits, maturity dates and disease resistance. Among the most popular are 'Early Girl' (small red fruit, early-ripening), 'Big Boy' (large, red fruit), 'Celebrity' (large, red fruit, very disease-resistant) and 'Jubilee' (large, yellow-orange fruit).

Currant tomato *L. pimpinellifolium* Has tiny, currant-sized fruit. Both red and yellow variants are available. The vigorous, indeterminate vines will need cages or stakes for support.

HARDINESS
Zones 3 and warmer; grow as a winter vegetable in warmer areas or indoors in pots almost anywhere.

DAYS TO MATURITY
120–150 days. In short-season areas, a newly established watercress bed may not produce a harvest in the first year.

COMMENTS
Named cultivars are not generally available.

WATERCRESS

AT ITS BEST IN AUTUMN AND EARLY SPRING, WATERCRESS IS A TASTY AND HEALTHFUL ADDITION TO SALADS AND SANDWICHES.

Position Plant in full sun or partial shade in wet, well-limed soil that is rich in humus, preferably at the edge of a stream or stream-fed pond; pH 6.0–7.0.

Cultivation Start indoors 4–8 weeks before the last spring frost, or sprinkle seeds as thinly as possible where they are to grow, about a month before the last frost, pressing them into the soil. Fill gaps in the planting by breaking off pieces of stem and pressing them into the soil, where they will root easily. Gardeners without access to constantly moist soil can grow watercress in pots, indoors or out. Set pots in pans of water and change the water daily to avoid the soil becoming sour and to prevent attracting breeding mosquitoes.

Pests and diseases Little troubled by pests and diseases.

Harvesting and storage Harvest the leaves as needed, midautumn through early spring, and including winter where the climate permits.

Special tips The flavor of the leaves deteriorates during the period the plants are flowering.

HARDINESS
All Zones.

DAYS TO MATURITY
126–140 days.

COMMENTS
Steam or bake parsnips as you would potatoes. Popular cultivars include 'Hollow Crown' and 'Harris Model'.

PARSNIP

PARSNIPS LOOK RATHER LIKE CREAMY WHITE CARROTS BUT HAVE A DISTINCTIVE FLAVOR.

Position Plant in full sun in friable, open, well-drained soil; pH 6.0–7.0.

Cultivation Sow after spring frosts have finished. Sow seeds directly where they are going to grow in a furrow 2½ inches (6 cm) deep and keep moist until germinated. Parsnip seeds take 21–28 days to germinate. Thin seedlings to 2–3 inches (5–7.5 cm) apart and control weeds by hand-weeding and cultivation. Do not overfeed with nitrogen fertilizers.

Pests and diseases Rarely troubled by pests. Shallow, heavy soil or fresh manure in the soil may result in misshapen roots. Remove stones and break up clods before planting.

Harvesting and storage Start pulling early to spread the harvest. Those left keep well in the soil. In winter cover crowns with a thick layer of straw mulch and mark the bed. Dig through mulch layer all winter for a continuous, fresh harvest. Roots store for up to 2 weeks on a shelf and a little longer in the refrigerator.

Special tips If parsnips are grown on a well-prepared and fertilized bed, extra fertilizer is rarely needed, but liquid feeds, such as compost tea, applied in midseason, will promote faster growth.

HARDINESS
Zones 9–10.

DAYS TO MATURITY
Leaves can be picked as soon as the plant is established.

COMMENTS
This plant grows 1–2 feet (30–60 cm) tall. Its other common names include laksa leaf, laksa plant and knotweed.

VIETNAMESE MINT

THE SPICY LEAVES OF THIS ATTRACTIVE PLANT HAVE RED MARKINGS TOWARD THE STEM, BUT THESE OFTEN DISAPPEAR IN WINTER OR WHEN THE PLANT IS GROWN IN SHADE.

Position Plant in a well-drained, moist position in partial shade to full sun; pH 6.0–7.0.

Cultivation Set out plants about 1⅓ feet (40 cm) apart. Given ideal conditions, Vietnamese mint can be invasive as the stems root wherever they touch the ground. However, these spreading stems are easily pulled out. Growing it in a pot or hanging basket overcomes this potential problem in warm, humid areas. In colder areas it is best grown as an annual as it does not tolerate frost.

Pests and diseases Little troubled by pests and diseases.

Harvesting and storage Cut the stems as needed. The older leaves are hotter, spicier and more flavorsome than younger ones and the strongly flavored stems can be removed before serving.

Special tips Cuttings are easily grown. Stems will quickly sprout roots if they are placed in water, or you can simply snip off the new plants where the stems have touched the soil and rooted.

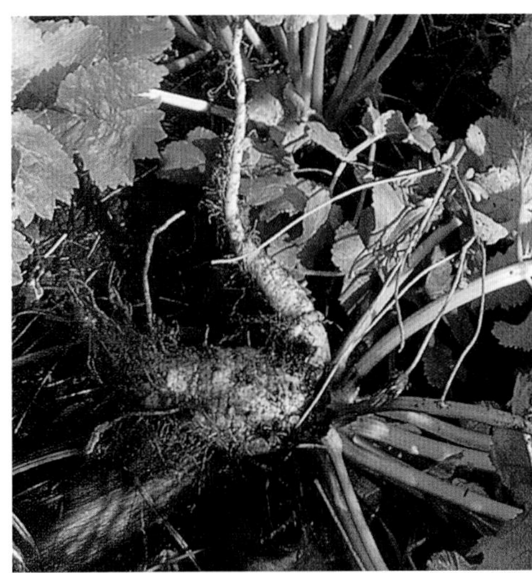

HARDINESS
Zones 4 and warmer.

DAYS TO MATURITY
78–90 days. Will withstand severe frost (frost actually sweetens the flavor).

COMMENTS
This plant is also commonly known as turnip-rooted parsley. 'Early Sugar' is a short-rooted cultivar.

PARSLEY, HAMBURG

GROWN FOR ITS THICK, WHITE TAPROOT RATHER THAN ITS LEAVES, HAMBURG PARSLEY IS ATTRACTIVE IN THE GARDEN AND TASTY AS WELL.

Position Plant in full sun in loose, deep, well-drained soil, free of stones; pH 6.0–7.0.

Cultivation Sow 4–6 weeks before the last spring frost and keep moist until germinated, which can take several weeks. Thin to stand 6–8 inches (15–20 cm) apart. If started indoors, set plants out while still small to avoid curled or forked roots. Cultivate or mulch to keep free of weeds. Water regularly in dry spells to produce large, more tender roots. Raised beds help.

Pests and diseases Shallow or heavy soil can result in misshapen roots. Break up clods, remove stones and don't step on seedbed. Handpick off any celery- or parsleyworms (green caterpillars with black and yellow stripes).

Harvesting and storage Dig up roots when large enough for you. The roots keep well in the ground (mulch to keep soil workable), or dig up before a hard freeze and store in a cool place in damp sand or sawdust.

Special tips Dig up overwintered plants before they begin to grow in spring. Roots shrink and toughen as the plants draw nutrients from them to set seed.

Phaseolus, Cicer, Lablab, Vigna spp. FABACEAE

HARDINESS
Zones 4 and warmer; use quick-maturing cultivars in colder areas.

DAYS TO MATURITY
90–150 frost-free days. The most popular quick-maturing garden cultivars are ready to harvest in 100 days or less.

COMMENTS
Native to India, the hyacinth bean (left) produces delicious pods and seeds.

BEANS, DRIED

MANY OF THE BEAN TYPES THAT DRY AND STORE WELL ARE PANTRY STAPLES IN THE WORLD'S VARIED CUISINES. WHILE YOU MAY NOT HAVE SPACE TO GROW EVERY BEAN YOU WILL USE EACH YEAR, EVEN A SMALL CROP GOES A LONG WAY AND IS FUN TO TRY.

Position Plant in full sun, in a site with good air circulation. Well-drained garden soil is acceptable; pH 6.0–7.0.

Cultivation Sow seed after the last frost and when soil has warmed, 1 inch (2.5 cm) deep and 3 inches (7.5 cm) apart in single or double rows. Cultivate shallowly until the plants are large enough to shade out weeds. Mulch between rows to help prevent pods from rotting if they touch the ground. Moisture is critical when the plants are in flower; when pods begin to mature, withhold water to hasten drying.

Pests and diseases Provide good air circulation to help prevent blights, mosaic disease and anthracnose; to avoid spreading rust, do not disturb plants when foliage is wet. Till or spade under all plant debris in autumn to destroy any disease organisms, and do not plant beans or other legumes in the same place more than once every 3 years. Damp weather late in the season, when the pods are maturing, can encourage beans to sprout in the pod. Pull plants when most of the

The black-eyed bean *Vigna unguiculata* subsp. *unguiculata* loves warmer climates. It is easy to grow and makes a wonderful, protein-rich addition to vegetable soups.

foliage has died and hang by the roots in a well-ventilated place to complete drying.

Harvesting and storage Harvest when pods are completely dry and the beans can barely be dented when bitten. Shell pods individually or thresh by placing in an old pillowcase and walking on it until pods are thoroughly crushed. Remove the resulting chaff by pouring the beans back and forth between two pans in a breezy area or in front of a fan. Store in airtight jars or bags in a dry, cool place.

Special tips To avoid potential problems with your crop being eaten by weevils, freeze the well-dried beans for several hours before storing. And remember that they will need to be soaked before cooking. One very good reason to grow beans is that they belong to the plant family that produces soil nitrogen by using the nitrogen in the atmosphere in cooperation with various soil bacteria. Grow a crop of beans in rotation with root and leafy green vegetables to ensure that your garden soil remains as healthy and productive as possible.

Related plants

Black bean *P. vulgaris* Sometimes called turtle bean or turtle soup bean, the black bean is especially popular in Caribbean and Latin

Pinto beans *Phaseolus vulgaris* are often used in Mexican cooking. You can either use them fresh, or dry the seeds.

American cuisines. The beans are small and shiny jet black.

Kidney bean *P. vulgaris* Historically the term "kidney bean" was used for all common beans, green and shelled as well as dry. But today it is usually used to refer to large, dry beans with the characteristic kidney shape—not just the dark, red-brown ones familiar from the supermarket shelf, but white, brown, yellow, black and mottled beans as well. Smaller kidney beans are often referred to as navy beans. Among firm favorite kidney bean cultivars are 'Jacob's Cattle', a red-speckled white bean popular in short-season areas, and 'Soldier', an "heirloom" bean that derives its name from a soldier-like marking on its edge.

Pinto bean *P. vulgaris* The pinto bean is a medium-sized, oval bean, usually mottled on a buff background. Its resistance to heat and drought makes it a favorite in arid areas. It is the standard bean in Mexican cooking.

Garbanzo bean *Cicer arietinum* Also called chickpea, the large, round, buff-colored garbanzo is native to southern Europe and India, where it is eaten boiled or roasted. It is the main ingredient in the popular hummus spread, in which its nutty flavor is combined with that of sesame seeds. It requires a relatively long growing season, 120 days or more.

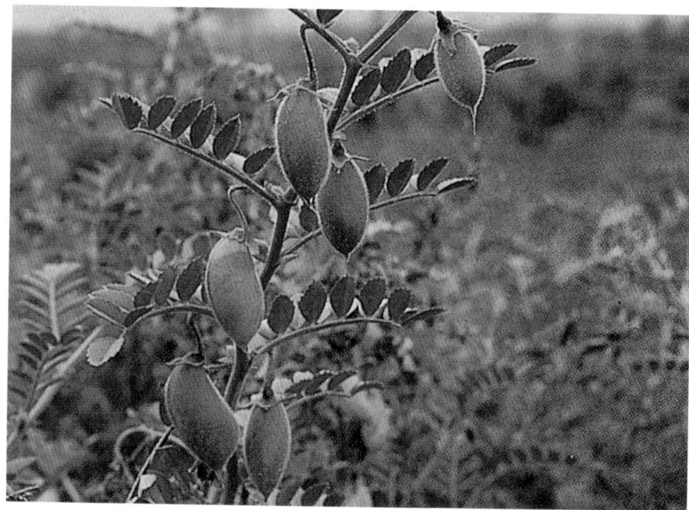

Soak garbanzo beans *Cicer arietinum* for two hours before cooking. They are delicious boiled or roasted.

Hyancinth bean *Lablab purpureus* This is a fast-growing, vining plant that is grown in its native tropics for both its pods and its seeds. It is a perennial in warm climates, but can also be grown in cooler areas as an annual. The wisteria-like blossoms are ornamental and the seeds can be dried and eaten like beans.

Adzuki bean *Vigna angularis* Small, dark red beans of Japanese origin. They are highly valued for their protein content. 'Express' is an early-maturing cultivar, requiring about 118 frost-free days.

Mung bean *V. radiata* The seeds are often sprouted for use as bean sprouts, but the dried beans are also edible after soaking and cooking. The pods can also be eaten when immature.

Black-eyed bean *V. unguiculata* subsp. *unguiculata* Also called black-eyed pea, this warm-region favorite is related to the asparagus bean (see page 213), but is grown for its seed rather than its pod. The round, off-white beans are marked with black. It does best in Zones 7 and warmer.

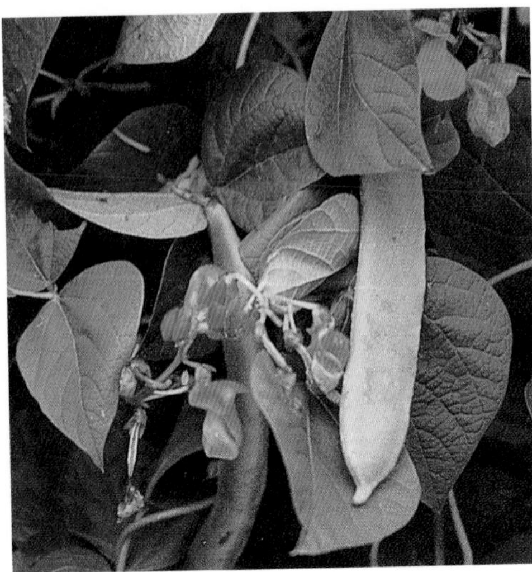

HARDINESS
Zones 3 and warmer; cold climates may require a quick-maturing cultivar.

DAYS TO MATURITY
A minimum of 42–55 frost-free days, depending on species/cultivar.

COMMENTS
The scarlet runner (left) has clusters of brilliant red edible flowers, edible pods and large seeds, used as fresh shelled beans.

BEANS, FRESH

EVERY GARDEN CAN ACCOMMODATE SOME FRESH BEANS, BE IT A FEW SMALL BUSH PLANTS OR A FULL CROP ON A TRELLIS.

Position Plant in full sun. Likes soil that is rich in humus but not excessively fertile; pH 6.0–7.5.

Cultivation Sow seed after frost danger is past. Sow bush snap beans about 1 inch (2.5 cm) deep and 3 inches (7.5 cm) apart in single or double rows. Keep well weeded or mulched. Regular watering will increase yield; thorough watering is critical when beans are in flower. Bush snap beans bear heavily but only for a few weeks. To assure a steady supply, make small plantings 3–4 weeks apart, ending 2 months before the first autumn frost date.

Pests and diseases Mexican bean beetles can be serious pests from midseason onward; early plantings are usually less troubled. Deter with row covers. Avoid the bean patch when the plants are wet to avoid spreading bean rust. Sown too early in cold, wet soil, bean seeds may rot before germinating. Small plantings for early harvest may be worth the risk, but larger plantings for freezing or bottling should be delayed until the weather is settled.

Harvesting and storage Pick at any size, but before seeds have begun to swell noticeably inside the pod.

Plant butterbeans *Phaseolus lunatus* successively for a regular supply. Water frequently when flowers appear for a heavy yield.

Tiny, fresh beans are a tender treat, but larger pods have a more characteristic "beany" flavor. Bottle, freeze or pickle snap beans, or leave pods on the plant to mature fully and then dry beans and use as you would other dried beans.

Special tips Increase yield by using an inoculant of nitrogen-fixing bacteria to help the plant make better use of nitrogen from the air. Add the inoculant to the seed or the soil at planting time.

Related plants

Scarlet runner bean *P. coccineus* Climbing bean grown as a perennial in subtropical areas and as an annual in areas as cool as Zone 4. Cold-tolerant cultivars include 'Prize Winner'.

Lima bean *P. lunatus* Climbing or pole limas require plenty of warm weather and a sturdy trellis, but are considered superior to the bush types in flavor. Require at least an 85-day growing season for the first beans to mature; a full harvest takes at least 100 days' favorable weather.

Bush lima bean *P. lunatus* Sometimes called butter or sugar bean, the bush lima is a heat-loving bean. It does best in Zones 7 and warmer. The seed, rather than the pod, is eaten, either as a fresh vegetable or as a dried bean. The beans are ready to pick when the pods are plump.

Romano beans *Phaseolus vulgaris* are flat-podded, tender beans, sometimes called Italian beans.

Butterbean *P. lunatus* Butterbeans are grown and used like limas but are flat, thin and much smaller. Also called Carolina bean.

Horticultural bean *P. vulgaris* Also called the shell bean, shelly bean, or cranberry bean, these plants are grown specifically for their seeds, which are eaten at the immature stage. Harvest horticultural beans when pods have started to turn rubbery but before the seeds inside have begun to harden. 'Tongue of Fire' is a striking bean, streaked with red on an off-white background; some seed suppliers may carry cultivars of French shelling beans, also known as "flageolets."

Pole bean *P. vulgaris* Also called runner beans, these beans require support for their long vines. They are often grown on a "teepee" framework, but can also be planted in a row and trellised. They bear over a longer period than bush beans and are a good choice where space is too limited for successive plantings to be made. They take longer to mature and some older cultivars will have strings that must be removed before eating. Cultivars include 'Kentucky Wonder', 'Case Knife' and 'Blue Lake'.

Purple-podded bean *P. vulgaris* Striking, quick-maturing purple bean that turns dark green when

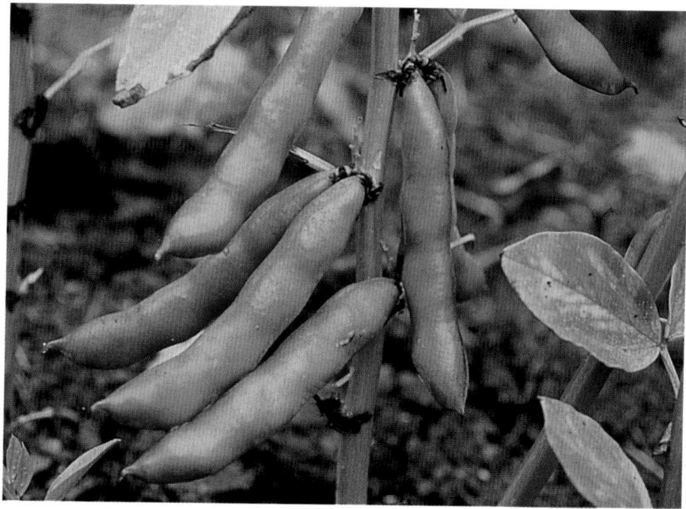

Pick fava beans *Vicia faba* when pods are plump, but before the outer skin becomes tough. Where winter abruptly turns to summer, blossoms may fall without setting pods.

cooked. Cultivars include 'Royal Burgundy' and 'Royalty Purple Pod'.

Romano bean *P. vulgaris* Tender, well flavored, early to mature. Cultivars include 'Romano II', 'Jumbo' and 'Greencrop'.

Wax bean *P. vulgaris* Also called yellow snap bean. Slender, pale to golden yellow pods that are picked, prepared, and eaten exactly as green snap beans. Cultivars include 'Yellow Pencil Pod' and 'Goldkist'.

Fava bean *Vicia faba* Also called broad bean, the fava is sometimes grown as a shell bean in place of limas in short-season areas. It is far more frost-tolerant than other beans and can be planted with the spring peas, 4–6 weeks before last frost of spring. It is best in areas with long, cool springs. 'Ipro' has some tolerance to hot weather; 'Windsor Long Pod' is widely available.

Asparagus bean *Vigna unguiculata* subsp. *sesquipedalis* Also known as Chinese long bean, dow guak, snake bean or yardlong bean, this relative of the southern cowpea produces long, thin, crunchy pods best eaten at 10–12 inches (20–30 cm). It requires a trellis, likes warm weather, and needs a longer growing season than regular beans—at least 75 days of frost-free weather. Named cultivars are hard to find, but some variants are identified by the color of their seed.

HARDINESS
Zones 6–9; hardiness varies among species. The "clumping" *Bambusa beecheyana* will grow in Zone 10.

DAYS TO MATURITY
Depending on species vigor, some shoots can be harvested in the second spring.

COMMENTS
Cut stalks for garden stakes when 3 years old or more.

BAMBOO SHOOT

WHERE GARDEN SPACE ALLOWS, BAMBOO PROVIDES EDIBLE YOUNG SHOOTS IN SPRING AS WELL AS USEFUL GARDEN STAKES LATER.

Position Plant in full sun in fertile, moist, well-drained soil; pH 6.0–7.0.

Cultivation Propagate by division in late winter or very early spring. Buy potted divisions by mail or in garden centers in areas where bamboo is hardy. Plant in early spring and water until established.

Pests and diseases Little troubled by pests. Most bamboos that produce edible shoots are "running" bamboos that spread by underground rhizomes. Build a strong underground barrier or mow frequently to keep the colony from getting out of hand.

Harvesting and storage Cut tender young shoots at ground level in early to midspring. Stir-fry or use fresh in salads.

Special tips Edible species vary widely in their mature height and hardiness. The smallest, *P. aurea*, also called fishpole or golden bamboo, grows to about 20 feet (6 m) tall. *P. bambusoides*, or timber bamboo, grows to 73 feet (22 m) tall and 6 inches (15 cm) in diameter. The hardiest bamboos include *P. aureosulcata*, *P. dulcis*, *P. nuda* and *P. viridiglaucescens*, all up to 30–35 feet (9–10.5 m) tall.

Pisum sativum

HARDINESS
Zones 2 and warmer; grow as a spring and autumn crop in most Zones, and as a winter vegetable in frost-free climates.

DAYS TO MATURITY
55–80 days. Young plants will tolerate moderate frost, but frost will halt the development of autumn crops.

COMMENTS
The pods of crisp snap peas (left) are edible.

PEA

TALL-GROWING PEAS WILL NEED THE SUPPORT OF SOME TYPE OF TRELLIS FOR THEIR CLIMBING STEMS.

Position Plant in full sun on a site with good air circulation. Prefers loose, well-drained soil; pH 6.0–7.0.

Cultivation Peas do poorly in hot weather, so plant spring crops early to beat the heat unless your springs are long and cool. In Zones 7 and warmer, seed planted in late autumn often overwinters and germinates in early spring. In colder Zones, plant 4–8 weeks before the last spring frost. Sow autumn crops 10–12 weeks before first autumn frost. Plant bush types 1 inch (2.5 cm) deep and about 1 inch (2.5 cm) apart in double rows spaced 6 inches (15 cm) apart. Planted in this way, the plants will help support each other and the yield will be greater in very little extra space. Plant tall types roughly 1 inch (2.5 cm) apart in single rows and provide a trellis for them to climb on. Do not thin. Cultivate carefully to avoid uprooting plants, or mulch to discourage weeds. Peas do not need supplementary fertilizer, especially if the soil has been sufficiently well dug and composted or manured during the previous season. If your soil tends to be acidic, apply a light dressing of lime to correct the pH level. Practice crop rotation with root

Keep your pea plants well watered during flowering and pod set and they will continue to produce for a considerable time, especially if the pods are picked regularly.

vegetables and leafy greens to avoid soilborne diseases.

Pests and diseases Rarely troubled by insects. Good air circulation and resistant cultivars help to prevent powdery mildew. If root rot is a problem in your area, do not plant where peas have been grown in the preceding 2 years. Autumn plantings in humid areas, even of resistant cultivars, are often plagued by powdery mildew. Spray the foliage thoroughly with a baking soda solution (1 teaspoon per quart [liter] of water).

Harvesting and storage Pick shelling-type peas when pods are full and plump and peas are tender. Pick snap peas when pods are rounded but still smooth, before the peas begin to bulge the sides of the pod. Pick snowpeas when pods are perfectly flat, showing only the tiniest hint of the pea inside. Peas are best eaten immediately or frozen or canned promptly, as their sugars begin to turn to starch quickly. Dry and store overmature crops as you would dried beans, for use in soups.

Special tips Make sure you provide adequate moisture when pea plants are in bloom. Even low-growing cultivars benefit from some vine support. Stick twiggy brush cuttings into the pea row to serve as what

If the space available for peas is limited, plant a variety such as 'Tall Telephone', which can be grown on a teepee-type support, or on a trellis.

old-time gardeners called "pea brush." Make plantings in late summer to extend the harvest, and remember to compost spent plants, as long as they are not diseased in any way. Time to maturity differs with the various cultivars, with the earlier ones generally producing a lower yield than those that grow taller and mature later.

Related plants

Shelling pea *P. sativum* var. *sativum*
Also called English pea or garden pea. Other cultivars include 'Laxton's Progress' (bush type), 'Tall Telephone' (trellis type) and 'Wando' (bush type, heat-resistant).

Snap pea *P. sativum* var. *sativum*
Pods are not fibrous like shelling peas and may be eaten cooked or raw in salads. They are best if the strings are removed before cooking. Cultivars include 'Sugar Snap' (trellis type), 'Sugar Ann' (bush type) and 'Sugar Daddy' (bush type, stringless).

Snowpea *P. sativum* var. *macro-carpon* Also called edible-podded or sugar pea. Favored in oriental cuisines. Cultivars include 'Oregon Sugar Pod' (trellis type), 'Mammoth Melting Sugar' (trellis type) and 'Little Sweetie' (bush type).

HARDINESS
Zones 4 and warmer.

DAYS TO MATURITY
60–70 days, although thinnings can be eaten sooner.

COMMENTS
Other common names include kitchen garden purslane, pourpier, pussley and verdolaga.

PURSLANE

POPULAR IN EUROPE AS A SALAD GREEN, CULTIVATED PURSLANE IS TALLER AND MORE SUCCULENT THAN ITS COUSIN, THE WEED.

Position Plant in full sun. Not fussy about soil and will even grow in sand; pH 6.0–7.0. Drought-resistant.

Cultivation Seed thinly in rows or broadcast in small beds after frost danger is past in spring. Do not cover seeds but firm gently into the soil with the back of a hoe. Keep the soil moist until the seeds germinate. Thin to 4–6 inches (10–15 cm) apart (the thinnings can be used in salads). Sow small successive crops up to 2 months before autumn frosts are expected. Water frequently.

Pests and diseases Little bothered by pests or diseases.

Harvesting and storage Harvest fresh leaves and stems with scissors as needed, leaving 1 inch (2.5 cm) or more above ground to sprout new leaves. May be harvested four or five times. Best used fresh as it does not store well.

Special tips Common purslane is also edible. Collect seeds of the best wild plants to grow in the garden, saving seed each year from plants with the best flavor and growth habit. Named cultivars are not generally available, but seed suppliers may offer variants based on leaf size or green or gold color.

Psophocarpus tetragonolobus FABACEAE

HARDINESS
Zones 7 and warmer; perennial in tropical climates.

DAYS TO MATURITY
120–150 frost-free days for edible pods; 180–210 days for tubers.

COMMENTS
Other common names are Goa bean, Manila bean, princess pea and winged bean.

ASPARAGUS PEA

ITS UNIQUE FLAVOR AND HIGH PROTEIN CONTENT MAKE THE ASPARAGUS PEA POPULAR IN ASIAN STIR-FRIES AND OTHER DISHES. IT ALSO PRODUCES EDIBLE TUBERS.

Position Plant in full sun near a trellis or fence in loose and well-drained soil; pH 7.3–8.0.

Cultivation Plant after frost danger is past, 1 inch (2.5 cm) deep and 2–4 inches (5–10 cm) apart. The vines grow to a height of 6–8 feet (1.8–2.4 m), so support with a sturdy trellis or fence. Cultivate shallowly or mulch to control weeds. The purplish red flowers form in loose clusters. The pods are four-sided, rather than round, with distinct flanges or "wings" at each corner.

Pests and diseases Do not grow where legumes, such as peas and beans, have grown the preceding year. Keep vines growing strongly with regular watering to deter aphids. Requires a long, warm growing season. Where the weather is not to its liking, it may die without flowering.

Harvesting and storage Harvest the pods at 6–8 inches (15–20 cm) long and eat steamed or stir-fried. Pick frequently, as pods can quickly become oversized. Dig up marble-sized tubers after frost has killed the plants; use in stir-fries or stews.

Special tips Named cultivars are not generally available.

Radish

FAST-GROWING RADISHES ADD A CRISP, COLORFUL TOUCH TO SPRING SALADS. HARVEST WHILE YOUNG AND TENDER.

Position Plant in loose, moisture-retentive soil; pH 5.5–6.8.

Cultivation Sow spring radishes 3–5 weeks before last spring frost, ½ inch (12 mm) deep in double or triple rows. Make the rows short and sow small crops every 2 weeks until a month after frost danger is past. Sow autumn crops starting 8 weeks before frost and continuing until frost. Thin spring radishes to 1–2 inches (2.5–5 cm) apart, or seed sparingly and thin by pulling radishes as they reach eating size. Sow winter radishes 8–10 weeks before autumn frost and thin to 4–6 inches (10–15 cm) apart. Keep moist to avoid strong flavor and toughness. Mulch between rows to keep soil moist in hot weather.

Pests and diseases Rotate radishes and other root crops to reduce damage from root maggots. Spring crops are more vulnerable than autumn crops. Spring radishes, especially slender French breakfast types, become woody and bitter when overmature. Plant small but frequent crops to keep tender radishes on the table. The roots of radishes planted in heavy soils are apt to be misshapen and have a number of branching side roots.

HARDINESS
All Zones; grow as a winter vegetable in mild areas.

DAYS TO MATURITY
21–35 days for spring radishes; 50–60 days for winter radishes. Will withstand moderate frost.

COMMENTS
Cultivars of the daikon (left) include 'Summer Cross' and 'Miyashige'.

Japanese radish *Raphanus sativus* is a white, carrot-shaped radish, up to 2 feet (60 cm) long. Also known as daikon, it is often grated as a condiment.

Harvesting and storage Pull spring and autumn crops when large enough for use. Pull winter radishes as needed when they reach eating size; harvest all roots before a hard frost. Store in damp sand or sawdust in a cool place, or pickle.

Special tips Interplant spring radishes with slower-growing crops such as broccoli and cabbage. Harvest the radishes before the companion crops needs the space. Radishes are frequently mixed with beet or carrot seeds: the radishes germinate first and so mark the rows of the slower-growing crops. Because they grow quickly, they are a good crop for children to plant.

Related plants

Black Spanish radish *R. sativus* Up to 4 inches (10 cm) in diameter, with black skin and white flesh. Pungent, keeps well.

Chinese radish *R. sativus* Also called lo bok or lo po. Long and white like the Japanese radish, but sweet, not pungent. Oriental seed suppliers offer named cultivars or variants based on skin color.

Winter radish *R. sativus* A catch-all term for radish cultivars that are suitable for at least short-term storage as a root vegetable. In addition to those above, the German beer radish, which is large, white, and turnip-shaped, is very popular in Europe.

HARDINESS
Zones 8 and cooler.

DAYS TO MATURITY
Harvest sparingly in the second year after planting and more heavily thereafter.

COMMENTS
Cultivars include 'MacDonald' and 'Valentine'. 'Victoria' is robust and green-stemmed rather than red.

RHUBARB

RHUBARB'S STOUT LEAF STALKS, COOKED BY THEMSELVES OR WITH OTHER SEASONAL FRUITS, MAKE DELICIOUS DESSERTS.

Position Plant in full sun in rich, deep, well-drained soil; pH 5.0–6.8.

Cultivation Can grow from seed, but it is quicker to use divisions of this hardy perennial. Plant in early spring, 1–2 months before last spring frost. Dig a hole big enough to accommodate roots and cover the crown with no more than 2 inches (5 cm) of soil. Mix a shovelful of compost or well-rotted manure into the soil to get the plant off to a good start. Cultivate or mulch. Heavy feeder; top-dress every spring with compost or rotted manure. Drought-tolerant, but provide adequate moisture to ensure abundant, tender stalks.

Pests and diseases Little troubled by pests. Plant in well-drained soil to avoid root rot.

Harvesting and storage To harvest large, outer leaf stalks, grasp them near the base and pull with a slight twisting motion. Remove the leaves, which are toxic. Harvest sparingly in autumn as well as in spring, but spring stalks are more tender. Chop and freeze uncooked stems.

Special tips Cut off flower stems that rob the plant of energy, resulting in stringy leaf stalks.

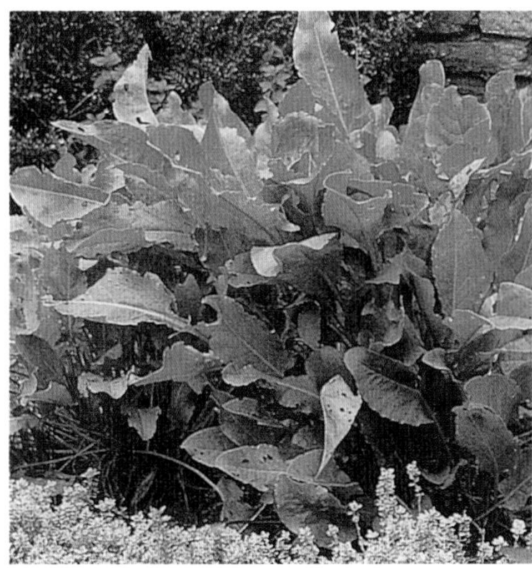

HARDINESS
All Zones.

DAYS TO MATURITY
60 days for first-year crop, although thinnings may be harvested sooner.

COMMENTS
Will withstand moderate frost. The leaves can be frozen for use in soup and sauces. Sheep's sorrel is also known as red sorrel.

SORREL, FRENCH

A TENDER GREEN SALAD PLANT WITH A DELICIOUS LEMONY FLAVOR. FRENCH SORREL WITHSTANDS DRY WEATHER BETTER THAN SOME OTHER SORRELS.

Position Plant in full sun or partial shade in rich, moist soil; pH 6.0–7.0.

Cultivation Start the seeds indoors or sow directly in the garden 2–4 weeks before last spring frost. Thin to stand 6–8 inches (15–20 cm) apart, using the thinnings in salads. Cultivate or mulch to discourage weeds and keep watered for best production. Top-dress the bed with compost or well-rotted manure each autumn or spring. Sorrel is a perennial plant, but will decline after 3–4 years. Start a new bed from seed or divide existing plants.

Pests and diseases Use row covers to protect plants from leaf-eating insects. Keep flower stems cut back to extend the spring harvest.

Harvesting and storage Pick fresh leaves as needed. Produces abundantly in spring and autumn; less productive in hot weather.

Related plants

Garden sorrel *R. acetosa* Also called sour dock. Pictured above, it has longer leaves and milder flavor than French sorrel.

Sheep's sorrel *R. acetosella* This is the most common "weed" sorrel. It is edible, but invasive in the garden.

HARDINESS
Zones 7 and warmer.

DAYS TO MATURITY
80–90 days for fruits; shoots and roots are harvested in the second year.

COMMENTS
Other common names for chayote are cho-cho, choko, chuchu, christophene, mirliton and vegetable pear.

CHAYOTE

CHAYOTE IS A SPACE-HUNGRY, AVID CLIMBER SUITED TO WARM CLIMATES. SHOOTS, ROOTS AND FRUITS ARE ALL EDIBLE.

Position Cooler areas may produce fruits only; roots are not harvested until the second year. Full sun, adjacent to a wall or fence for climbing. Deep, fertile, moist, but well-drained soil; pH 5.5–6.5.

Cultivation After last spring frost, plant the entire fruit (about 4 inches [10 cm] long, containing one seed), with 1 inch (2.5 cm) of narrow end exposed. One plant will satisfy most gardeners' needs. Plant near a fence or trellis, or provide 12 feet (3.6 m) of growing space. Keep well watered. Perennial in mild areas; may overwinter in cooler climates with protection. Cut back after frost and mulch roots; pull back mulch after frost danger is past next spring.

Pests and diseases Provide good air circulation to avoid fungal disease and mildew.

Harvesting and storage Pick immature fruits at 4–6 inches (10–15 cm) long and use like summer squash. Harvest mature fruits before frost; store and use like winter squash (see page 175). Cut second-year shoots in spring; marinate or steam as you would asparagus. Dig up roots in autumn of the second year; store and use like potatoes.

HARDINESS
Zones 5 and warmer.

DAYS TO MATURITY
50–75 frost-free days.

COMMENTS
Eggplant can be grown in large pots in disease-free soil. Provide adequate soil moisture and calcium to prevent blossom-end rot, which shows up as a soft, brown spot at the blossom end of the fruit.

EGGPLANT (AUBERGINE)

EGGPLANT THRIVES IN HOT WEATHER. IT NEEDS AMPLE AMOUNTS OF WATER AND FERTILIZER TO PRODUCE ITS FRUITS.

Position Plant in full sun in light, rich, well-drained, warm soil; pH 5.5–6.8.

Cultivation It does not pay to start the plants too early in the season or set them out too early. Start 8 weeks before night temperatures can be counted on to stay above 50°F (10°C). Night covers may be needed in colder climates. Space the plants 1½–2 feet (45–60 cm) apart. Eggplant needs plenty of water and food to produce well. Apply fish emulsion or compost tea at least once a month.

Pests and diseases Use row covers to deter flea beetles. Pick off Colorado potato beetles by hand; a light dusting of ground limestone helps to repel this pest. To avoid soilborne diseases such as Fusarium and Verticillium wilt, rotate eggplant and other members of the nightshade (Solanaceae) family, such as tomatoes and potatoes.

Harvesting and storage Clip the fruit with some stem attached; harvest often to encourage further fruiting. Standard eggplant cultivars, such as 'Black Beauty', will bear 4–10 full-sized fruits, or more if picked small. Oriental cultivars, such as 'Sanshi', bear more but smaller fruits. It is

The white eggplant is as delicious as it is decorative. Harvest the glossy fruits at any size and keep picking regularly to keep the plants bearing.

better to harvest when a little small than to let eggplant become bitter and overmature. When frost threatens, harvest all fruits, leaving 2 inches (5 cm) of stem attached, and store in a cool, moist, well-ventilated place. They will keep for a month or longer.

Special tips Where the growing season permits, try making two small plantings a month apart.

Related plants

Baby eggplant *S. melongena*
A gourmet item, usually slender or egg-shaped, up to 4 inches (10 cm) long. Quick-maturing, good for short-season areas. Cultivars include 'Pirouette' and 'Little Fingers'.

Italian eggplant *S. melongena* There are many fine cultivars with tender, nonbitter white flesh and dazzling skin color. 'Rosa Bianca' is rosy lavender and white; 'Violetta di Firenze' has dark lavender, somewhat ridged fruit.

Oriental eggplant *S. melongena*
Also called Japanese eggplant. Long, thin, purple-black fruits, but also light green and white-lavender. Cultivars include 'Orient Express' and 'Kurume'.

White eggplant *S. melongena* This variety has an attractive white skin, but may be less prolific than its purple siblings. 'Casper' has full-sized fruit; 'Osterei' and 'White Egg' bear smaller fruits.

HARDINESS
Zones 3 and warmer.

DAYS TO MATURITY
55–80 days.

COMMENTS
Young plants will withstand a light frost. Fingerling potatoes (left) are long and slender, with a waxy texture that makes them ideal for use in salads.

POTATO

POTATOES THRIVE IN RICH, LOOSE, WELL-DRAINED, SLIGHTLY ACID SOIL. ALL POTATOES CAN BE STORED FOR LATER USE.

Position Plant in full sun in loose, well-drained, slightly acid soil with plenty of potash; ideal pH 5.2–5.7, but will also do well at pH 5.8–6.5.

Cultivation Most potatoes do not come true from seed and are planted from pieces of tuber called "seed potatoes." Each piece should be about the size of an egg and contain one or more "eyes," or dormant buds. Cut seed potatoes to size and let the pieces dry for 1 day to avoid having them rot in the ground. Plant 2–4 weeks before last spring frost, about 1 foot (30 cm) apart in a trench 3–4 inches (7.5–10 cm) deep. Rake the soil level over the seed potatoes. Tubers will form above the seed potato, not below it, so plants must be "hilled" to get good yields. With a hoe or rake, draw soil up around the plant when it is 6–8 inches (15–20 cm) tall, burying all but the topmost leaves. Repeat at least once more as the plant grows. Hilling also supports the plants and protects new potatoes from exposure to light. On level or slightly sloping beds, the furrow between rows can be used for irrigating. You can also grow potatoes under straw or leaf mulch, adding layers as the plant grows.

Potato continued

White potatoes are good for all-purpose use. For easy harvesting, incorporate loose compost, leaves and straw into the hills and the potatoes will pull up readily.

In well-prepared and fertilized soil, no extra fertilizer is needed, but water regularly to promote smooth-skinned, well-developed potatoes.

Pests and diseases Rotate plantings of potato and its nightshade relatives, such as tomato and eggplant. Potatoes like soil that has recently been under sod, but prepare the area the autumn before planting and turn it over once during the winter, if possible, to destroy grubs. Do not use fresh manure on potato beds as it encourages scab. Covering plants with row covers or dusting them with ground limestone helps to deter flea beetles and Colorado potato beetles. A special strain of BT, a microbial insecticide, is available to control potato beetle larvae where the insect is a serious problem. If exposed to light, potato tubers develop green patches that contain the toxic alkaloid solanine. Hill or mulch deeply to prevent sunlight from reaching the tubers; store harvested potatoes in a dark place (never eat greened potatoes).

Harvesting and storage Blooming is usually the signal that the plant has begun to form tubers. Check by gently probing the soil around the base of the plant, taking no more than a few tubers per plant for early use. "New potatoes" are those that

When blossoms appear on the plants, you can harvest some small new potatoes. When the leaves die down, the mature potatoes are ready to harvest.

have been freshly harvested and eaten within a day, before the skin toughens and the sugars begin to be converted to starches. When foliage dies back, the potatoes are mature. Dig up as needed, completing the harvest before a hard freeze, because potatoes that have been frozen will rot in storage. Dry, without washing, and store in well-ventilated boxes or mesh bags in a cool to cold place, ideally about 40°F (4°C).

Special tips To speed up your harvest, try presprouting your seed potatoes. Set whole tubers in a cool, bright spot. Once they have developed short, bright sprouts (in about 4–6 weeks), plant the whole potatoes out into the garden as you would normally.

Related plants

Fingerling potatoes *S. tuberosum* Also called German potatoes, this variety (pictured on page 227) has long, slender tubers, often with a waxy texture that makes them ideal for potato salad. They are more prolific than standard potatoes. Dig up soon after they mature, because potatoes left in the ground tend to become knobby. Cultivars include 'German Fingerling', 'Yellow Fingerling' and 'Larota'.

Red potatoes *S. tuberosum* A red-skinned potato, usually with moist,

Red potatoes are good for boiling or baking in their skins. Set aside any tubers that are nicked or damaged during harvesting and use them first.

white flesh, but some cultivars have cream-colored or yellow flesh. Small ones are often sold commercially as "new potatoes." Cultivars include 'Red Pontiac', 'Red Norland', 'Red Bliss' and 'Red Gold' (yellow flesh).

Russet potatoes *S. tuberosum* Usually oblong potatoes with netted skin, this variety has a mealy texture ideal for baking. Cultivars include 'Russet Burbank'.

White potatoes *S. tuberosum* With white- or buff-colored skin and white flesh, this variety is an all-purpose potato. 'Irish Cobbler' is a very thin-skinned and early cultivar. 'Kennebec' is well adapted to many areas. 'Green Mountain' is an old and reliable cultivar.

Yellow potatoes *S. tuberosum* Yellow-fleshed potatoes are gaining popularity for their delicate flavor, beauty and their appealing waxy texture. Some popular cultivars include 'Bintje', 'Yukon Gold' and 'Yellow Finn'.

HARDINESS
All Zones.

DAYS TO MATURITY
40–53 days, although thinnings can be harvested sooner. Spinach will withstand moderate frost.

COMMENTS
Good, reliable cultivars are 'Longstanding Bloomsdale', 'Melody' and 'Tyee'.

SPINACH

FRESH OR COOKED, SPINACH IS DELICIOUS AND NUTRITIOUS. IT NEEDS COOL WEATHER AND PLENTY OF WATER TO PRODUCE ABUNDANT, CRISP LEAVES.

Position Plant in full sun or partial shade in moist, fertile, well-limed soil; pH 6.0–7.0.

Cultivation Sow seed ½ inch (12 mm) deep, 4–6 weeks before the last spring frost. In very short-season areas, or where hot weather sets in abruptly, start spinach indoors. Set out or thin seedlings to 4–6 inches (10–15 cm) apart. Keep free of weeds and water regularly. Sow autumn crops 4–6 weeks before the first frost, or later for overwintering. Seed autumn crops heavily, because spinach germinates poorly in warm soil.

Pests and diseases Use row covers to protect from leaf miners and chewing insects.

Harvesting and storage Pick larger outside leaves or harvest the whole plant at its base. Spinach freezes well for use as a cooked vegetable.

Special tips Hot weather and lengthening days can cause spinach plants to bolt to seed. Choose heat-resistant cultivars and sow spring crops early to avoid this problem.

Tetragonia tetragonioides AIZOACEAE

HARDINESS
Zones 4 and warmer.

DAYS TO MATURITY
55–70 days.

COMMENTS
Named cultivars are not generally available.

SPINACH, NEW ZEALAND

NEW ZEALAND SPINACH IS A BRANCHING, MATLIKE PLANT THAT THRIVES IN WEATHER THAT IS TOO HOT FOR TRUE SPINACH.

Position Plant in full sun in rich, well-drained soil; pH 6.5–7.5.

Cultivation Soak seed overnight to hasten germination and sow directly in the garden 1–2 weeks before the last spring frost. In warm climates, prechill seed in the refrigerator for 1–2 days. In short-season areas, start indoors 4–6 weeks before the last frost. Set plants 1–1½ feet (30–45 cm) apart when the danger of frost is past.

Pests and diseases New Zealand spinach is rarely troubled by pests. Seed can be slow to germinate. Mark the row well to avoid weeding out young plants.

Harvesting and storage Pick about 4–6 inches (10–15 cm) of the branch tips, together with the leaves, which are small and brittle. Whole plants may be cut above the ground when they are small; the stem will resprout. Cook as you would true spinach.

Special tips New Zealand spinach is good for hot, dry climates where true spinach does poorly. It will tolerate saline soils.

HARDINESS
Zones 4 and warmer; grow as a winter vegetable in mild climates.

DAYS TO MATURITY
120–150 days.

COMMENTS
Other common names include oyster plant and vegetable oyster, a reference to the unusual flavor of this easily grown vegetable.

SALSIFY

A HARDY ROOT VEGETABLE, SALSIFY LOOKS LIKE A SLENDER PARSNIP WITH NARROW, GRASSY LEAVES, BUT HAS A DELICATE, OYSTER-LIKE FLAVOR.

Position Plant in full sun in deep, light and rich soil; pH 6.0–8.0.

Cultivation Sow seed ½ inch (12 mm) deep 2–4 weeks before the last spring frost, or in autumn in mild climates. Thin to stand 3–4 inches (7.5–10 cm) apart. Water regularly and mulch to maintain the soil moisture and produce smoother, more tender roots.

Pests and diseases Salsify is little troubled by pests or diseases. Spotty or slow germination may indicate that the seed is old. Purchase fresh salsify seed each year.

Harvesting and storage Dig roots as needed when large enough, but mulch the bed before a hard freeze. Store the harvested roots in damp sand or sawdust in a cool place.

Special tips Young plants can tolerate light frost; mature ones, severe frost.

Related plants

Black salsify *Scorzonera hispanica*
Cream root with black skin. Leaves can be eaten in salads.

Spanish salsify *Scolymus hispanicus*
Also called golden thistle, this variety is quite mild in flavor.

Valerianella locusta VALERIANACEAE

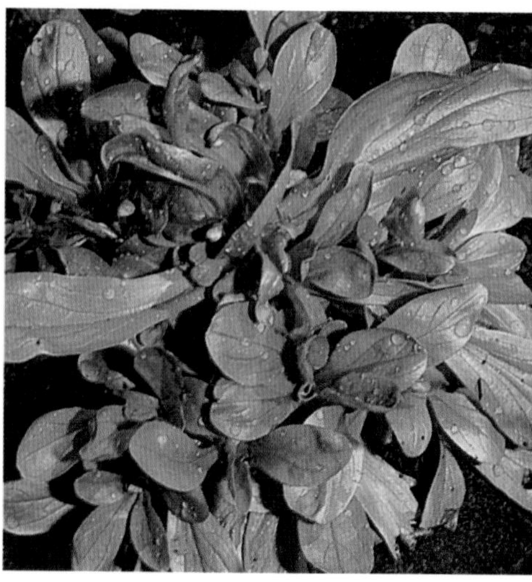

HARDINESS
Zones 2 and warmer. Over-winters in Zones 5 and warmer; in mild areas, grow as a winter vegetable.

DAYS TO MATURITY
45–60 days from spring seeding; thinnings can be harvested earlier.

COMMENTS
Other common names are fetticus, lamb's lettuce and mâche. Reliable cultivars are 'Elan', 'Piedmont' and 'Vit'.

CORN SALAD

SMALL, TENDER, GREEN CORN SALAD CAN BE PLANTED IN AUTUMN TO GRACE SPRING'S EARLIEST SALADS. IT'S EXPENSIVE TO BUY, BUT EASY TO GROW.

Position Full sun or partial shade. Not fussy about soil, but prefers it rich with humus; pH 6.0–7.0. Will withstand light frosts.

Cultivation Sow seed in early spring, 2–4 weeks before last frost; just cover with fine soil and firm with the back of a hoe. Plant thickly in rows or more thinly in wide beds; keep moist. Thin to stand 2 inches (5 cm) apart; use thinnings in salads. Avoid plantings that will mature in hot weather. Plant in autumn near first frost date; mulch lightly after a hard freeze. Remove mulch in early spring.

Pests and diseases Little troubled by pests or diseases. In colder areas, mulch more heavily over winter to avoid plants being "heaved" up above ground as the soil freezes.

Harvesting and storage Harvest entire rosettes by pinching off at ground level. Some cultivars remain sweet even when in flower, but taste to check.

Special tips In wide-bed plantings, thin and weed simultaneously by raking shallowly in two directions.

Hardiness
Zones 3 and warmer.

Days to maturity
54–94 frost-free days. Early cultivars (54–70 days) include 'Seneca Horizon' and 'Earlivee'. Longer-season cultivars include 'Tuxedo', the super-sweet 'Honey 'n Pearl', and 'Silver Queen'.

Comments
Use short-season cultivars in colder areas.

Corn

Tender and succulent, fresh sweet corn is a classic summer treat from the garden. It's well worth growing.

Position Plant in full sun, avoiding areas subject to high winds. Accepts many soil textures; prefers deep, well-manured soil with high organic content; pH 6.0–6.8.

Cultivation Sow seed after last spring frost, or 1–2 weeks earlier if soil has first been warmed by covering with black plastic for a week or more in sunny weather. Seed germinates poorly in cold, wet soil and may rot. Plant 1 inch (2.5 cm) deep and 4 inches (10 cm) apart in blocks at least four rows wide, rather than in long, single rows, to ensure good wind-pollination. Rows should be 1½–2 feet (45–60 cm) apart. Thin seedlings to stand 8–12 inches (20–30 cm) apart; mulch or cultivate shallowly to avoid damaging roots near the soil surface. Corn grows rapidly and needs adequate feeding and water. Apply fish emulsion or compost tea after 1 month and again when the tassels appear. Water is most critical when corn is in tassel. Plant successive crops every 10–14 days through midsummer, or until about 90 days before first frost. Choose an early-maturing cultivar for the last planting. Modern corn cultivars include some known as "super-sweet," which have been genetically

Corn continued

Colorful ears of ornamental corn are very easy to grow. Hang them upside-down to finish drying and use for dramatic decorative effects.

modified to slow the conversion of sugar to starch. But if these cultivars cross-pollinate with other sweet corn cultivars, tough kernels will result. It is recommended that corn plots be separated by 25 feet (7.5 m) or more, but this is not always practicable in home gardens. Instead, time the plantings to ensure that at least 10 days elapse between pollination periods for the cultivars. For example, you could plant a super-sweet cultivar that matures in 82 days at the same time as a regular cultivar that matures in 72 days. Or you could plant an 82-day super-sweet cultivar next to an 82-day regular cultivar, as long as you sow it 10 days earlier or later.

Pests and diseases Plant in warm soil to avoid wireworms, which destroy seed. Late plantings are less prone to corn borers; early plantings are less susceptible to corn earworms. Help control earworms by dropping mineral oil into the immature ears as soon as you see the pests' sticky frass on the silks. Rotate corn plantings and shred or bury crop debris to reduce overwintering pests. Patchy spots on kernels, or poorly filled ears, indicate poor pollination.

Harvesting and storage Harvest when silks have turned brown and dry and ears feel full, usually about 3 weeks after the silks appear.

Plant corn in blocks rather than rows to get more effective pollination. To hand-pollinate corn, strip the pollen from the tassels and sprinkle it onto the silks.

Check by pulling back a husk and pressing a thumbnail into a kernel. It should squirt back a milky liquid. Holding the stalk firmly, snap the ear downward, then up. Bottle or freeze corn that cannot be eaten immediately after picking, as it begins to turn starchy within hours.

Special tips If space is limited, interplant a fast-growing crop such as lettuce between rows of corn. The lettuce can be used before the corn casts too much shade.

Related plants

Miniature corn *Z. mays* var. *rugosa* Pick baby ears a day or two after silks appear and use whole in stir-fries or for pickling. 'Baby' and 'Baby Asian' are grown specifically for miniature corn, but any sweet corn cultivar will do.

Ornamental corn *Z. mays* var. *indurata* Also called Indian corn. These cultivars of field corn have colorful kernels. Many cultivars, such as 'Hopi Blue' and 'Mandan Bride', are ground as cornmeal or flour.

Popcorn *Z. mays* var. *praecox* The dense kernels explode into crisp puffs when heated. Harvest as dry as possible, pull back the husks, and hang in an airy place to "cure." Test-pop a few kernels to determine when the corn is dry enough to be shucked and stored in bags or jars. Cultivars include 'Matinee', 'White Cloud' and 'Strawberry'.

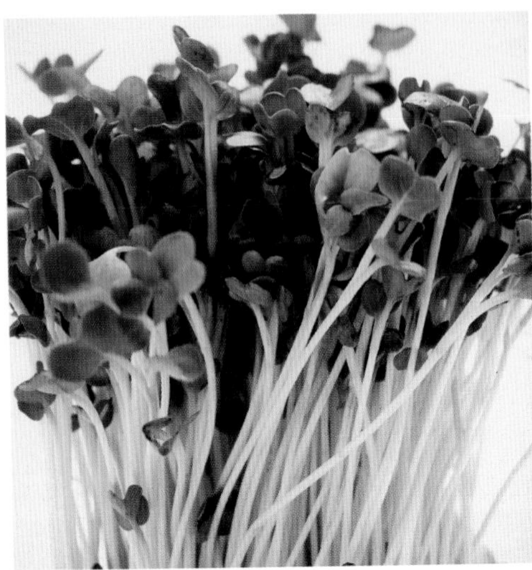

DAYS TO MATURITY
This varies with the type of seed you are sprouting and the temperature.

COMMENTS
Many vegetable and grain seeds are excellent for sprouting, including wheat, barley, rye, oats, peas, millet, sunflowers, beans, radishes and broccoli. Flavor and texture vary widely; experiment to find out what you like best.

SPROUTS

A WIDE VARIETY OF SEEDS, INCLUDING ALFALFA AND LENTILS, ARE EASY TO SPROUT WITHOUT SOIL. THEY ARE TASTY EATEN RAW IN SALADS AND SANDWICHES, OR SPRINKLED OVER STIR-FRIES AT THE LAST MINUTE.

Position Sprouts are grown indoors and no soil is required.

Cultivation Use only seeds that have not been treated with fungicides or other chemicals; natural food stores often carry seeds packaged especially for sprouting. Use fresh seeds to ensure good germination. Soak large seeds overnight in water, or smaller ones for an hour or two. Pick out any broken seeds and rinse the rest several times in warm water in a strainer or colander. (Don't waste the rinse water. Some potplants, for example African violets, thrive on it, but test with small diluted amounts until you are sure.) You will find several styles of sprouting systems at natural food stores, but you can simply put the seeds in a wide-mouthed jar, cover it with cheesecloth and invert it over a dish to catch any remaining rinse water. Good air circulation is very important. Keep the container in a warm place, rinsing the seeds twice daily with tepid water. In hot weather, rinse more often.

Harvesting and storage Sprouts are ready to eat in 3–5 days, or slightly longer if you are sprouting some of

SOME OF THE MANY SYSTEMS FOR GROWING SPROUTS

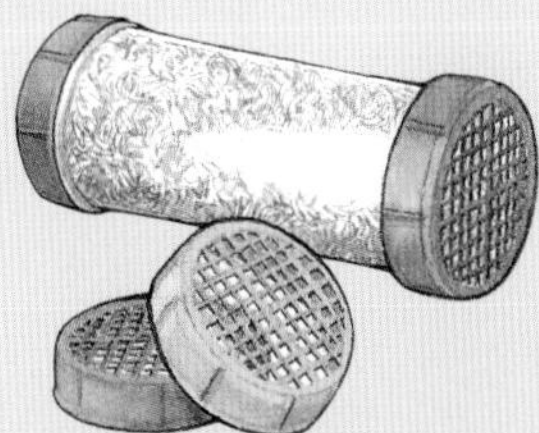

1. **The tube system** is, after a screw-top jar, perhaps the simplest of all. It has three screen lids and one solid lid for transportation. Made from clear plastic, it affords excellent drainage and air circulation.

2. **The SproutMaster** is a system of stackable trays that come in two tray sizes. Excellent drainage and air circulation and perhaps the best choice if you like to have a few types of sprouts on the go at the same time.

3. **The hemp bag system** has excellent drainage and air circulation. It is very good for beans, grains and the larger seeds, but it's fine for smaller seeds, too. It really comes into its own when you are traveling.

4. **The miniature garden** is perfect for baby greens. It's so small you can keep it on your desk at work to supply fresh sprouts for your lunch. Simply sprinkle small seeds on the moist felt pads for a mini-crop.

the hard-seeded vegetables. Store sprouted seeds in the refrigerator and use promptly; many sprouts become moldy quite quickly, especially in hot weather.

Special tips Old seeds may not germinate or do so only slowly. Visit www.sproutpeople.com for more information on the types of sprouting systems that are available.

emon Balm
Scented Thyme

Part Six

Plant Directory

Fruits

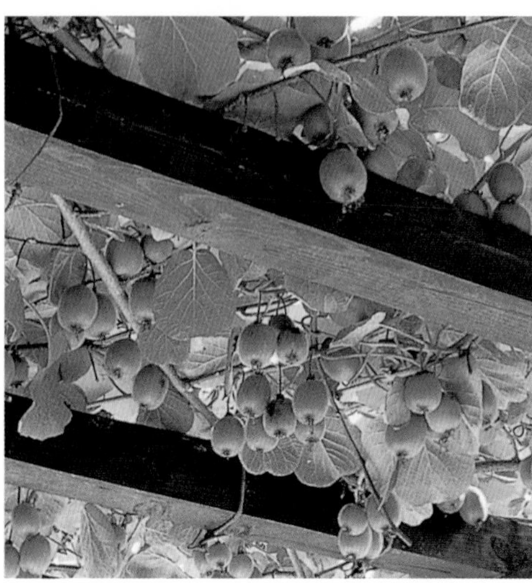

HARDINESS
Zones 7–9. In the colder parts of this range, protect plants from late-spring frosts.

HEIGHT
4–6 feet (1.2–1.8 m)

SPREAD
15 feet (4.5 m)

COMMENTS
You'll need to control enthusiastic kiwi growth so the vine won't tangle or shade itself out.

KIWI FRUIT

KIWI VINES MAKE EXCELLENT COVERING FOR TRELLISES AND ARBORS. WHILE YOU ENJOY THE SHADE, REACH UP TO PICK THE FRUIT.

Position Plant in full sun to light shade in average to poor, well-drained soil.

Cultivation With the exception of a few self-fertile cultivars, such as 'Issai' and 'Blake', kiwi vines have either male or female flowers. For pollination, plant a male vine within about 40 feet (12 m) of females—closer if possible. One male will pollinate up to eight female vines. Keep the soil moist up to harvest time, but water less as winter approaches. Mulch well, but fertilize lightly, if at all.

Pruning Before planting, install a sturdy post-and-wire trellis (as you would for grapes). Insert a stake next to the vine at planting time, and cut out all but one stem. Prune off sideshoots from the remaining stem and train it up the stake.

Propagation Propagate using cuttings or by grafting.

Pests and diseases Surround young plants with a circle of wire mesh fencing to prevent cats from rolling or chewing on leaves and stems.

Harvesting and storage Pick kiwi fruit in autumn, when the seeds are black and most of the fruit is still firm. Peel before eating.

HARDINESS
Zones 4–8.

HEIGHT
10–20 feet (3–6 m)

SPREAD
15–20 feet (4.5–6 m)

COMMENTS
The fruit has a mild flavor reminiscent of watermelon.

AKEBIA

AKEBIA VINES PRODUCE BLUISH OR PURPLE FRUITS WITH NUMEROUS DARK SEEDS EMBEDDED IN THEIR EDIBLE, JELLY-LIKE FLESH.

Position Akebia grows best in full sun but tolerates light shade. The plants are not finicky about soil, as long as it is well drained. The flowers appear early, so choose a site not prone to late-spring frosts.

Cultivation Plant container-grown vines anytime the ground isn't frozen, or set out bareroot plants in spring or autumn, while they are dormant. Space plants 10 feet (3 m) apart to spread out on a trellis or an arbor. If fruit set is poor, try hand-pollination: Transfer pollen with a paintbrush from the male flowers (the ones toward the end of each flower stalk) to the female flowers (near the base of each flower stalk).

Pruning Just before spring growth, thin out spindly or tangled stems.

Propagation Mix seed with moist peat moss and keep at temperatures just above freezing for 1–2 months; sow seed in a warm, bright place. Or root from softwood cuttings.

Pests and diseases Generally no significant problems.

Harvesting and storage When fruit is ripe, the skin splits lengthwise. Pick the fruit at this point for fresh eating, or just as it starts to split along its seam for storage.

HARDINESS
Zone 10.

HEIGHT
3–6 feet
(90–180 cm)

SPREAD
3–6 feet
(90–180 cm)

COMMENTS
Inside the pineapple's inedible and tough outer covering, the edible flesh is yellow or almost white, with a tangy and sweet flavor.

PINEAPPLE

PINEAPPLE FLOWERS FUSE TO FORM A WARTY, GREEN-AND-YELLOW SKIN OVER THE FRUIT.

Position Pineapples need full sun and well-drained, acid soil; pH 4.5–6.5. They are reasonably tolerant of dry conditions.

Cultivation Plant anytime, setting out plants 1 foot (30 cm) apart in double rows 2 feet (60 cm) apart. No pollination needed. In areas cooler than Zone 10, grow plants in containers, with a growing mix that contains extra sand or perlite for good drainage. Avoid overwatering. When plant is about 2 years old, induce flowering by covering the crown for a few days with a paper bag containing a slice of apple.

Pruning Prune 1–2 months after harvest, cutting off sideshoots arising near ground level as well as those originating along or at the base of the fruit stalk. If remaining sideshoots along the stem are crowded, thin them out.

Propagation Pull off and plant sideshoots. Or twist the crown of leaves off the top of the fruit, let it dry for a few days, and plant it.

Pests and diseases Control mealybugs with oil sprays.

Harvesting and storage Cut or snap fruit from stem when color changes; slight softening and aroma indicate ripeness. Store above 50°F (10°C).

HARDINESS
Zone 10, with a period of cool, but not cold, winter weather.

HEIGHT
15–30 feet (4.5–9 m)

SPREAD
10–25 feet (3–7.5 m)

COMMENTS
Cherimoya is a rich-textured, luxurious fruit that can be frozen and eaten with a spoon, like ice cream.

CHERIMOYA (CUSTARD APPLE)

INSIDE THE PALE GREEN SKIN, CHERIMOYA FLESH IS WHITE AND CUSTARDY, WITH A COMBINATION OF BANANA, PINEAPPLE AND PAPAYA FLAVORS. EAT THE FLESH BUT NOT THE SEEDS OR SKIN.

Position Plant in a sheltered spot in full sun and well-drained, slightly acid soil.

Cultivation Plant container-grown stock anytime, or set out bareroot plants in spring or autumn, while they are dormant. Space plants 10–25 feet (3–7.5 m) apart. Hand-pollinate flowers with a fine brush for best yields of large fruits. Water less in winter to encourage the plants to go dormant.

Pruning Prune just before the new-season growth begins, while the plant is leafless. Keep fruiting branches close to main stems by removing a moderate amount of wood each year.

Propagation For the best-tasting fruits, graft cultivars to seedling rootstock just as buds are swelling.

Pests and diseases Generally no significant problems.

Harvesting and storage Clip firm fruits from the tree when their color changes to pale green or yellow; let them soften at room temperature. Store harvested fruits at 50°F (10°C) before ripening at room temperature.

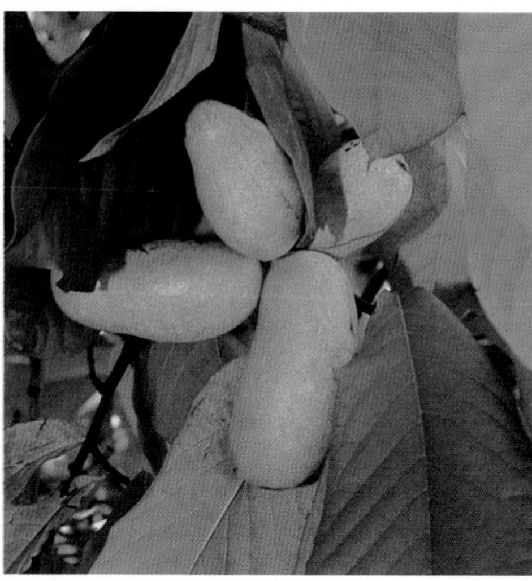

HARDINESS
Zones 4–8.

HEIGHT
10–25 feet
(3–7.5 m)

SPREAD
5–15 feet
(1.5–4.5 m)

COMMENTS
Papayas are delicious raw or cooked into puddings and pies. Use only slight heat while cooking so as to preserve the delicate flavor. Eat the flesh only.

PAPAYA (PAWPAW)

RIPE PAPAYA FRUIT HAS GREENISH YELLOW SKIN SPECKLED WITH BROWN. THE ORANGE, CUSTARDY FLESH TASTES LIKE BANANA, WITH HINTS OF PINEAPPLE, MANGO AND VANILLA.

Position Papayas prefer full sunlight but aren't finicky about soil, as long as it is well drained.

Cultivation Plant young trees in spring, 15 feet (4.5 m) apart. Papayas need cross-pollination, so plant at least two seedlings, a seedling and a named cultivar, or two different cultivars. Papayas sometimes need hand-pollination for good fruit set.

Pruning Little or no pruning is necessary for papayas.

Propagation Seed germinates easily after you keep it cool and moist for 2–3 months. Growth is very slow for the first 3 years and it takes 6 years or more for fruits to appear. For quicker fruit of more reliable quality, graft selected cultivars onto seedling papayas just as the buds are swelling in spring.

Pests and diseases Generally no significant problems.

Harvesting and storage Ripe papayas are slightly soft and have black specks on their skin. Either let the fruits ripen on the tree, or pick slightly underripe for refrigerated storage. When ready to use, ripen the fruits at room temperature.

Averrhoa carambola OXALIDACEAE

HARDINESS
Zone 10.

HEIGHT
20–30 feet (6–9 m)

SPREAD
15–25 feet (4.5–7.5 m)

COMMENTS
Carambolas come in either sweet or sour types. For jelly, use slightly underripe sweet types or fully ripe sour types. Ripe carambolas can be cooked in tarts and puddings or added to curries.

CARAMBOLA (STAR FRUIT)

CARAMBOLA TREES PRODUCE FLESHY FRUITS THAT ARE STAR-SHAPED IN CROSS SECTION AND ENCLOSED WITHIN A WAXY, YELLOW SKIN. BOTH THE SKIN AND THE CRISP FLESH ARE EDIBLE.

Position Plant in full sun and well-drained, slightly acid soil with low salt content. Avoid sites that are subject to hot, dry winds.

Cultivation Work compost into the soil before planting, and also use it as a mulch to prevent nutrient deficiencies. Set out container-grown plants anytime. Space trees 15–25 feet (4.5–7.5 m) apart. Better yields can usually be obtained with cross-pollination.

Pruning Carambola needs little pruning beyond the removal of vigorous, upright shoots.

Propagation Seed germinates readily when fresh. However, grafted plants bear more quickly, and their fruit quality is more predictable.

Pests and diseases Plants have no significant pest or disease problems.

Harvesting and storage Pick the fruits when they are pale green with some yellow. Ripe fruits often fall to the ground. Fruits will keep for a few weeks at 50°F (10°C). Pickle underripe fruits or cook them as you would a vegetable.

HARDINESS
Zones 3–9.

HEIGHT
3–12 feet
(90–360 cm)

SPREAD
3–12 feet
(90–360 cm)

COMMENTS
Common barberry *Berberis vulgaris* and other species, including raisin barberry *B. asiatica* and Nepal barberry *B. aristata*, are used for their fruits.

BARBERRY

BARBERRIES PRODUCE RED, YELLOW OR BLACK BERRIES; BOTH THE FLESH AND SKIN OF THE BERRIES ARE EDIBLE. THE FLAVOR IS USUALLY TART, BUT IN SOME SPECIES THE FRUITS HAVE ENOUGH SUGAR TO BE DRIED INTO "RAISINS."

Position Barberries prefer full sun and moist, well-drained soil. (Evergreen species are generally less hardy than deciduous species.)

Cultivation Set out container-grown plants anytime the soil isn't frozen, or plant bareroot shrubs in spring or autumn, while they are still dormant. Space plants 3–12 feet (90–360 cm) apart, depending on how big the particular species gets.

Pruning Cut a few of the oldest stems to the ground in winter. Also shorten spindly stems and thin out suckers if the stems are crowded.

Propagation Mix seed with moist peat moss and refrigerate it for 2–3 months before sowing in a warm, bright place. Or dig up and transplant suckers from the base of a bush.

Pests and diseases Generally no significant problems.

Harvesting and storage Harvest the berries after they are fully colored. Make the fruit into conserves, jams or pickles for storage, or dry them and store in airtight jars.

HARDINESS
Zone 10.

HEIGHT
2–18 feet (60–540 cm), but cultivars vary in their eventual height and spread.

COMMENTS
Natal plum fruit is usually cooked into jellies, sauces and pies.

NATAL PLUM

THE ROUNDISH FRUIT OF NATAL PLUM IS THE SIZE OF A PING-PONG BALL, WITH A CRIMSON SKIN AND STRAWBERRY-RED FLESH. THE WHOLE FRUIT IS EDIBLE; SOME PEOPLE PREFER TO REMOVE THE SMALL SEEDS.

Position Plant in full sun or partial shade in well-drained soil. Natal plum withstands salt spray and is moderately drought-tolerant.

Cultivation Set out container-grown plants anytime, spacing them roughly 10 feet (3 m) apart, depending on the eventual size of the particular cultivar. Natal plum generally needs cross-pollination, so plant at least two seedlings or cultivars. Hand-pollination often helps when fruiting is poor. In areas where Natal plum is not hardy, grow it indoors in a container.

Pruning Prune only as needed to shape the plant and to remove dead or crossing branches. You can even shear this plant as a hedge.

Propagation Take cuttings of semi-woody shoots, or layer a branch from an established plant.

Pests and diseases Generally no significant problems.

Harvesting and storage For fresh eating, pick fruit when fully ripe (fully colored); pick fruits slightly underripe for cooking. Plants produce fruit almost year-round, so pick it as you need it.

HARDINESS
Zones 6–9.

HEIGHT
50–150 feet
(15–45 m)

SPREAD
35–50 feet
(10.5–15 m)

COMMENTS
If the growing season in your area is closer to the 150-day range, choose extra-hardy and early-maturing cultivars such as 'Major' or 'Giles'.

PECAN

LARGE, RICH-FLAVORED NUTS EMERGE EASILY FROM THEIR SHELLS—A BIG TIME-SAVER.

Position Plant in full sun in average to rich, well-drained soil.

Cultivation Male (pollen-providing) and female (nut-producing) flowers on pecan trees usually don't open at the same time. For this reason, you usually need to plant another tree that can provide pollen when the main crop tree is ready. Space trees 35–50 feet (10.5–15 m) apart. Mulch with compost and irrigate during dry periods.

Pruning Pecans naturally take on a central-leader shape, so established pecans seldom need much pruning. Remove any branches that are competing with the main trunk and trim out dead or damaged branches as you spot them. Call an arborist to remove large limbs.

Propagation Propagate by grafting.

Pests and diseases Diseases such as scab can be a problem in humid areas. Pecan weevils lay their eggs in almost-mature nuts. Rake up and destroy damaged nuts.

Harvesting and storage Grafted trees will begin bearing nuts in 4–7 years. Tap limbs with a padded stick or pick up fallen nuts. Remove the husks and dry the nuts for several weeks. Store in a cool place.

Casimiroa edulis

RUTACEAE

HARDINESS
Zone 10.

HEIGHT
15–50 feet
(4.5–15 m)

SPREAD
15–50 feet
(4.5–15 m)

COMMENTS
Only the flesh is edible, not the seeds or skin. (The seeds are poisonous.)

SAPOTE, WHITE

THE ROUND OR OVAL FRUIT OF WHITE SAPOTE IS COVERED WITH A THIN, PALE GREEN OR GOLDEN YELLOW SKIN. THE BUTTERY FLESH IS WHITE OR YELLOW AND IT HAS A SWEET AND SLIGHTLY RESINOUS FLAVOR.

Position White sapote needs full sun and well-drained soil.

Cultivation Set out container-grown plants anytime, spacing them 15–50 feet (4.5–15 m) apart. Many, but not all, cultivars are self-fruitful. Do not plant where the fallen fruit will be a nuisance. The trees require very little care.

Pruning Shorten stems on young trees to promote branching. Prune mature trees to keep them from growing too large.

Propagation Propagate cultivars by grafting onto seedling rootstock.

Pests and diseases Generally no significant problems.

Harvesting and storage Watch for the color change, which is subtle on green-skinned cultivars. This signals that it is time to clip fruits from the tree. Leave a piece of stem attached and allow the harvested fruit to ripen at room temperature.

HARDINESS
Zones 9–10.

HEIGHT
25–50 feet (7.5–15 m)

SPREAD
15–35 feet (4.5–10.5 m)

COMMENTS
The pods have a rather chocolate-like flavor. Munch on raw pods, or remove the seeds and roast and grind the pods, for use as a substitute for chocolate.

CAROB

CAROB TREES YIELD FLAT, BROWN, EDIBLE PODS THAT ARE FILLED WITH A ROW OF SEEDS AND SOFT, SWEET, BROWN FLESH.

Position Carob prefers climates with a hot, dry summer; plant in full sun and alkaline, well-drained soil.

Cultivation Transplant young plants or set out container-grown stock carefully. Plant potted plants anytime, or set out bareroot plants in spring or autumn, while they are dormant. Space plants 15–35 feet (4.5–10.5 m) apart. Male trees are usually needed to pollinate female trees; either plant a male for every 25–30 females, or graft a single male branch onto a female tree.

Pruning No regular pruning needed.

Propagation Fresh seed germinates readily, but dry seed germinates slowly and at a low rate even when helped along by being nicked with a file. Propagate cultivars by budding or grafting scions onto seedling rootstock.

Pests and diseases Keep deer and rabbits from trees with traps and fences. Where scale insects are a problem, spray with horticultural oil.

Harvesting and storage Pods turn dark brown when ripe. Pick before wet weather or even heavy dew. Shake or knock ripe pods from the branches and dry them in the sun.

HARDINESS
Zones 9–10 for outdoor culture.

HEIGHT
6–24 feet (1.8–7.2 m)

SPREAD
3–12 feet (90–360 cm)

COMMENTS
The sweet, edible rind easily peels away from the segmented flesh, which is juicy, but too tart to eat plain. Use fruits to flavor drinks or to make marmalade.

CALAMONDIN

CALAMONDINS GROW AS BUSHES OR SMALL TREES, PRODUCING BOUNTIFUL HARVESTS OF SMALL, ROUND, REDDISH ORANGE FRUITS.

Position Give calamondins full sun and slightly acid, well-drained soil.

Cultivation Set out container-grown plants anytime, spaced 3–12 feet (90–360 cm) apart, depending on whether you want a hedge or individual plants. Calamondins are self-fruitful, so you need only one plant. They are easy to grow in containers. Water your tree regularly to keep the soil evenly moist, especially during bloom.

Pruning Calamondins don't need regular pruning, unless you want to keep the plant small. Plants can be sheared as hedges.

Propagation Propagate calamondins by sowing fresh seed, taking stem cuttings, or grafting. Trifoliate orange *Poncirus trifoliata* is a good disease-resistant, dwarfing rootstock to use for grafting.

Pests and diseases Problems are usually minimal if soil drainage is good, but keep an eye out for scale, mealybugs, mites and whiteflies.

Harvesting and storage Harvest when fruits are fully colored, or let them hang on the tree until you are ready to use them. Store in a refrigerator crisper.

Citrus

One factor common to all citrus fruits is their rich vitamin C content. Lemons and limes have the power to perk up the flavor of most dishes; oranges and grapefruit are refreshing as snacks and in salads.

Position Frost will damage the fruit of any citrus plants and sometimes the rest of the tree. Plant in full sun to light shade in average to rich, well-drained soil. If your area gets surprise frosts, plant these trees near a sunny wall that will radiate heat on cold nights.

Cultivation Citrus trees are nearly all self-fertile, so you need to plant only one to get a good harvest. Space large citrus trees at least 25 feet (7.5 m) apart and dwarf trees 10 feet (3 m) apart. Paint the trunk with white latex paint (diluted with an equal amount of water) to prevent sunburn. Keep the soil moist to prevent early fruit drop. Mulch with compost, adding a fresh layer several times during the year as the old layer breaks down. Fertilize lightly but often to encourage good tree vigor.

Pruning Remove damaged or diseased branches and upright-growing shoots that emerge from the roots. Trim back long branches to shape the plant. Wear gloves when pruning thorny types to protect your hands.

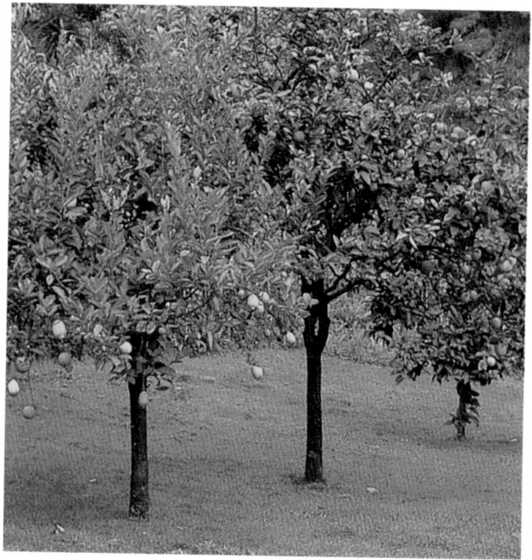

HARDINESS
Zones 8–10.

HEIGHT
10–30 feet (3–9 m)

SPREAD
10–30 feet (3–9 m)

COMMENTS
If you need a smaller tree, choose one that has been grafted onto a dwarfing rootstock, or look for dwarf cultivars such as 'Meyer' and 'Snow' lemons or 'Valencia' oranges.

Citrus make attractive garden features, but if space is limited, consider planting just one tree grafted with two or three types of citrus fruits.

Propagation Propagate by bud grafting onto disease-resistant stock.

Pests and diseases Start with virus-free, disease-resistant plants and provide good growing conditions to minimize problems. Keep an eye out for scale (small, hard-shelled insects on leaves and stems), whiteflies (small, white flies on leaf undersides), thrips (tiny insects that cause scarring on leaves and fruits), and mites (tiny insects that cause yellow-stippled leaves). Use beneficial insects, traps and insecticidal soap to prevent infestations and control diseases.

Harvesting and storage Most citrus trees produce fruit 3–4 years after planting. Finding out when the fruit is ripe can be tricky, since you can't rely on the skin color as an indicator. For example, some oranges remain green when they are ripe unless the temperature falls to below 45°F (7°C). Other cultivars color up early, well before the fruit is ready. The only way to really know if the fruit is ripe is to taste it. Even when they're ripe, many citrus fruits can linger on the tree for weeks without loss of quality. The exception is mandarin oranges; pick these fruits promptly before the flavor deteriorates. Store citrus fruit in the refrigerator for up to two weeks.

HARDINESS
Zones 4–8.

HEIGHT
15–25 feet (4.5–7.5 m)

SPREAD
10–20 feet (3–6 m)

COMMENTS
You can enjoy the fruits out of hand, although they are normally used to make a drink, preserves, or a thickened, sweet syrup called *rob de cornis.*

CHERRY, CORNELIAN

THE RED FRUITS OF CORNELIAN CHERRY LOOK LIKE TRUE CHERRIES. THE FLAVOR IS TART—RATHER LIKE A SOUR CHERRY. YOU CAN EAT THE WHOLE FRUIT, BUT NOT THE SEED.

Position Give plants full sun and average, well-drained soil.

Cultivation Set out container-grown plants anytime, as long as the ground is not frozen, or plant bareroot stock in spring or autumn, while it is still dormant. Space plants 10–20 feet (3–6 m) apart. The flowers are partially self-fertile, but cross-pollination increases yields.

Pruning No regular pruning needed.

Propagation Cornelian cherry is easy to graft onto seedling rootstock. To grow seedlings, either nick the seed with a file or keep it warm and moist for 4 months. Then pot the seed and move to a cool, moist spot for 1–4 months before putting the pots in a warm, bright place so the seeds will sprout.

Pests and diseases Generally no significant problems.

Harvesting and storage Harvest the fruits anytime after they are fully colored. (Most turn red; a few kinds ripen yellow or white.) The longer they hang on the tree, the more mellow they become in flavor. Harvested fruits also mellow if kept at room temperature.

HARDINESS
American and beaked hazels are hardy in Zones 2–8. Turkish filberts are hardy in Zones 4–9. European hazels are hardy in Zones 4–8.

HEIGHT
6–70 feet (1.8–21 m)

SPREAD
Up to 20 feet (6 m)

COMMENTS
Destroy damaged nuts to eliminate filbertworms.

HAZELNUT

HAZELNUTS, OR FILBERTS, ARE SMALL, PLUMP NUTS PRODUCED ON TREES AND SHRUBS.

Position Hazelnuts do best in full sun (or light afternoon shade in hot climates) in well-drained, loamy soil.

Cultivation Mulch to reduce weeds. Water mature trees during dry times or grow drought-tolerant cultivars.

Pruning European, beaked and American hazels naturally grow into dense bushes that make good hedges; thin out the older wood each winter to encourage new growth. Turkish hazels grow into tall trees that need little pruning.

Propagation Grow from seed, or by layering or grafting.

Pests and diseases If eastern filbert blight is a problem, plant less-susceptible American hazels, or moderately resistant European cultivars such as 'Hall's Giant' and 'Barcelona'. Net shrub forms to keep animal pests away from the nuts.

Harvesting and storage Hazels begin bearing nuts in 2–3 years. They ripen in autumn and are ready to pick when nuts come free from the husks easily. Pluck them or tap the limbs with a padded stick to make the nuts drop onto a cloth. The European cultivar 'Barcelona' drops its nuts without tapping. Let the nuts dry until crunchy. Store in a cool place for up to a year.

MELON

VINE-RIPENED MELONS ARE A GREAT FLAVOR TREAT, WELL WORTH THE LITTLE EXTRA CARE THEY DEMAND FOR A SUCCESSFUL CROP.

Position Full sun in a site with good air circulation. Plant in well-drained, well-manured soil, not too acid; pH 6.0–7.0.

Cultivation Set out plants 2–3 weeks after germination into soil that has first been warmed with black plastic mulch. Use row covers to increase warmth and protect from cucumber beetles; remove covers when the plants bloom. Cultivate shallowly to reduce competition from weeds until plants begin to vine. Water weekly with compost tea or fish emulsion to maintain growth.

Pruning Trim to confine only.

Propagation In long-season areas, sow seed directly into the ground when the soil is thoroughly warm. Plant three or four seeds to a hill and site hills 4–5 feet (1.2–1.5 m) apart. In colder areas, start indoors in individual pots, two seeds to a pot, around the time of last frost.

Pests and diseases Plant radishes or basil in the hill with melons to help deter cucumber beetles. Or protect plants with row covers; remove covers when plants start to flower to aid pollination. Spray foliage thoroughly with a baking soda solution (1 teaspoon per quart [liter] of water) to control mildew. Rotate

HARDINESS
Zones 4 and warmer. In colder areas, grow short-season cultivars.

SPREAD
If space is limited, melon vines can be supported on a frame or trellis.

COMMENTS
Melons do not tolerate frost. Most cantaloupes and muskmelons mature in about 68 days, watermelons and honeydews take up to 95 days.

Muskmelon *Cucumis melo*, also called Persian melon or nutmeg melon. Melons do not ripen after picking, so for the best flavor leave on the vine until fully ripe.

plantings of melons and relatives, such as squash and cucumber, to reduce pest populations. Wilt spread by cucumber beetles causes plants to collapse before fruit ripens. Do not allow plants to become stressed from lack of water or nutrients. In warm areas, successive plantings increase the odds of a good harvest.

Harvesting and storage Pick muskmelons when cracks appear where fruit is attached to the stem. They should "slip" from the stem easily with a slight tug. Let them sit for 1–2 days at room temperature to ripen perfectly. Watermelons are ripe when the tendril closest to the fruit is brown and shriveled. When ripe, hard-rind melons, such as honeydews, casabas and true cantaloupes, will show a subtle change of rind color. Most melons have a short storage life; some late-season melons will keep up to 2 months in a cool, dry place.

Related plants

Apple melon *C. melo*, Chito Group Also called mango melon, vegetable orange, garden lemon or vine peach. Small yellow or orange fruit, used in preserves and pickles. No named cultivars.

Cantaloupe *C. melo*, Cantalupensis Group Also called rockmelon. Most commercial cantaloupes are muskmelons. Widely grown in

Watermelon *Citrullus lanatus*. The cultivars 'Charleston Gray' and 'Jubilee' are both resistant to Fusarium wilt, which is spread by the striped cucumber beetle.

Europe, true cantaloupes don't have a netted rind. Try 'Charentais'.

Casaba melon *C. melo*, Inodorus Group Large, football- or banana-shaped fruit with gold skin and white flesh. Late-maturing, good keeper. Cultivars include 'Juan Canary' and 'Santa Claus'.

Crenshaw melon *C. melo*, Inodorus Group Pear-shaped with pale tan skin, delicately flavored, light pink or salmon flesh. Cultivars include 'Burpee Early Hybrid Crenshaw'.

Honeydew melon *C. melo*, Inodorus Group Smooth rind, usually pale green or ivory, with green flesh. Generally late-maturing; early cultivars include 'Earlidew' and 'Venus Hybrid'.

Muskmelon *C. melo*, Reticulatus Group Also called Persian melon, nutmeg melon, and, incorrectly, cantaloupe. Rind is netted and usually ridged, flesh is orange or green, sweet and fragrant. Cultivars include 'Harper Hybrid' (small, early melon), 'Ambrosia' and 'Iroquois'.

Watermelon *Citrullus lanatus* More drought-tolerant than other melons and less vulnerable to insect pests. Rind can be dark to light green, solid, striped or mottled. Usually red-fleshed, but some orange-, yellow- and white-fleshed cultivars. Cultivars include 'Sugar Baby' (a small melon), 'Charleston Gray' (large, long season), and 'Yellow Doll' (yellow-fleshed).

Cydonia oblonga ROSACEAE

HARDINESS
Zones 5–9.

HEIGHT
15–20 feet
(4.5–6 m)

SPREAD
15–20 feet
(4.5–6 m)

COMMENTS
The skin and spicy, white or yellowish flesh are edible cooked, but the flesh is too astringent to be eaten raw. Quince adds pizzazz to an apple pie.

QUINCE

QUINCE TREES PRODUCE YELLOW FRUIT COVERED WITH DOWNY HAIRS.

Position Plant in full sun in well-drained and moderately fertile soil.

Cultivation Plant container-grown stock anytime, as long as the ground is not frozen; or set out bareroot plants in spring or autumn, while they are dormant. Space plants 15–20 feet (4.5–6 m) apart. Quinces are self-fertile, so you need only one plant.

Pruning Train as a small tree or large shrub. Each winter, prune off enough wood to keep the plant open to sunlight and air, removing any diseased or misplaced branches.

Propagation Graft cultivars onto quince rootstock, propagated by layering or from seed.

Pests and diseases In summer, watch for blackened leaves and curled-over stems—signs of fireblight, which is a big problem in many areas.

Harvesting and storage Pick fruits when they are scented and fully colored. Handle ripe fruit gently. It can be stored for 2–3 months at temperatures near freezing with high humidity, such as in a refrigerator. Alternatively, make it into a fine, clear, pink jelly or a dense paste for use with cheese and crackers.

Diospyros spp.

EBENACEAE

HARDINESS
Zones 7–10 for most oriental persimmons; Zones 4–9 for American persimmons.

HEIGHT
25–60 feet (7.5–18 m)

SPREAD
20–35 feet (6–10.5 m)

COMMENTS
Fresh persimmons will keep for about 2 months in the refrigerator. Eat fresh, or freeze or dry them.

PERSIMMON

PERSIMMON FLESH HAS A HONEY-LIKE SWEETNESS, SMOOTH AS SILK IN ORIENTAL PERSIMMON *DIOSPYROS KAKI*, BUT DRIER AND RICHER IN THE CASE OF THE AMERICAN PERSIMMON *D. VIRGINIANA*.

Position Give persimmons full sun and well-drained soil.

Cultivation Plant in spring, preserving as much of the taproot as possible. Space plants 20–35 feet (6–10.5 m) apart. The pollination needs vary with the cultivar. Thin oriental persimmon fruits by hand if they seem too crowded.

Pruning Shorten long, willowy growth on young trees to stimulate branching. Prune mature trees only enough to stimulate new growth for regular fruiting and to keep bearing wood near the main branches.

Propagation Graft selected cultivars onto *D. virginiana*, *D. kaki* or *D. lotus* rootstocks in spring, just as the buds are swelling.

Pests and diseases Where persimmon girdler is a problem, pick up and burn fallen twigs regularly in autumn.

Harvesting and storage Clip ripe persimmons from trees. Harvest non-astringent oriental types when fully colored and firm. Astringent oriental and American types are not edible until very soft.

HARDINESS
Zones 8–10.

HEIGHT
20–30 feet (6–9 m)

SPREAD
25–35 feet (7.5–10.5 m)

COMMENTS
Eat loquats fresh, cook them into a sauce or cut them in half and dry them. Fresh fruits will keep in the refrigerator for 1–2 weeks.

LOQUAT

LOQUAT TREES PRODUCE YELLOW, PLUM-SIZED, ROUND, OVAL OR PEAR-SHAPED FRUIT WITH SCENTED WHITE PULP THAT IS SWEET WITH A BIT OF A TANG. REMOVE THE SKIN AND SEEDS BEFORE EATING LOQUATS.

Position Plant in full sun or partial shade in well-drained soil. Loquats are somewhat drought-resistant.

Cultivation Set out container-grown plants anytime, spacing them 20–30 feet (6–9 m) apart. Most cultivars are self-fruitful. Thin fruits in winter by clipping off some of the clusters or individual fruitlets. Mulch to protect the shallow roots. Fertilize regularly. To grow loquats in containers, choose a dwarf cultivar and repot annually.

Pruning Thinning the fruits by removing clusters takes care of much of the pruning. Shorten additional stems to let in light.

Propagation Graft cultivars onto seedling loquat rootstock. Both quince and pyracantha have been used as dwarfing rootstocks.

Pests and diseases Watch for blackened leaves and curled-over shoots—signs of fireblight, a big problem in many areas. Enclose fruits in paper bags to protect them from sunburn if plants are growing in full sun.

Harvesting and storage Clip off fruits when fully colored and slightly soft.

HARDINESS
Zones 9–10; possibly Zone 8.

HEIGHT
15–20 feet (4.5–6 m)

SPREAD
15–20 feet (4.5–6 m)

COMMENTS
The fleshy flower petals, white with a tinge of purple, are also sweet and edible.

FEIJOA

THE GREEN FRUIT OF FEIJOA FORMS ON A LARGE, BUSHY PLANT. THE EDIBLE, GREENISH FLESH, EMBEDDED WITH SMALL, EDIBLE SEEDS, HAS A FLAVOR COMBINING THE BEST OF PINEAPPLE, STRAWBERRY AND MINT.

Position Feijoa needs some winter chilling to flower and fruit. Plant in well-drained soil and full sun, except in desert areas, where some midday shade is needed.

Cultivation Set out container-grown plants anytime. Space them at least 3 feet (90 cm) apart. Most feijoas need cross-pollination, but a number of cultivars are self-fertile. In cool climates, you can grow feijoas in pots; move them indoors to a cool, bright location in winter.

Pruning Train as a shrub, small tree or sheared hedge. Train grafted plants as single-trunked trees, removing all shoots that come off the base of the stem. Feijoas don't require much pruning, but can be tidied up after harvest.

Propagation Propagate cultivars by taking cuttings or by grafting them onto seedling rootstock.

Pests and diseases Generally no significant problems.

Harvesting and storage Ripe fruits drop to the ground; gather them every few days. Nearly ripe fruits will ripen indoors. Fruits keep well refrigerated with high humidity.

HARDINESS
Grow figs outdoors in Zones 8–10 or in protected areas up to Zone 6.

HEIGHT
10–25 feet (3–8 m)

SPREAD
10–25 feet (3–8 m)

COMMENTS
Figs such as 'Conadria', 'Genoa' and 'Panachee' need long, hot summers; cultivars such as 'Venture' and 'Osborne Prolific' do best with cool summers.

FIG

FIGS ARE PRODUCTIVE AND GENERALLY EASY TO GROW. THEY ARE SELDOM TROUBLED BY PESTS, EXCEPT FOR BIRDS. NET THE TREE TO DISCOURAGE THESE GREEDY FIG-LOVERS.

Position Plant in full sun in average, well-drained soil. In cool climates, plant figs in large containers and move them inside for winter.

Cultivation Select self-pollinating cultivars. Space large cultivars up to 25 feet (8 m) apart; smaller trees can be as close as 5 feet (1.5 m) apart. Mulch generously with compost as needed.

Pruning Thin out excess growth as needed to control plant size and allow for good light penetration into the center of the plant. You can also train figs as espaliers to grow on sun-warmed walls.

Propagation Propagate by cutting rooted suckers off the roots or taking hardwood cuttings.

Pests and diseases Place netting over trees to discourage birds, or grow green-fruited cultivars, which are less appealing to birds.

Harvesting and storage Fig trees produce their first crop a year after planting. Ripe figs are soft, with a slightly flexible "neck;" sometimes the skin splits. You can keep figs for a few days in the refrigerator, or cut them in halves and dry them.

HARDINESS
Zones 9–10.

HEIGHT
8–15 feet (2.4–4.5 m)

SPREAD
6–12 feet (1.8–3.6 m)

COMMENTS
Fruits are tasty fresh, candied or cooked into a marmalade or a sauce. They keep well in the refrigerator.

KUMQUAT

THE FRUIT OF THE KUMQUAT LOOKS LIKE A MINIATURE ORANGE—ABOUT THE SIZE OF A CHERRY AND EITHER ROUND OR ELONGATED. THE SKIN IS EDIBLE AND SWEET, AND THE JUICY FLESH RANGES FROM TART TO SWEET.

Position Plant in full sun in well-drained, slightly acid soil. Kumquat tolerates winter weather as cold as 18°F (–7.7°C), but without sufficient heat in summer, the fruits will be few and of poor quality.

Cultivation Plant container-grown stock anytime, or set out bareroot plants in spring or autumn, while they are dormant. Space plants 6–12 feet (1.8–3.6 m) apart. Kumquats make beautiful potted plants that fruit reliably. Put in a cool, sunny room in winter and repot every year.

Pruning Kumquats need no pruning other than to shape the plants and thin out crowded branches.

Propagation Kumquats are usually grafted onto the rootstock of trifoliate orange *Poncirus trifoliata*, which also dwarfs the tree, or onto sour orange *Citrus aurantium* or grapefruit rootstocks.

Pests and diseases Problems are usually minimal if soil drainage is good, but look out for scale, mealybugs, mites and whiteflies.

Harvesting and storage Harvest fruits when fully colored.

HARDINESS
Zones 3–10.

HEIGHT
10 inches (25 cm)

SPREAD
1–2 feet
(30–60 cm)

COMMENTS
Strawberries are self-fruitful. For the longest possible harvest, grow plants of more than one type (June-bearers, ever-bearers and day-neutrals).

STRAWBERRY

YOU'LL AVOID MOST PROBLEMS BY STARTING WITH CERTIFIED DISEASE-FREE PLANTS OF DISEASE-RESISTANT CULTIVARS.

Position Choose cultivars that are appropriate for your climate. For warmer areas, try 'Apollo', 'Arking', 'Chandler' and 'Sequoia'. In cooler climes, try 'Crimson King' or 'Fort Laramie'. Of the day-neutral types, 'Tristar', 'Tribute', 'Fern' and 'Selva' can grow well in a fairly wide range of climates; 'Brighton' and 'Heckler' are best in cooler, temperate areas. Plant in an area of full sun (or light afternoon shade for day-neutral strawberries) free from late-spring frosts. The soil should be fertile and well drained. If possible, avoid garden areas previously used to grow bell peppers (capsicum), tomatoes, potatoes, eggplant (aubergine), melons, okra, mints, raspberries or blackberries, mums or roses—crops that may leave behind problems that can attack strawberries. Add extra organic matter before planting to make the soil rich and moist.

Cultivation For an easy-care strawberry bed, mound your garden soil in a bed about 6 inches (15 cm) tall and 2 feet (60 cm) wide, install drip irrigation, and cover it all with plastic mulch before planting. Cut X-shaped slits in the plastic, and plant through the slits into the soil.

Strawberries do well in containers, such as special strawberry pots or hanging baskets. A bonus with such ways of growing is that the fruits are easier to protect from birds.

This hill system is especially good for ever-bearing or day-neutral strawberries. If planting in a flat bed, space plants 1–2 feet (30–60 cm) apart and keep the soil moist until berries are almost ripe. In early winter, cover plants with 2 inches (5 cm) of straw to prevent cold damage. Pull back the mulch as soon as plants begin to grow again in spring. If frost threatens new growth, cover the plants overnight with a floating row cover.

Pruning Weed, pinch out unwanted runners and mow along edge of bed as needed to keep walkways clear.

Propagation Propagate by transplanting disease-free rooted runners.

Pests and diseases Pick ripe fruit regularly to keep gray mold (botrytis blight) at bay. Remove and destroy damaged flowers and fruits as you spot them. Several problems can cause wilted plants. To determine the cause, dig up a few plants. If there are few or no side roots and the roots are reddish inside when cut lengthwise, red stele is the problem. If the roots are black and rotting, the culprit is root rot. Destroy all wilted plants.

Harvesting and storage Pick berries, leaving some stem on for better storage, when fully colored, tender and sweet. Eat fruit fresh, or make into jam or freeze immediately.

Fragaria vesca 'Semperflorens'

ROSACEAE

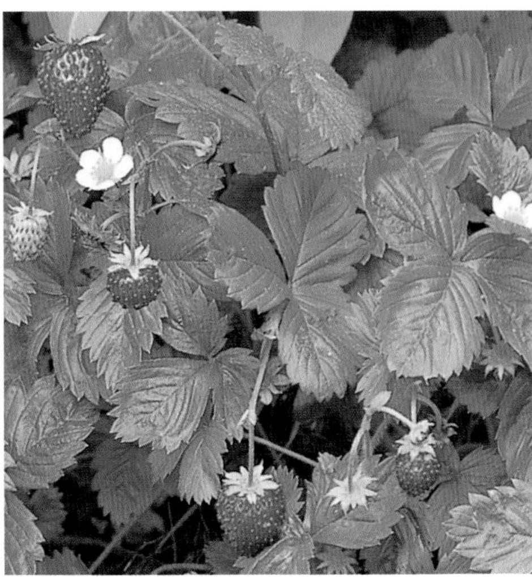

HARDINESS
Zones 3–10.

HEIGHT
6 inches (15 cm)

SPREAD
6–12 inches (15–30 cm)

COMMENTS
Plants will fruit generously, even in small pots. Eat the fruits fresh as they do not store well.

STRAWBERRY, ALPINE

ALPINE STRAWBERRIES PRODUCE POINTED FRUITS ON LOW, CLUMP-FORMING PLANTS. THE RIPE FRUITS ARE USUALLY RED, ALTHOUGH SOME WHITE CULTIVARS EXIST. THE WHOLE FRUIT IS EDIBLE.

Position Plant in full sun or partial shade, with well-drained soil that is rich in humus.

Cultivation Set out container-grown plants anytime the ground isn't frozen, or plant bareroot stock in spring or autumn, while the plants are dormant. Set plants 6–12 inches (15–30 cm) apart, planting so that the ground level is just below the lowest leaves on the crown. Alpine strawberries are self-fruitful, so you will get fruit from just one plant.

Pruning None is necessary.

Propagation To divide old plants, dig them up and cut off young crown pieces (with attached roots) from the outside of the clump. Throw away the old center part and replant the divisions immediately. To grow alpine strawberries from seed, scatter the fine seed on the surface of potting soil in a container. Transplant seedlings when large enough to handle.

Pests and diseases Keep birds at bay with netting, or grow white-fruited cultivars, which birds leave alone.

Harvesting and storage Harvest the fruits when soft and scented.

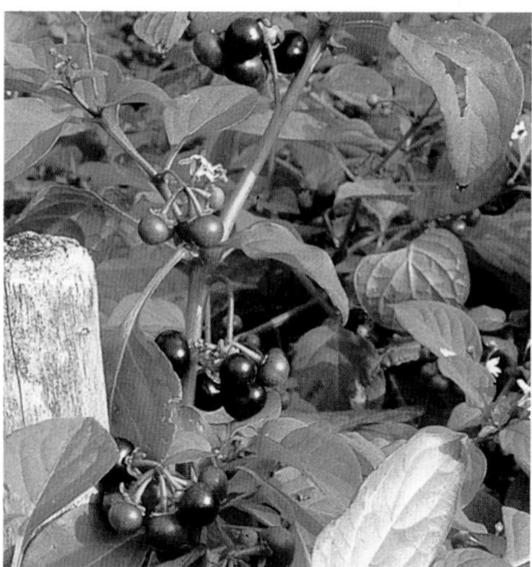

HARDINESS
Plants vary in adaptability, according to origin, but generally Zones 5–8.

HEIGHT
1–6 feet (30–180 cm)

SPREAD
3 feet (90 cm) or more (some spread via underground stems).

COMMENTS
The whole fruit is edible, including the seeds.

HUCKLEBERRY

HUCKLEBERRY FRUIT LOOKS AND TASTES SIMILAR TO A BLUEBERRY. YOU'LL KNOW WHAT YOU'RE EATING, HOWEVER, BY THE CRUNCH OF HUCKLEBERRY'S SMALL SEEDS.

Position *G. frondosa* and *G. dumosa* enjoy wet sites; *G. baccata* prefers drier sites. All huckleberries like full sun and very acid soil; pH 4.5–5.5.

Cultivation Plant container-grown shrubs anytime the ground isn't frozen, or set out bareroot plants in spring or autumn, while dormant. Space plants 3 feet (90 cm) apart. Before planting, make sure the soil is very acid and rich in humus. Dig acid peat moss into the soil to meet both of these needs.

Pruning No regular pruning needed.

Propagation Fresh seed germinates fairly well, but for best results, keep the seed warm and moist for a month, then cool and moist for 1–2 months. Cuttings taken from late summer through autumn root well in a mix of peat and either sand or perlite.

Pests and diseases Generally no significant problems.

Harvesting and storage Pick fruits when fully colored. One way to harvest is to spread a clean cloth on the ground and shake the plant; ripe fruits fall on the cloth. Store in the refrigerator with high humidity.

HARDINESS
Zones 3–7.

HEIGHT
40–60 feet
(12–18 m)

SPREAD
30–50 feet
(9–15 m)

COMMENTS
Other members of this nut-producing family include English walnuts *Juglans regia* (also called Persian walnuts) and black walnuts *J. nigra*.

BUTTERNUT

BUTTERNUTS ARE LARGE TREES THAT PRODUCE EDIBLE NUTS ENCASED IN A HUSK AND SHELL. THE HARD SHELL IS SOMEWHAT ELONGATED AND ENDS IN A POINT. THE MEAT WITHIN IS RICH AND BUTTERY.

Position Full sun and deep, moist, rich soil is best, but plants will tolerate dry, rocky soil, especially on limestone.

Cultivation Transplant in spring, taking care to preserve as much of the taproot as possible if the plant is not growing in a container. Space plants 30–50 feet (9–15 m) apart.

Pruning Train young trees to form a sturdy framework of well-spaced, wide-angled branches. On mature trees, just cut out diseased or dead wood and odd untidy branches.

Propagation Mix seed with damp peat moss and refrigerate for 3–4 months before sowing in a warm, bright place. Graft cultivars onto black walnut rootstock.

Pests and diseases Small, black pustules and dying limbs indicate butternut dieback disease. Cut diseased branches back to healthy wood, and fertilize and water trees.

Harvesting and storage Harvest nuts after they fall. Allow husks to dry, so they crumble off when you are ready to crack the nut. Store kernels in the refrigerator at high humidity.

APPLE

TO GET HIGH YIELDS FROM YOUR APPLES, YOU'LL NEED TO GROW AT LEAST TWO CULTIVARS THAT FLOWER AT THE SAME TIME SO THEY CAN CROSS-POLLINATE.

Position Plant apple trees in full sun and well-drained soil.

Cultivation There are more than 1,000 different apple cultivars available. For extra-high yields, you can choose spur-type trees, which are so heavily loaded with short fruit-bearing spur branches that they stay about 25 percent smaller than the same cultivar without spurs. You can also choose grafted trees with different combinations of rootstocks, interstems (short pieces of trunk) and tops to make just about any kind of apple tree you can imagine. Plant full-sized apple trees 25–30 feet (7.5–9 m) apart, semidwarfs 12–15 feet (3.6–4.5 m) apart and dwarfs 6–8 feet (1.8–2.4 m) apart. Provide plenty of moisture and nutrients to keep young trees growing quickly. Mulch with compost in spring, and make sure the soil is moist around mature trees when they're in bloom.

Pruning Apple trees grow best when trained into a pyramidal, central leader form, with one trunk and several sets of branches off it. Start pruning young trees just after spring planting (or in the spring following autumn planting).

HARDINESS
Zones 3–9, but choose a cultivar that's suited to your area.

HEIGHT
8–30 feet (2.4–9 m)

SPREAD
8–30 feet (2.4–9 m)

COMMENTS
Support the brittle trunks of young apple trees by tying carefully to a strong stake.

A mulch of marigold roots has been found to suppress populations of parasitic nematodes in the soil around apple trees.

Continue thinning and pruning each year until the trees mature.

Propagation Propagate by grafting.

Pests and diseases Some problems that might occur are apple maggots, codling moths, plum curculios, rust, scab, mildew and fireblight. You can prevent many problems by planting disease-resistant cultivars. Among these, 'Prima', 'Dayton' and 'William's Pride' are early ripening; 'Jonafree', 'Freedom' and 'Liberty' ripen in midseason; and 'Enterprise' ripens late. When rust, mildew or scab do strike, carefully rake up all dropped leaves in autumn. If the diseases were a major problem last year, spray sulfur as often as once a week from the time growth begins until midsummer. Fireblight is a difficult-to-control disease that has become an epidemic across the United States and elsewhere. Use blight-resistant cultivars or you'll have problems.

Harvesting and storage Depending on the rootstock, apples will start producing fruit in 2–5 years. Pick apples when they develop full color and flavor but are still crunchy and crisp. You can leave late-maturing apples on the tree as long as the temperature remains above 28°F (–2°C). Use bruised fruit at once. Store unblemished apples at 32°F (0°C) and 90 percent humidity.

HARDINESS
Zones 3–9.

HEIGHT
8–25 feet
(2.4–7.5 m)

SPREAD
8–25 feet
(2.4–7.5 m)

COMMENTS
Fruits of most crab apples are used for cooking, but a few cultivars are also excellent for eating.

CRAB APPLE

SOME CRAB APPLES TASTE DELICIOUS OUT OF HAND, WHILE OTHERS TASTE GOOD ONLY WHEN COOKED WITH SWEETENER INTO JELLIES. YOU CAN EAT THE WHOLE FRUIT, EXCEPT FOR THE SEEDS.

Position Plant in full sun and well-drained soil.

Cultivation Plant container-grown stock anytime the ground isn't frozen, or set out bareroot plants in spring or autumn, while dormant. Space plants 8–25 feet (2.4–7.5 m) apart. The plants need cross-pollination, but the pollinator can be an apple or a crab apple.

Pruning Train young plants to a sturdy framework of wide-angled, well-spaced main limbs. Mature plants need little pruning beyond removing water sprouts and thinning congested growth.

Propagation Graft or bud cultivars onto seedling apple or crab apple rootstock. Seed, for seedling rootstocks, germinates readily if kept cool and moist for 2–3 months.

Pests and diseases Crab apples can have the same pest and disease problems as apples but are usually less troubled by them.

Harvesting and storage Pick fruits when fully colored and they pull off the plant easily. Store, refrigerated, in a plastic bag with air holes in it.

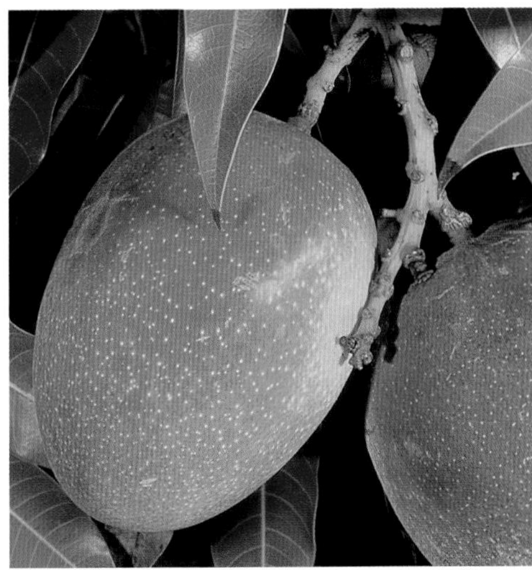

HARDINESS
Zone 10.

HEIGHT
50–90 feet (15–27 m)

SPREAD
30–125 feet (9–37.5 m)

COMMENTS
Remove the seed and skin before eating the pulp. The fruits are good fresh or when used for chutney, sauces and ice cream.

MANGO

THE RIPE FRUIT OF MANGO TREES IS LARGE AND ELONGATED WITH SKIN IN SHADES OF RED, YELLOW AND GREEN. INSIDE, THE JUICY, ORANGE PULP HAS A SWEET, RICH FLAVOR.

Position Mangoes need full sun and well-drained soil that is not too rich.

Cultivation Set out container-grown plants anytime, spacing them 30–60 feet (9–18 m) apart. Plants are self-fruitful, so you need only one to get a harvest. Thin fruits and fertilize during years of good production; otherwise, the tree tends to bear only every other year.

Pruning Remove dead and crowded wood to keep the tree within bounds. In late summer, shorten some of the stems and remove any vigorous, upright ones.

Propagation Some cultivars come true from seed, which should be sown fresh, with the top of the seed at soil level. A more reliable way to propagate any cultivar is to graft or bud it onto a mango seedling while the tree is actively growing.

Pests and diseases In areas where anthracnose disease is a problem, rake up and dispose of infected leaves and fruit.

Harvesting and storage Pick fruits when they soften slightly and change color. To store, pick them firm and ripen at room temperature.

Mespilus germanica

ROSACEAE

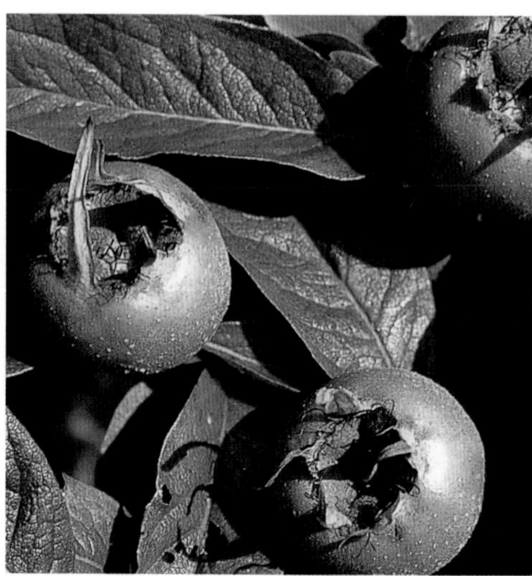

HARDINESS
Zones 4–8.

HEIGHT
9–20 feet
(2.7–6 m)

SPREAD
9–20 feet
(2.7–6 m)

COMMENTS
The ripening process takes more than 2 weeks in cool temperatures. Eat the flesh but not the seeds or the skin.

MEDLAR

MEDLAR FRUIT LOOKS LIKE A SMALL, RUSSETED APPLE, TINGED WITH DULL YELLOW OR RED. THE FLESH IS SOFT AND BROWN AND TASTES LIKE THICK APPLESAUCE.

Position Give medlars full sun and moderately rich, well-drained soil.

Cultivation Plant container-grown stock anytime the ground isn't frozen, or set out bareroot plants in spring or autumn, while they are dormant. Space plants 12–25 feet (3.6–7.5 m) apart. Plant with the graft union below ground level so the scion also takes root. Medlars are self-fertile, and virtually every blossom sets fruit. On young trees, pinch off some blossoms to channel more energy into shoot growth.

Pruning This small tree needs very little pruning; simply trim as needed to shape and to remove odd dead or diseased branches.

Propagation Graft medlar onto pear, hawthorn, quince or medlar seedling rootstock.

Pests and diseases No pest or disease problems worth noting.

Harvesting and storage Harvest the fruits as the leaves begin to drop in autumn. Although the fruits may feel rock-hard, handle them carefully to avoid bruising. Place them on a shelf in a cool room to "blet," or soften. Fruits will be soft and ready to eat in about 2 weeks.

Morus spp.

MORACEAE

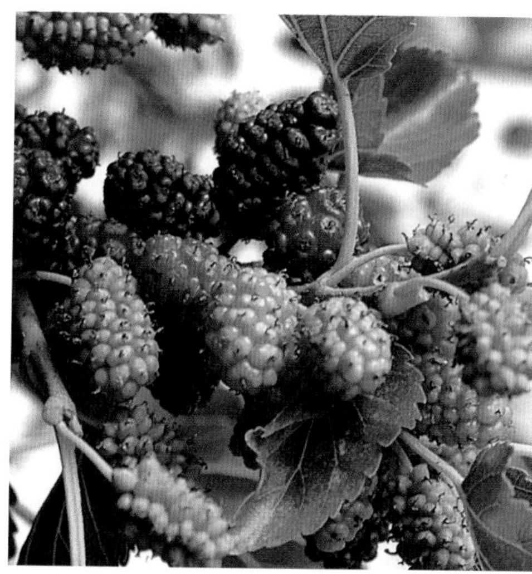

HARDINESS
Zones 5–10.

HEIGHT
15–30 feet (4.5–9 m)

SPREAD
10–20 feet (3–6 m)

COMMENTS
Do not plant mulberries where falling fruits will cause problems with staining. For cooking, pick the fruit when it is still firm and slightly underripe.

MULBERRY

MULBERRY TREES PRODUCE BLACK, RED OR WHITE BLACKBERRY-SHAPED FRUITS. FLAVOR RANGES FROM SWEET WITH A SHARP TANG TO PURELY SWEET. EAT THE WHOLE FRUIT.

Position Plant in full sun and average, well-drained soil.

Cultivation Plant container-grown stock anytime the ground isn't frozen, or set out bareroot plants in spring or autumn, while dormant. Space plants 10–30 feet (3–9 m) apart. Cultivars selected for fruit production generally do not need cross-pollination.

Pruning No regular pruning needed.

Propagation Russian mulberry *M. alba* 'Tartarica' makes a good rootstock for most other mulberries. Softwood or hardwood cuttings of most species usually root readily. With hardwood cuttings, either split the lower end or take a small "heel" of 2-year-old wood along with the 1-year-old wood used for the cutting.

Pests and diseases Control scale insects with dormant oil, and handle dieback by cutting off infected portions.

Harvesting and storage To harvest in quantity, spread a clean sheet under the tree and shake the branches. Ripe fruits do not keep well fresh but can be frozen or dried.

HARDINESS
Zone 10.

HEIGHT
8–30 feet (2.4–9 m)

SPREAD
8–20 feet (2.4–6 m)

COMMENTS
The edible flesh of all bananas is creamy-yellow, with a smooth texture and a sweet, rich flavor.

BANANA

BANANAS ARE PRODUCED ON LARGE, SOFT, PERENNIAL PLANTS THAT GROW TO THE PROPORTIONS OF A SMALL TREE.

Position Give bananas full sun and well-drained, slightly acid soil.

Cultivation Plant anytime of year, spacing plants 10–20 feet (3–6 m) apart. Bananas do not need cross-pollination, so you can get fruit from just one plant. The "stem" is really a pseudostem, a tightly wound sheath of leaves, which dies to the ground after fruiting but is replaced by others growing up from the rhizome (a thick underground stem). Cut off male flowers, which form at the far end of the fruit stalk. These plants are heavy feeders, so fertilize regularly, and provide abundant water in warm weather.

Pruning Remove all but three pseudostems—one fruiting, one ready to follow and one just peeking up from below. Cut down the fruiting pseudostem at harvest.

Propagation Divide rhizomes or dig up suckers with some attached roots.

Pests and diseases Generally no significant problems.

Harvesting and storage Cut off the entire stalk when some fruits begin to change color. Ripen fruits at room temperature to yellow. Bananas are best eaten fresh, but can also be dried for storage.

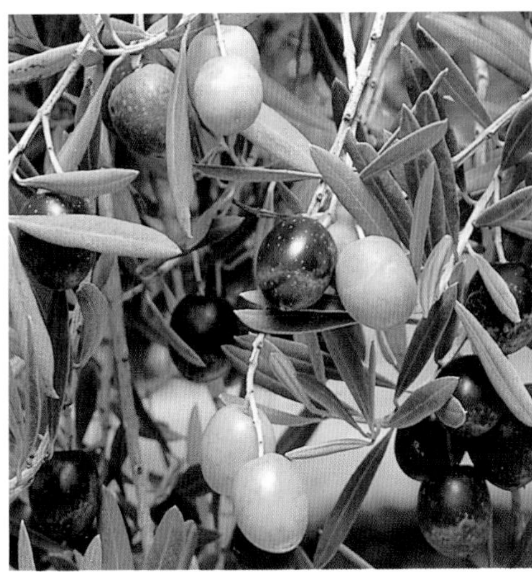

HARDINESS
Zones 9–10.

HEIGHT
30 feet (9 m)

SPREAD
Up to 30 feet (9 m)

COMMENTS
Do not plant olives along walkways, driveways or patios, where fallen fruit will be a nuisance.

OLIVE

OLIVE TREES PRODUCE GRAPE-SIZED FRUIT WITH EDIBLE FLESH AND SKIN (DON'T EAT THE SEEDS). THE FRUITS HAVE A RICH, OILY TASTE, ESPECIALLY WHEN THEY ARE RIPE.

Position Give olives full sun and well-drained soil. They bear best where summers are long and hot, with low humidity.

Cultivation Plant container-grown stock anytime, or set out bareroot plants in spring or autumn, while dormant. Space plants 20–80 feet (6–24 m) apart, with the greater distances reserved for drier climates where the trees will not be irrigated. Cross-pollination usually increases yield. Where fruits are close together on a stem, thin by just cutting back the stem, or removing excess fruits individually.

Pruning Young trees need little pruning. Prune mature trees to keep them from growing too large.

Propagation Propagate olives by hardwood or softwood cuttings.

Pests and diseases Where olive knot disease is a threat, prune in summer to prevent problems. Cut away galls produced by this disease.

Harvesting and storage Harvest fruit when it is green (unripe) or black (ripe). Don't expose olives intended for eating to cool temperatures. Olives are usually brined for storage after bitterness has been removed.

Opuntia spp. CACTACEAE

HARDINESS
Zones 5–10, depending on the species.

HEIGHT
1–15 feet (30–450 cm)

SPREAD
3–15 feet (90–450 cm)

COMMENTS
Both the fruit and the fleshy green pads are edible. Eat the fruits raw. Slice the pads and cook as you would string beans.

PRICKLY PEAR

PRICKLY PEAR FRUITS ARE ABOUT THE SIZE OF AN EGG WITH RED (OR SOMETIMES YELLOW OR GREEN) SKIN. THE EDIBLE PULP IS USUALLY RED, WITH A MILD FLAVOR AND MANY SMALL, EDIBLE SEEDS.

Position Prickly pear needs full sun and very well-drained soil.

Cultivation Plant anytime, unless the ground is frozen, spacing plants 3–15 feet (90–450 cm) apart (depending on their mature size).

Pruning No pruning is necessary.

Propagation Sow seed and keep it in the dark until sprouts appear. You can also use the fleshy pads to start new plants. Cut a pad from the mother plant and let it dry for a few days before setting it upright with the bottom part in well-drained soil. Water sparingly until roots form and growth begins.

Pests and diseases Generally no significant problems.

Harvesting and storage Wear thick leather gloves to harvest the flat, green pads, then remove the spines (and the tiny hairlike needles at the base of the spines) by rubbing them off with a rough cloth or peeling them off with a vegetable peeler. Also wear gloves when harvesting the fruits, which are ripe when fully colored. Rub off the needles and peel away the skin before eating.

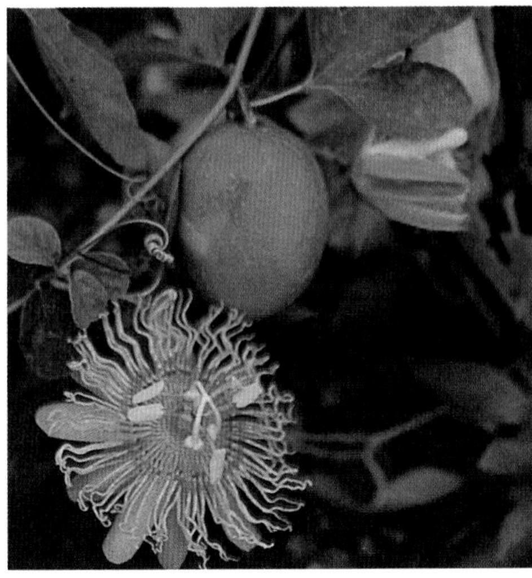

HARDINESS
Zone 4–10.

HEIGHT
20 feet (6 m)

SPREAD
Up to 20 feet (6 m) or more, if unrestricted.

COMMENTS
Eat the fleshy seed covering with or without the seeds.

MAYPOP

MAYPOP FRUITS ARE YELLOW TO YELLOW-GREEN WITH MANY SEEDS, EACH ENCASED IN GELATINOUS PULP WITH A TROPICAL FLAVOR.

Position Plant in full sun in well-drained soil.

Cultivation Plant container-grown vines anytime the ground isn't frozen, or set out dormant bareroot plants in spring or autumn. Space plants 6–18 feet (1.8–5.4 m) apart, depending on whether you plan to train vines upward or outward. This vine likes to have a fence, arbor or deciduous shrub to climb on. The roots spread fast and far, so contain them with a barrier strip or mowed lawn. Maypops are cross-pollinators; hand-pollination may help fruit set.

Pruning Cut the whole plant to the ground each year at the end of the growing season.

Propagation Suckers root readily if dug from the mother plant when a few inches high. To grow maypops from seed, first soak the seed in water for 24 hours. After sowing, provide a warm, dark environment until sprouts appear.

Pests and diseases No significant pest or disease problems.

Harvesting and storage Fruit drops to the ground when ripe; gather it as soon as possible. Store in high humidity, such as in a plastic bag, in cool, not cold, temperatures.

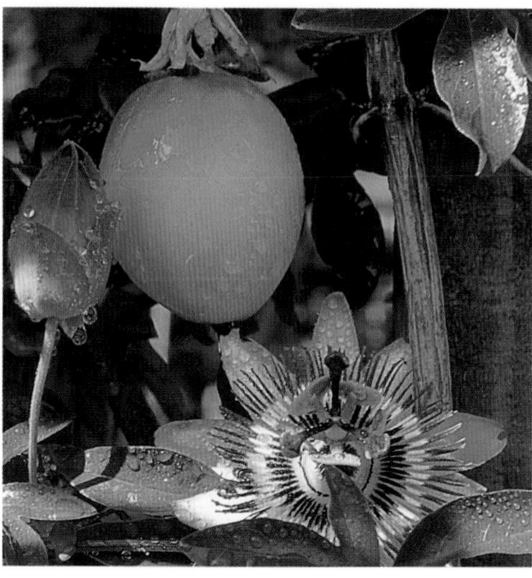

Hardiness
Zone 10.

Spread
A sprawling vine, spreading 20 feet (6 m) or more in a season, unless pruned.

Comments
Passionfruit are filled with many seeds, each enclosed in a membrane with a sweet-tart, tangy flavor. You can eat both the seeds and the fleshy covering around them.

Passionfruit

A GRAFTED VINE WILL BEAR FRUIT, AS IT HAS BOTH MALE AND FEMALE CHARACTERISTICS.

Position Grow in full sun or, in very hot areas, partial shade. The vines need well-drained soil, rich in humus and low in salts.

Cultivation Set out container-grown plants anytime, spacing them about 9 feet (3 m) apart. Some need cross-pollination, so it's smart to plant at least two seedlings or cultivars to be on the safe side. The vines need some support, such as a fence or trellis, on which to climb. Where they are not cold-hardy, grow passionfruit vines in a well-drained soil mix in containers. The plants can wait out winter without full sun in a cool room; in spring, trim and provide full sunlight.

Pruning Regular pruning is not a necessity, but it will help to keep the vine untangled. For the neatest growth, train one or two permanent "arms" along the top of the support. Each winter, cut all sideshoots to within a few inches of these arms.

Propagation Sow fresh seed, take cuttings (or buy a grafted plant).

Pests and diseases Generally no significant problems.

Harvesting and storage Pick up ripe fruits from the ground. Fruit can be stored for a few weeks in a plastic bag at about 50°F (10°C).

HARDINESS
Zones 9–10.

HEIGHT
20–60 feet
(6–18 m)

SPREAD
25–35 feet
(7.5–10.5 m)

COMMENTS
Because of its rough skin and green, sometimes almost black, color, the avocado was once called the "alligator pear."

AVOCADO

THE AVOCADO'S PALE GREEN, EDIBLE FLESH IS BUTTERY SMOOTH, WITH A RICH FLAVOR.

Position Plant in full sun. Avocado grows best in well-drained soil with a pH between 5.5 and 6.5.

Cultivation Plant in spring, with the base of the trunk slightly higher out of the ground than it was in the nursery. Space plants 25–35 feet (7.5–10.5 m) apart. Avocados can self-pollinate (so you can get fruit from just one plant), but cross-pollination may improve yields.

Pruning Prune as necessary after harvest to limit the size of the tree.

Propagation Graft onto seedlings or rootstocks grown from cuttings.

Pests and diseases Avocado root rot can occur where drainage is poor. Avoid this problem by planting certified disease-free plants in a good site. There is no cure for infected trees. In humid areas, watch for leaf diseases. Minimize damage by keeping trees fertilized and watered as needed, pruning to promote air circulation among branches, and cleaning up infected leaves that fall to the ground.

Harvesting and storage When fruit is mature but still hard, clip it off with a piece of stem attached. Dark-skinned cultivars turn dark when mature; green cultivars yellow slightly. Allow fruit to soften slightly.

HARDINESS
All Zones.

HEIGHT
3–6 feet (90–180 cm). There is a larger-growing variety, *Physalis peruviana.*

SPREAD
3–6 feet (90–180 cm)

COMMENTS
Eat the ripe fruit fresh, cook the berries into jams, or dry them like raisins. Unripe fruit is poisonous.

CAPE GOOSEBERRY, DWARF

THE PALE YELLOW BERRIES OF DWARF CAPE GOOSEBERRY RIPEN WITHIN A HUSK ON A SMALL, SPREADING BUSH.

Position Cape gooseberry is a perennial in the tropics, but you can grow it as an annual wherever you can grow tomatoes. It needs full sun and well-drained soil that is not overly rich in nitrogen.

Cultivation Start seed indoors about 8 weeks before the average date of your last killing spring frost. Transplant outdoors 1 week after that last frost date. Space plants 3 feet (90 cm) apart.

Pruning No pruning is necessary, but in year-round warm climates, cut plants back hard after the first harvest to reduce pest problems.

Propagation Grow from seed sown indoors in early spring. Even where Cape gooseberries are perennial, yields are better if you start new plants every 2–3 years.

Pests and diseases Plants usually have no significant problems in temperate climates.

Harvesting and storage Harvest fruits when the husks are dry and papery. Pick them individually, or shake the plant and gather those that drop. Fruit can be stored for months if kept dry and intact in their husks. The husk is not edible.

HARDINESS
Zones 3–8, depending on the species.

HEIGHT
25–150 feet (7.5–45 m)

SPREAD
10–75 feet (3–22.5 m). Eventual size varies with species.

COMMENTS
The dry-textured, delicate-flavored, cream-colored nuts are usually about ½ inch (12 mm) long.

PINE NUT

MANY PINE SPECIES YIELD ELONGATED, EDIBLE NUTS, HELD WITHIN THE CONES.

Position Plant in full sun in well-drained soil. Grows best in rich soil, but will tolerate infertile conditions.

Cultivation Plant container-grown stock anytime the ground isn't frozen, or set out small bareroot plants between spring and autumn where winters are mild, or in spring where winters are severe. Space plants 10–75 feet (3–22.5 m) apart, depending on the eventual size of the plant, which varies with species.

Pruning Pines need little pruning. If desired, pinch out the shoot tips in spring for bushier growth.

Propagation Enhance germination by keeping sown seed warm for 2–3 months, then cool for a few months. Graft pines using a side graft indoors in winter or, where winters are mild, outdoors in late summer or early autumn.

Pests and diseases Generally no significant problems.

Harvesting and storage Gather cones of species that drop ripe seed just before the cones open. With other pines, open the fallen cones either by heating them in the oven or smashing them with a hammer. Store nuts in cool, dry conditions.

HARDINESS
Zones 8–10.

HEIGHT
20–25 feet (6–7.5 m)

SPREAD
25–30 feet (7.5–9 m)

COMMENTS
One male tree can pollinate 8–12 female trees. At maturity, the nut shell is pale (perhaps blushed with pink) and the nut loosens within.

PISTACHIO

PISTACHIO PLANTS GROW AS SHRUBS OR TREES AND PRODUCE EDIBLE NUTS.

Position Pistachios prefer full sun and average, well-drained soil, although they tolerate alkaline and saline conditions. They need some winter cold (about 1,000 total hours below 45°F [7.2°C]), as well as summers that are long, hot and dry.

Cultivation Set out container-grown plants anytime, spacing them at least 25 feet (7.5 m) apart. You'll need both male (nonfruiting) and female (fruiting) trees to get nuts.

Pruning Prune young plants to make them bushy, shortening stems by about 8 inches (20 cm) when they are 3 feet (90 cm) long. Prune mature plants lightly, shortening some of the branches in winter.

Propagation Propagate by grafting onto selected rootstock, depending on climate and soil conditions. *Pistacia terebinthus* is cold-resistant; *P. integerrima* is resistant to Verticillium fungi; and *P. terebinthus* and *P. atlantica* resist nematodes.

Pests and diseases Avoid root diseases by selecting a suitable site and rootstock.

Harvesting and storage Shake the branches to dislodge ripe nuts. Rub off the hulls and dry the nuts at 150°F (65.5°C) for 8–10 hours.

Prunus armeniaca ROSACEAE

HARDINESS
Zones 5–9.

HEIGHT
8–24 feet
(2.4–7.2 m)

SPREAD
16–24 feet
(4.8–7.2 m)

COMMENTS
In frost-prone areas, select later-blooming cultivars, such as 'Harglow', or the more frost-tolerant 'Alfred' and 'Manchurian Bush Apricot'.

APRICOT

FULLY RIPE APRICOTS ARE SO SOFT THAT THEY DON'T SHIP WELL, SO THE BEST WAY TO ENJOY THEM AT THEIR PEAK IS TO GROW YOUR OWN.

Position Plant in full sun in average to poor, well-drained soil. Early-opening flowers should be sheltered from frost.

Cultivation Many apricots are self-fertile and will produce some fruit if planted alone. But with most, yields will increase if you plant a second cultivar for cross-pollination. Plant dwarf trees 12–15 feet (3.6–4.5 m) apart and full-sized trees 25 feet (7.5 m) apart. Mulch with compost to keep the soil moist in spring and fertilize as needed.

Pruning Some cultivars will fruit only every other year unless the fruits are thinned out to leave them 2 inches (5 cm) apart. Apricot trees should be pruned using the open-center system where the leader branch is removed and the tree is pruned to an open vase shape.

Propagation Propagate by bud graft.

Pests and diseases Susceptible to Eutypa dieback, a disease that attacks through pruning cuts. Treat scale, mite and aphid infestations with oil sprays.

Harvesting and storage Pluck the fruits when they're soft and sweet. Can be made into jam or frozen.

HARDINESS
Zones 4–9.

HEIGHT
15–30 feet
(4.5–9 m)

SPREAD
15–30 feet
(4.5–9 m)

COMMENTS
Sweet cherries often need a compatible partner for cross-pollination. Sour cherries *Prunus cerasus* are self-fertile, so you can get a harvest from just one tree.

CHERRY, SWEET

CHERRIES ARE IN SEASON FOR ONLY ABOUT 6 WEEKS SO CAN BE VERY EXPENSIVE. IT'S A LUXURY TO HAVE A TREE IN THE GARDEN.

Position Plant in full sun in average to poor, well-drained soil. Cherries prefer arid climates.

Cultivation Space standard sweet cherry trees 20–30 feet (6–9 m) apart, sour cherries 20 feet (6 m) apart, and dwarf cherries 10 feet (3 m) apart. Mulch with compost in early spring. In cooler climates, plant from valleys to protect cherry flowers from frost.

Pruning Train naturally spreading cherry trees to an open-center form; for more upright growing trees, prune to a central leader form. Ask the nursery for specific information.

Propagation Propagate by grafting.

Pests and diseases The main predator with cherries is birds. Be prepared to net the trees once the fruit starts to ripen to keep the birds away. Choose cultivars that are resistant to the diseases most prevalent in your area.

Harvesting and storage Cherries begin to bear fruit 3–7 years after planting. If the weather is dry, let cherries ripen on the trees for best flavor. They should be fairly soft and very sweet.

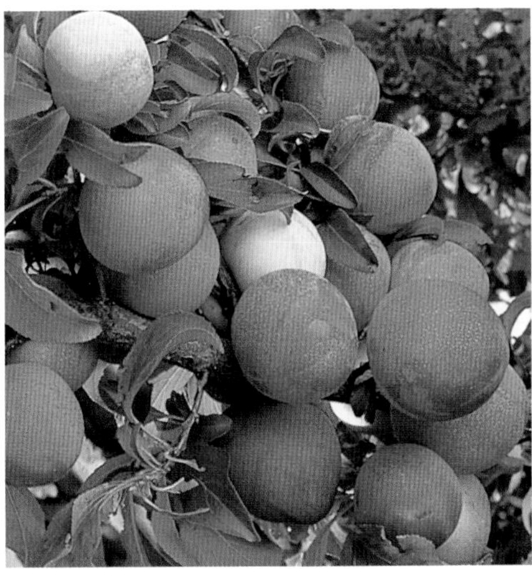

HARDINESS
Zones 4–10.

HEIGHT
8–20 feet
(2.4–6 m)

SPREAD
8–20 feet
(2.4–6 m)

COMMENTS
'Santa Rosa' is a Japanese plum *Prunus salicina* with large, high-quality fruit. It yields best when planted with other Japanese plums.

PLUM, EUROPEAN

PLUMS COME IN A WIDE RANGE OF COLORS, FLAVORS AND SIZES, SOME FRUITING EARLIER THAN OTHERS. SPEND SOME TIME CHOOSING THE ONE BEST SUITED TO YOUR NEEDS.

Position Plant plum trees in full sun in average to rich soil.

Cultivation Many European plums and damson plums will self-pollinate, so one tree is enough. But if you plant two compatible cultivars, they may set more fruit. Space full-sized plum trees 20–25 feet (6–7.5 m) apart and dwarf trees 8–12 feet (2.4–3.6 m) apart. Mulch with compost in spring and keep the soil moist through the growing season. Apply a complete fertilizer when the petals drop.

Pruning Train upright-growing cultivars to a central leader. Open-center training works better for more spreading plums, including most Japanese types. Thin the fruit on trees that are overburdened.

Propagation Propagate by bud graft.

Pests and diseases Plums are prone to black knot, a fungus that causes dark swellings on tree limbs. If black knot was a problem in the previous year, spray with lime-sulfur when the buds swell, then reapply a week later.

Harvesting and storage Plum trees start to bear 3–4 years after planting. Pick the fruit when soft and sweet.

HARDINESS
Zones 6–9.

HEIGHT
15–30 feet
(4.5–9 m)

SPREAD
15–30 feet
(4.5–9 m)

COMMENTS
To spread out your harvest, choose early- and later-maturing almonds. One of the earliest-producing cultivars is 'Nonpareil'; 'Monterey' and 'Fritz' bear a month or so later.

ALMOND

MOST ALMONDS NEED CROSS-POLLINATION TO SET THEIR CROP, SO CHECK THE CATALOG DESCRIPTIONS TO MAKE SURE YOU PLANT THE BEST COMPANIONS.

Position Grow in full sun in average to fertile, well-drained soil.

Cultivation Most almonds require another tree to pollinate them. Plant trees 25 feet (7.5 m) apart and mulch with compost each spring. Water plants regularly when the weather is hot.

Pruning Train almonds to an open-center form, but as you prune each year, do more heading and less thinning than you would for trees such as peaches. The aim is to develop a thick branch network, which will promote better fruiting.

Propagation Propagate by grafting.

Pests and diseases Unfortunately, disease resistance is minimal in almonds so they're best grown in a dry climate. Keep mulch away from the trunk to discourage rodent activity. Pick up all fallen nuts and destroy bad ones to reduce problems with navel orangeworms—the white caterpillars with brown heads that feed on the nut meat.

Harvesting and storage Most almond trees begin to produce nuts after 3–4 years. Use a padded stick to knock the nuts off the tree.

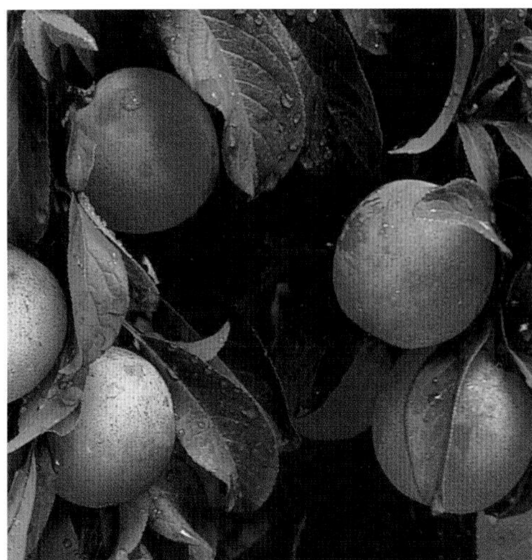

HARDINESS
Zones 6–9.

HEIGHT
8–20 feet
(2.4–6 m)

SPREAD
8–20 feet
(2.4–6 m)

COMMENTS
Dwarf cultivars can be grown successfully in containers.

PLUMCOT

IN BOTH APPEARANCE AND FLAVOR, PLUMCOTS RESEMBLE THEIR PARENTS, PLUMS AND APRICOTS. THE FLESH AND SKIN OF THE FRUIT ARE EDIBLE, BUT NOT THE SEED.

Position Plant in full sun and well-drained soil. Avoid sites subject to late frost early in the season.

Cultivation In colder regions, plant only in spring; elsewhere, plant in either spring or autumn. Plumcots need cross-pollination, although the pollinator can vary, depending on the cultivar. (Ask the nursery or check catalog descriptions to get the right pollinator for your plant.)

Pruning Prune out a moderate amount of wood each year, just before the blossoms open, to keep the plant open to light and air at the center.

Propagation Graft cultivars onto either seedling or cutting-grown apricot or plum rootstock.

Pests and diseases Brown rot may damage the fruit. Remove and destroy any shriveled fruit left hanging on the tree at the end of the season.

Harvesting and storage Pick the fruits when they are fully colored and slightly soft. They can be stored for up to a couple of weeks at high humidity and temperatures just above freezing.

HARDINESS
Zones 5–9.

HEIGHT
8–15 feet (2.4–4.5 m)

SPREAD
10–20 feet (3–6 m)

COMMENTS
Genetic dwarfs with especially good fruit flavor include 'Nectar Babe', 'Bonanza' and 'Southern Flame'. Trees that are grafted onto dwarfing roots grow to 8–10 feet (2.4–3 m) tall.

PEACH AND NECTARINE

BOTH PEACHES AND NECTARINES ARE ATTRACTIVE WHEN GROWN AS FAN-SHAPED ESPALIERS. GROWING THEM ON A WALL ALSO PROVIDES THEM WITH EXTRA WARMTH.

Position Plant in full sun in average to poor, well-drained soil.

Cultivation Most peaches and nectarines are self-pollinating, so you can get a full crop from just one tree. Fertilize with compost in early spring and again with a balanced organic fertilizer when the fruit first forms. Spray the leaves with liquid kelp every 3–4 weeks during the growing season.

Pruning Train peach trees to an open-center form. Thin young trees lightly in summer to remove excess branches. With mature trees, cut half the older branches back by about half of their total length during the dormant season so they resprout productive new wood.

Propagation Propagate by bud graft.

Pests and diseases If you live in an area that is prone to peach tree diseases, start with disease-resistant cultivars. Otherwise, you may have to spray to control diseases.

Harvesting and storage Peach and nectarine trees begin producing fruit 2–4 years after planting. Harvest when fruit is soft and sweet. Can be made into jam or frozen.

HARDINESS
Zones 3–6.

HEIGHT
9–15 feet
(2.7–4.5 m)

SPREAD
9–15 feet
(2.7–4.5 m)

COMMENTS
Although it has a delicate beauty, Nanking cherry is a tough shrub. Its blossoms resist frost, and the plants tolerate drought, extremely cold winters and hot summers.

CHERRY, NANKING

NANKING CHERRIES GROW AS LARGE BUSHES WITH SMALL RED OR YELLOW FRUIT. DEPENDING ON THE PLANT, THE FRUIT MAY TASTE LIKE SWEET CHERRIES OR SOUR CHERRIES. EXCEPT FOR THE SEED, THE WHOLE FRUIT IS EDIBLE.

Position Nanking cherries need full sun but tolerate a wide range of soil types as long as they are provided with good drainage.

Cultivation Set new plants out in spring, spacing them 6–16 feet (1.8–4.8 m) apart. Nanking cherries generally need cross-pollination, so grow at least two plants. This shrub thrives with little or no care.

Pruning No pruning is needed, but you can keep the plants smaller or even train them as hedges with regular, late-winter pruning.

Propagation Keep the seed moist and cold for 3 months before sowing it in a warm, bright place. Seedlings typically begin to bear fruit by their third season.

Pests and diseases Twigs or stems occasionally die back; cut them back to healthy wood.

Harvesting and storage Harvest the fruit as soon as it fully turns color. Harvested fruits store poorly, so just pick and eat them fresh.

HARDINESS
Zone 10.

HEIGHT
10–25 feet
(3–7.5 m)

SPREAD
7–15 feet
(2.1–4.5 m)

COMMENTS
Tropical guava *Psidium guajava* has larger fruits than strawberry, or Cattley, guava *P. littorale.* The flesh of both is edible. Both make excellent jelly, jam or juice.

GUAVA

WHEN RIPE, THE TROPICAL GUAVA GIVES OFF A MUSKY AROMA BUT THE FLAVOR IS SOMEWHAT INSIPID; THE STRAWBERRY GUAVA HAS A SPICY FLAVOR.

Position Plant in full sun. Well-drained, slightly acid soil rich in organic matter is ideal.

Cultivation Set out container-grown plants anytime, spacing them 9–15 feet (2.7–4.5 m) apart. Plants are partly self-fruitful, so growing two or more seedlings or cultivars may increase yields. Fertilize often to keep your plants vigorous.

Pruning Prune heavily to stimulate new growth and keep fruits close to the center of the plant.

Propagation Dig suckers from around the base of an established bush, or take stem cuttings. The seed germinates fairly easily.

Pests and diseases Generally not a problem in home plantings.

Harvesting and storage The aroma and color change tell you when the fruits are ripe. Tropical guava turns yellow when ripe. It is usually stored just below 50°F (10°C). Strawberry guava turns yellow or red when ripe and is best stored at temperatures just above freezing. Slightly underripe fruit will keep for a few weeks at cool temperatures with high humidity.

HARDINESS
Will grow in Zone 8 but fruits best in Zones 9–10.

HEIGHT
10–20 feet (3–6 m)

SPREAD
6–8 feet (1.8–2.4 m)

COMMENTS
Dwarf cultivars are good in pots in colder climates. Besides eating fresh pomegranate seeds and flesh, use the juice for jelly, or in punch.

POMEGRANATE

POMEGRANATE FRUIT IS USUALLY RED AND THE SIZE OF A SOFTBALL. INSIDE, THE SEEDS ARE SUPPORTED WITHIN MEMBRANES. EAT BOTH SEEDS AND FLESHY SEED COVERING.

Position Pomegranates prefer a hot, dry climate. Give the plants full sun. They tolerate a wide range of well-drained soil types.

Cultivation Set out container-grown plants anytime, or plant bareroot stock from spring to autumn. Space plants 18 feet (5.4 m) apart. Cross-pollination sometimes increases yields, so grow at least two plants if you have room.

Pruning Train the plant as a multiple-stemmed bush or as a single-stemmed tree. Prune mature plants lightly each winter—just enough to stimulate some new growth and thin out excess fruit. Also remove suckers, unless they are needed to replace a damaged trunk.

Propagation Seed germinates readily. Propagate cultivars by hardwood cuttings.

Pests and diseases Generally no significant problems.

Harvesting and storage Clip fruits from the plant as soon as they are fully colored. Fruits refrigerated at high humidity keep well for several months. For grenadine syrup, cook juice with an equal weight of sugar.

HARDINESS
Zones 4–9.

HEIGHT
8–20 feet (2.4–6 m)

SPREAD
8–20 feet (2.4–6 m)

COMMENTS
Plant cultivars that mature at different times. For example, 'Clapp's Favorite' and 'Moonglow' (ripen mid-August), 'Bartlett' (early September), 'Seckel' and 'Magness' (mid-September), 'Comice' and 'Kieffer' (October).

PEAR

MOST PEARS REQUIRE CROSS-POLLINATION TO SET FRUIT, SO YOU'LL NEED TO PLANT AT LEAST ONE COMPATIBLE COMPANION TO GET A GOOD CROP.

Position Plant in full sun in average to poor, well-drained soil.

Cultivation Space full-sized trees 15–20 feet (4.5–6 m) apart and dwarfs 8–12 feet (2.4–3.6 m) apart. Water and mulch as necessary to keep the soil moist and prevent damage to foliage and fruit. Mulch with compost in spring.

Pruning Use the central leader system to shape upright-growing European pears. Heavy-bearing trees will need some fruit thinning. In late spring, remove the smaller fruits, leaving one or two of the best fruit per cluster.

Propagation Propagate by grafting.

Pests and diseases Keep an eye out for pear psyllas, tiny insects that suck sap from tender shoot tips and fruit, spreading diseases as they go. During the growing season, use insecticidal soap or horticultural oil sprays to control psyllas. Select pear cultivars resistant to fireblight.

Harvesting and storage Pear trees generally begin to produce fruit 3–5 years after planting. Pick European pears when they are mature but not quite ripe.

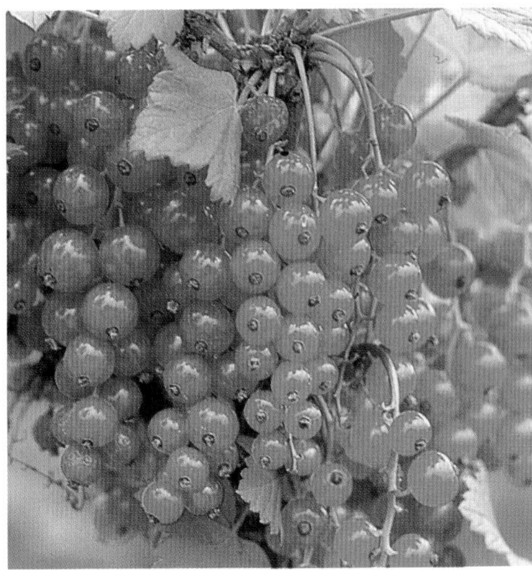

HARDINESS
Zones 3–7.

HEIGHT
3–7 feet
(90–210 cm)

SPREAD
3–7 feet
(90–210 cm)

COMMENTS
Buy gooseberry cultivars that are resistant to mildew. Mildew-resistant currant cultivars are also available.

CURRANT AND GOOSEBERRY

THE TART BERRIES OF CURRANTS ARE EXCELLENT FOR JAMS OR JUICE. IF POSSIBLE, PLANT TWO OR MORE CULTIVARS, AS CROSS-POLLINATION WILL INCREASE YIELDS.

Position Plant in full sun to light shade in average soil.

Cultivation Most currants and gooseberries are self-pollinating; however, if interplanted with two or three other culivars, they'll produce higher yields. Space the plants 6 feet (1.8 m) apart and mulch well. Add compost and a potassium-rich fertilizer in early spring. Water regularly in dry weather.

Pruning At planting time, select one branch as the main trunk and remove the rest. Each winter, remove all shoots that are more than 3 years old (or more than 2 years old on blackcurrants); then remove all but six of the remaining shoots.

Propagation By hardwood cuttings.

Pests and diseases Powdery mildew can devastate gooseberries, and sulfur sprays are not always an effective treatment.

Harvesting and storage For cooking or making jelly, pick currants and gooseberries when they are not quite ripe. For fresh eating, let them ripen on the bush until they taste right to you.

HARDINESS
Zones 5–9.

HEIGHT
4–7 feet
(1.2–2.1 m)

SPREAD
3–6 feet
(90–180 cm)

COMMENTS
Look for thornless, highly productive cultivars, such as 'Navaho Erect' and 'Arapaho', which stand erect with no support necessary.

BLACKBERRY

THE FLAVOR OF BLACKBERRIES IS AT ITS BEST WHEN THE FRUITS TURN DARK AND LOSE SOME OF THEIR GLOSSINESS. SOME THORNLESS CULTIVARS NEED SUPPORT.

Position Plant in full sun in average to rich soil.

Cultivation Buy blackberries as bareroot plants, or as tissue-cultured plantlets. They need plenty of space and good air circulation. Plant thorny cultivars 3–4 feet (90–120 cm) apart and thornless cultivars 4–6 feet (1.2–1.8 m) apart. Make paths between the rows for good sun exposure and adequate air circulation. Keep the soil evenly moist and mulch with compost in early spring.

Pruning Cut fruit-bearing canes to the ground right after harvest. In early spring, thin to leave only seven strong canes per plant. Shorten side branches to about 1 foot (30 cm) long. For maximum yields, train blackberries to a trellis.

Propagation By division or layering.

Pests and diseases Watch for distorted growth, sterile canes or orange-spotted leaves that drop early. These are all symptoms of incurable viral or orange rust diseases. Remove infected plants.

Harvesting and storage Eat soft, sweet blackberries as soon as possible after picking, or freeze.

HARDINESS
Zones 3–9.

HEIGHT
4–6 feet
(1.2–1.8 m)

SPREAD
2–4 feet
(60–120 cm)

COMMENTS
Raspberries ripen from summer on. Summer-bearing cultivars, such as 'Boyne', fruit on 2-year-old canes. 'Heritage' and 'Redwing' bear a second autumn crop on new canes.

RASPBERRY

IF BIRDS ARE BEATING YOU TO YOUR BERRIES, COVER THE PLANTS WITH NETTING. ROLL BACK THE COVER AS NEEDED TO HARVEST.

Position Plant in full sun in average to poor soil.

Cultivation If possible, buy bareroot plants and plant them 2 feet (60 cm) apart in a row. They'll fill in within a year or two. Apply compost and a little balanced organic fertilizer in late winter, if needed, for good growth. Water during dry spells and mulch to discourage weeds and keep the soil evenly moist.

Pruning Cut off all the old canes at ground level when they have finished fruiting. Leave the new current-season canes to produce berries next year.

Propagation Propagate by division or layering, but only if you are sure your plants are healthy.

Pests and diseases Buy only certified disease-free plants. Several fungal diseases may attack raspberries: powdery mildew, anthracnose and cane blight. If these diseases were a problem in the previous year, spray with lime-sulfur when the buds begin to turn green. Remove and destroy plants affected by disease.

Harvesting and storage Harvest berries when they're sweet and ripe. Eat fresh or freeze for later.

HARDINESS
Zones 8–9.

HEIGHT
8–12 feet
(2.4–3.6 m)

SPREAD
8–12 feet
(2.4–3.6 m)

COMMENTS
Completely ripe fruits have a delectable flavor and aroma. Use quickly, as they are very soft and fragile.

BOYSENBERRY

RIPE BOYSENBERRY FRUITS ARE LARGE, MAROON AND ALMOST SEEDLESS.

Position Plant canes in full sun in well-drained soil, rich in humus.

Cultivation Plant container-grown stock anytime the ground isn't frozen, or set out bareroot plants in spring or autumn, while dormant. Boysenberries are self-fruitful, so you can get fruit from just one plant. Space plants 3–6 feet (90–180 cm) apart. Set up a post next to each plant or erect a one- or two-wire trellis on which to support the canes. The canes are biennial, bearing fruit in their second season.

Pruning In winter, cut canes that fruited the previous summer to the ground—they are dead anyway. Thin remaining canes, leaving eight to 10 of the most vigorous ones per plant. Shorten these to 7 feet (2.1 m), and cut back any sideshoots to 1–1½ feet (30–45 cm).

Propagation Propagate by layering.

Pests and diseases Given good growing conditions, boysenberries usually have few major problems.

Harvesting and storage For full flavor, harvest when the fruit practically drops off into your hand. Even at cool temperatures and high humidity, fruit keeps only 2–3 days.

HARDINESS
Zones 2–9.

HEIGHT
6–10 feet
(1.8–3 m)

SPREAD
3–6 feet
(90–180 cm)

COMMENTS
Edible species include blueberry elder *Sambucus caerulea*, American elder *S. canadensis* and European elder *S. nigra*. But some species (such as *S. ebulus*) have poisonous berries.

ELDERBERRY

ELDERBERRIES PRODUCE CLUSTERS OF SMALL BLUE-BLACK BERRIES. THE FLAVOR IS VERY MILD, SO ELDERBERRIES TASTE BEST COOKED WITH A SWEETENER AND ANOTHER, MORE ACIDIC FRUIT. THE WHOLE FRUIT IS EDIBLE.

Position Plant in full sun or partial shade and evenly moist soil.

Cultivation Plant container-grown shrubs anytime, or set out bareroot plants in spring or autumn, while they are dormant. Space plants 6 feet (1.8 m) apart. Plant two seedlings or two different cultivars for best yields.

Pruning On established bushes, cut stems that are more than 3 years old to ground level each winter. Also prune away suckers to control the spread of the plants.

Propagation Dig up and transplant suckers from around the base of the plant. You also can take cuttings or sow seed.

Pests and diseases If necessary, cover the bushes with netting to keep birds at bay.

Harvesting and storage Harvest the berries when they are fully colored. An easy way to pick fruit from the clusters is to pop it off with the tines of a dinner fork. Store the fruit in a covered container in the refrigerator. The fruit is most often used in jams, pies and preserves.

Vaccinium corymbosum

ERICACEAE

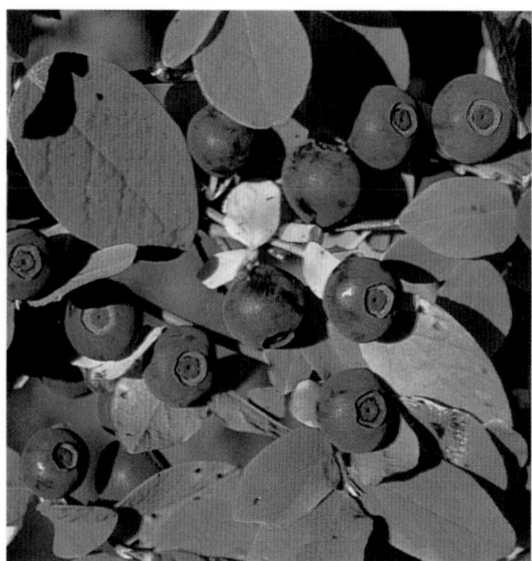

HARDINESS
Lowbush cultivars grow well in Zones 3–7. Midhighs grow up to Zone 4. Highbush types thrive in Zones 5–7. Rabbiteyes are normally adapted to Zones 6–9, but cultivars, such as 'Briteblue', can also grow in Zone 10.

HEIGHT
2–15 feet (60–450 cm)

SPREAD
3–10 feet (90–300 cm)

BLUEBERRY

SOME BLUEBERRIES NEED CROSS-POLLINATION, SO MAKE SURE YOU CHECK CATALOG DESCRIPTIONS TO GET THE APPROPRIATE PARTNERS.

Position Plant in full sun in average to rich, well-drained soil.

Cultivation Depending on whether you're growing lowbush, highbush, midhigh or rabbiteye blueberries, plant them 2–8 feet (60–240 cm) apart. Apply a thick layer of mulch to keep the soil evenly moist. Add compost each spring.

Pruning Pinch off all the flowers on a young blueberry bush the first year after planting so the bush will grow strong. The next year you'll have to remove only dead or damaged wood. Let plenty of sun and air penetrate the entire plant.

Propagation Propagate by hardwood or softwood cuttings, or by division, depending on cultivar.

Pests and diseases If stems begin to die back or show unusual cankers or cracks, cut them back to healthy tissue. Use sticky red balls (such as apple maggot traps) to catch blueberry maggots before they can tunnel into the ripening berries.

Harvesting and storage Harvest after the berries turn blue. Don't pick underripe berries; they won't ripen. Eat immediately or freeze.

Vaccinium macrocarpon ERICACEAE

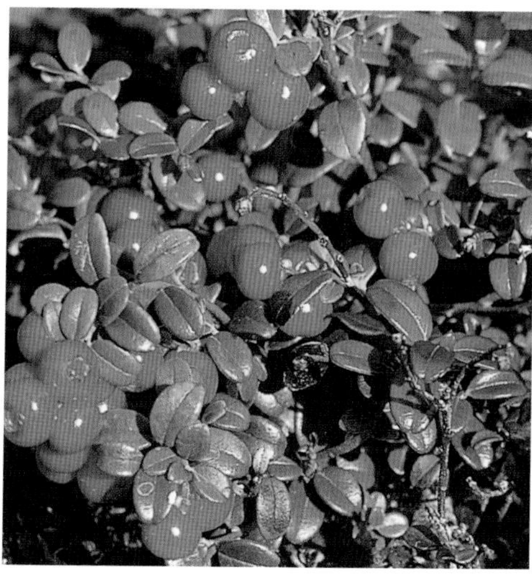

HARDINESS
Zones 2–6.

HEIGHT
Up to 1 foot (30 cm)

SPREAD
Unlimited. (The sprawling stems root where they touch the ground and continue to grow outward.)

COMMENTS
The tart berries are completely edible.

CRANBERRY

CRANBERRIES GROW AS LOW, CREEPING BUSHES. THEIR WHITE FLOWERS ARE FOLLOWED BY HARD, RED BERRIES, EACH ABOUT THE SIZE OF A THUMBNAIL.

Position Cranberries thrive in sun and moist, well-drained, humus-rich and very acid soil; pH 4.0–5.5. The plants do not tolerate dry soil, but they can withstand flooding in cold weather.

Cultivation Plant in spring or autumn where winters are mild or in spring where winters are severe. Space plants 1–2 feet (30–60 cm) apart. Mix plenty of acid peat into the soil before planting. Mulch with sawdust or sand, renewing the mulch periodically.

Pruning Cut away some of the sprawling stems and some of the upright fruiting stems when they become overcrowded.

Propagation Summer stem cuttings root readily. Where winters are mild, set rooted cuttings outdoors in autumn; otherwise, set them out as early as possible in spring.

Pests and diseases Generally no significant problems.

Harvesting and storage Pick berries in autumn, after they are fully colored. Cranberries will keep for 2–4 months at high humidity and temperatures just above freezing. They can also be dried.

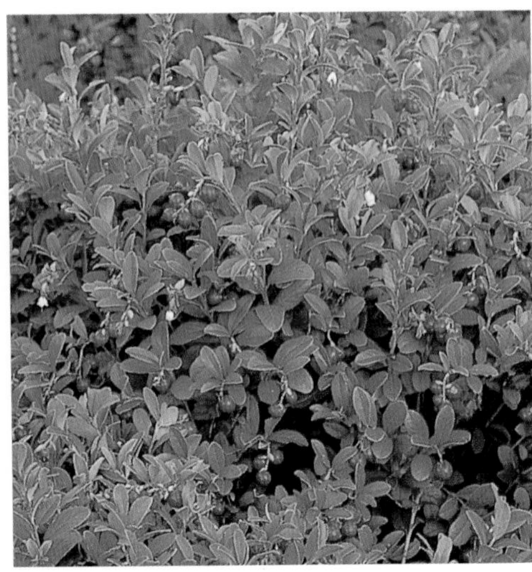

HARDINESS
Zones 2–6.

HEIGHT
6–24 inches (15–60 cm)

SPREAD
Unlimited. (Plants send up shoots from creeping underground stems.)

COMMENTS
The round, red berries are a little larger than peas and have a flavor similar to, but less sharp than that of true cranberries.

LINGONBERRY

LINGONBERRY IS A LOW, CREEPING BUSH THAT PRODUCES WHOLLY EDIBLE FRUIT.

Position Give lingonberries full sun or partial shade and well-drained, humus-rich, acid soil; pH 4.5–5.5.

Cultivation Set out container-grown plants anytime the ground isn't frozen, or plant bareroot stock in spring or autumn, while dormant. Space plants of the species *vitis-idaea* 1½ feet (45 cm) apart and those of the variety *minus* 10 inches (25 cm) apart. Lingonberries compete poorly with weeds, so weed thoroughly before planting. Also dig in plenty of acid peat moss. Mulch with sand or sawdust to further suppress weeds and to keep the shallow roots cool and moist. Plants are partially self-fertile, but planting at least two seedlings or cultivars may increase yields.

Pruning Once plants are a few years old, mow a different third or quarter of the planting in late autumn each year (so each part gets mowed every 3–4 years) to about 1 inch (2.5 cm) high.

Propagation Take cuttings in spring.

Pests and diseases Generally no significant problems.

Harvesting and storage Delay harvest until fruit is thoroughly red and ripe. Store fruit at temperatures just above freezing with high humidity.

HARDINESS
Zones 4–9.

HEIGHT
8–12 feet
(2.4–3.6 m)

SPREAD
8–12 feet
(2.4–3.6 m)

COMMENTS
The seeds must be strained out when you make jam or jelly. There is an offensive odor while the fruit is cooking, but it is not present in the finished product.

CRANBERRY, HIGHBUSH

THE SHINY, BRIGHT RED BERRIES OF HIGHBUSH CRANBERRY RIPEN IN DROOPING CLUSTERS. THE TART FRUITS CONTAIN A SINGLE, LARGE SEED. EAT THE WHOLE FRUIT, EXCEPT FOR THE SEED.

Position Plant in full sun or partial shade in moist, well-drained soil.

Cultivation Plant container-grown shrubs anytime the ground isn't frozen, or set out bareroot plants in spring or autumn, while they are dormant. Space plants 6–9 feet (1.8–2.7 m) apart. Plant several of them close together for a bright spot when they are in fruit, or along a border as an informal hedge, or grow just one as a specimen shrub.

Pruning Cut off old, nonproductive stems at ground level in winter.

Propagation Take hardwood or softwood cuttings. Seed does not germinate until it has been kept warm and moist for 4 months, then cool and moist for 3 months.

Pests and diseases Generally no significant problems.

Harvesting and storage Harvest anytime after the berries turn fully red. Fruits not harvested hang on the bush well into winter, shriveling with time. Store at cool temperatures and high humidity, such as in a covered container in the refrigerator.

HARDINESS
Zones 4–10.

HEIGHT
4–6 feet
(1.2–1.8 m)

SPREAD
8–15 feet
(2.4–4.5 m)

COMMENTS
Grapes come in a variety of different types. The hardiest are American, or fox, grapes *Vitis labrusca*, robust growers with rich flavor for fresh eating, or making jelly or juice.

GRAPE

TO PREVENT GROWING CLUSTERS FROM RIPENING UNEVENLY, THIN IN EARLY SUMMER, WHEN FRUITS ARE SMALL AND HARD.

Position Plant in full sun in average to rich soil.

Cultivation Start with 1-year-old plants that are virus-indexed and certified disease-free. Set up a support system before planting for the vines to cling to. After planting, let the grapevine grow untrained for a year to develop strong roots. Pinch off grape flowers during that year. Keep the soil moist and mulch well. Feed with compost in spring.

Pruning Train the vine over wire strung between posts. In late winter, cut the vine back to a stump with two buds. When the buds start growing, leave the stronger shoot and remove the other one.

Propagation Propagate by cuttings, grafting or, for some types, layering.

Pests and diseases Black rot causes reddish brown leaf spots and hard, shriveled fruit. Botrytis bunch rot causes a fluffy gray-brown coating on the fruit. Anthracnose infection produces sunken, dark-ringed spots on leaves and fruit. Remove and destroy all infected fruit and leaves.

Harvesting and storage Harvest the bunches of grapes by clipping them off the vine with clean secateurs.

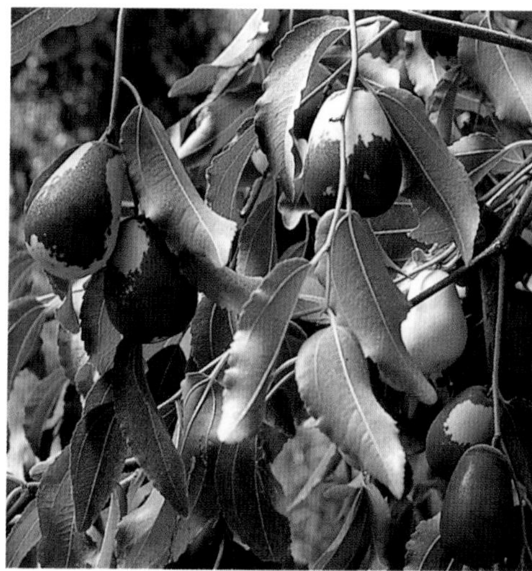

HARDINESS
Zones 5–8.

HEIGHT
Up to 30 feet (9 m)

SPREAD
Up to 20 feet (6 m)

COMMENTS
The skin is pale green, mottled with brown. You can eat the skin and flesh but not the seed. Dried fruits taste rather like dates.

JUJUBE

FRESH JUJUBE FRUITS HAVE A CRUNCHY TEXTURE AND A FLAVOR SIMILAR TO APPLES.

Position Jujube needs full sun and abundant summer heat but grows in almost any soil, and will tolerate even very wet or dry conditions.

Cultivation Plant container-grown trees anytime the ground isn't frozen, or set out bareroot plants in spring or autumn, while dormant. Space plants 20 feet (6 m) apart. Pollination needs are not well defined, but cross-pollination generally increases fruit size and yield. The trees tend to sucker, especially when young.

Pruning No regular pruning needed.

Propagation Increase cultivars by grafting or, if the mother tree is not grafted, by digging up suckers. To grow a seedling for a rootstock, open the seed lengthwise to extract the two kernels, then keep the kernels cool and barely moist for 2 months to assist germination.

Pests and diseases Generally no significant pest or disease problems.

Harvesting and storage Harvest fruits for fresh eating just as they become mottled with brown. Will store for a month or more at 50°F (10°C). Fruits left hanging on the tree turn completely brown, then shrivel and lose moisture. Dried fruits keep for over a year at cool temperatures.

Plant Hardiness Zone Maps

These maps of the United States, Canada and Europe are divided into ten zones. Each zone is based on a 10°F (5.6°C) difference in average annual minimum temperature. Some areas are considered too high in elevation for plant cultivation and so are not assigned to any zone. There are also island zones that are warmer or cooler than surrounding areas because of differences in elevation; they have been given a zone different from the surrounding areas. Many large urban areas, for example, are in a warmer zone than the surrounding land. Plants grow best within an optimum range of temperatures. The range may be wide for some species and narrow for others. Plants also differ in their ability to survive frost and in their sun or shade requirements.

PACIFIC OCEAN

Average Annual Minimum Temperature °F (°C)

ZONE 1	Below -50°F (Below -45°C)	**ZONE 6**	-10° to 0°F (-23° to -18°C)
ZONE 2	-50° to -40°F (-45° to -40°C)	**ZONE 7**	0° to 10°F (-18° to -12°C)
ZONE 3	-40° to -30°F (-40° to -34°C)	**ZONE 8**	10° to 20°F (-12° to -7°C)
ZONE 4	-30° to -20°F (-34° to -29°C)	**ZONE 9**	20° to 30°F (-7° to -1°C)
ZONE 5	-20° to -10°F (-29° to -23°C)	**ZONE 10**	30° to 40°F (-1° to 4°C)

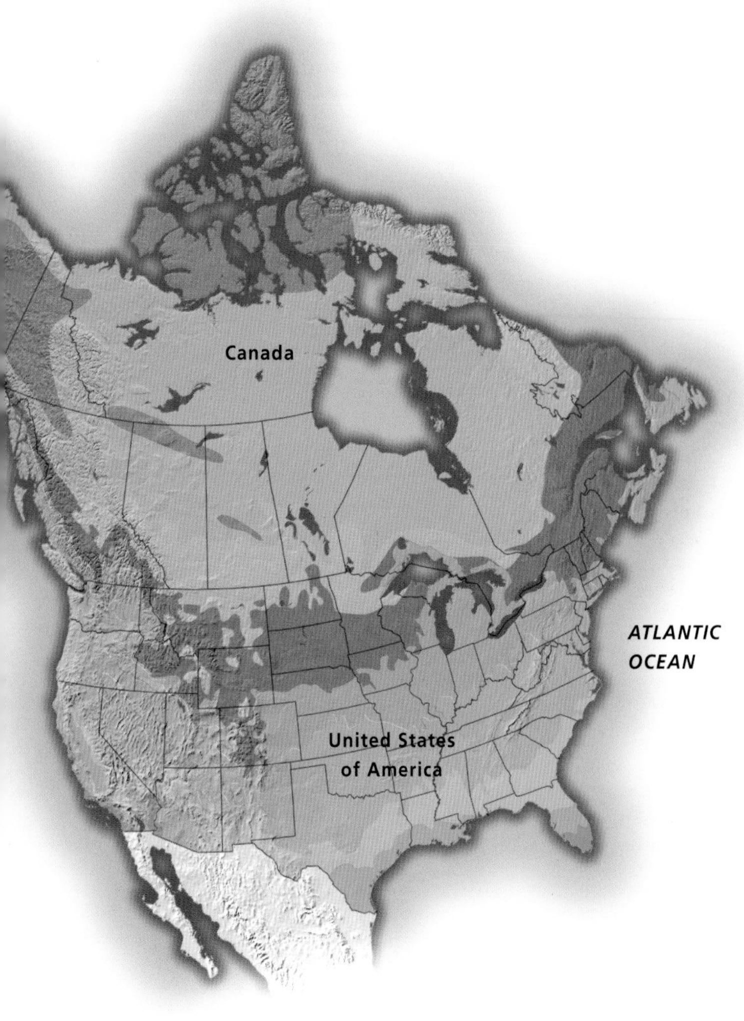
Canada
ATLANTIC
OCEAN
United States
of America

The zone ratings indicate conditions in which designated plants will grow well, and not merely survive. Many plants may survive in zones that are warmer or colder than their recommended zone range. Remember that other factors, including wind, soil type, soil moisture, humidity, snow and winter sunshine, may have a great effect on growth.

Keep in mind that some nursery plants have been grown in greenhouses, so they might not survive in your garden. It's a waste of time and money, and a cause of heartache, to buy plants that aren't suitable for your climate zone.

Australia and New Zealand

These maps divide Australia and New Zealand into seven climate zones which, as near as possible, correspond to the USDA climate zones used in the United States, Britain and Europe and in this book. The zones are based on the minimum temperatures usually, or possibly, experienced within each zone. This book is designed mainly for cool-climate gardens, but the information in it can be adapted for those in hotter climates. In this book, the ideal zones in which to grow particular plants are indicated and when you read that a plant is suitable for any of the zones 7 through to 10, you will know that it should grow successfully in those zones in Australia and New Zealand. There are other factors that affect plant growth, but temperature is one of the most important. Plants listed as being suitable for zone 10 may also grow in hotter zones, but to be sure, consult a gardening guide specific to your area.

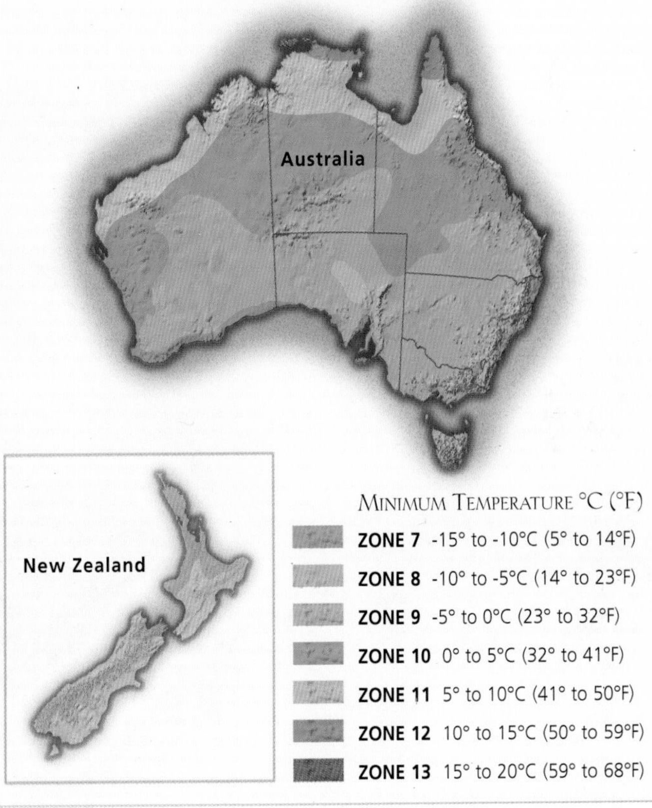

INDEX

Page references in *italics* indicate photos and illustrations.

A

B

C

F

G

H

I

J, K

L

M

N

O

P

Q

R

S

T

U, V

W, Z

Acknowledgments

KEY l=left, r=right, c=center, t=top, b=bottom

APL=Australian Picture Library; AZ=A–Z Botanical Collection; BCL=Bruce Coleman Ltd; CM=Cheryl Maddocks; CN= Clive Nichols; DF=Derek Fell; DW=David Wallace; GDR=G.R. "Dick" Roberts; GP.com=gardenphotos.com; GPL=Garden Picture Library; HA=Heather Angel; HSC=Harry Smith Collection; HSI=Holt Studios International; IH=Ivy Hansen; JP=Jerry Pavia; JY=James Young; LC=Leigh Clapp; LR=Lorna Rose; OSF=Oxford Scientific Films; PD=PhotoDisc; PH=Photos Horticultural; SM=Stirling Macoboy; SOM=S. & O. Mathews; TE=Thomas Eltzroth; TPL=photolibrary.com; WO=Weldon Owen; WR=Weldon Russell

1t OSF/Steffen Hauser; c WO/JY; b WR/John Callanan **2**c WO **5**c LC **6**t WO/JY; c WO/JY; b APL/ Corbis/Lynda Richardson **7**t JY; c OSF/Richard Kolar; b GPL/Howard Rice **10**c APL/Corbis/Michael Boys **13**b GPL/Eric Crichton **15**b LR **16**tl DF **17**tr PH **20**tr HSC **21**bl TE **23**c GPL/Howard Rice **24**t GPL/John Millar **25**b PH **26**c APL/Corbis/Michael Boys **28–29**b WR **30**b GPL/Joanne Pavia **31**t GPL/Michael Howes **33**c, b DW **37**t DF **38**b WO **39**tl WO; br GP.com/Judy White **41**c HSC **42**t PH; b HSI/Nigel Cattlin **43**b PH **44**t HSI/Nigel Cattlin **45**tr PH **46**b TE **47**t WO **48**t HSI/Nigel Cattlin **49**b BCL/Jane Burton **50**br WR **51**br PH **52**t APL/Corbis/Patrick Johns; c, b TE **53**l WR **54**c GPL/John Glover **56**tl WO; br WR **57**r WO/Kevin Candland **59**t PD **61**b PD **62**bl John Callanan **63** DW **67** DW **70**t Andrew Lawson; b TE **71**b CN **74–75**b PH **75**tr GPL/Mel Watson **76**tl GPL/John Glover; br GPL/Stephen Robson **77**t TE **78**b GP.com/Judy White **80**c LC **82**tl Denise Greig **83**c CN **84**t APL/Corbis/Eric Crichton **84–85**b GPL/Juliette Wade **86–87**b APL/Corbis/Eric Crichton **87**t GPL/John Glover **88**t, b TE **89**t APL/Corbis/Bohemian Nomad Picture Makers **90**tl TE **91**b GPL/Howard Rice **92**bl GPL/Mayer/Le Scanff **93**tr TE **95**t GPL/Michael Howes **96**b GPL/ Mel Watson **97**tr Corbis **99**t GPL/Mel Watson **100**cl DF; bl GPL/Robert Estall **102**tl GPL/Marijke Heuff **103**b **105**t APL/Corbis/Michael Boys **106**t PH **106–107**b Denise Greig **107**t AZ/Anthony Cooper **108**t PH **109**t Artville; b GPL/Ron Sutherland **110**tr AZ/Bjorn Svensson **110–111**b GPL/JP **111**t PH **112**t GPL/JP **114**t JY **115**t PH **116**t JP **117**t GPL/Sunniva Harte **118**t TE **119**t DW **120**t GDR **121**t DF **122**t GDR **123**t WO/JY **124**t WR **125**t DW **126**t PH **127**t Ardea London/Don Hadden **128**t HA **129**t HA **130**t WR **131**t CM **132**t PH **133**t DF **134**t WO/JY **135**t GDR **136**t DW **137**t BCL **138**t GDR **139**t DF **140**t **141**t TE **142**t GDR **143**t GPL/John Glover **144**t GDR **145**t DW **146**t JY **147**t DW **148**t WO **149**t GDR **150**t GPL/Jacqui Hurst **151**t GDR **152**t WR **153**t DW **154**t GPL/Christi Carter **155**t TE **156**t TE **157**t WO/Michael Freeman **158**t TE **159**t WO/JY **160**t WR **161**t WO/JY **162**t WO/JY **163**t AZ **164**t DW **165**t TE **166**t WO/JY **167**t BCL **168**t JY **169**t PH **170**t GPL/John Glover **171**t GDR **172**t JY **173**t DW **174**t WO **175**t DW **176**t GPL/Lamontagne **177**t APL/Corbis/Michael Boys **178**t HA

179t CM **180**t SM **181**t PH **182**t DW **183**t GDR **184**t DW **185**t DW **186**t DW **187**t HSC **188**t IH **189**t DW **190**t WO/JY **191**t WO **192**t PH **193**t DW **194**t HSC **195**t HSC **196**t DW **197**t TE **198**t GPL/Lamontagne **199**t Auscape/ C. Andrew Henley **200**t PH **201**t JY **202**t DW **203**t TE **204**t LR **205**t DW **206**t DW **207**t TE **208**t SM **209**t Tony Rodd **210**t CM **211**t DW **212**t Rodale Stock Images **213**t GDR **214**t DW **215**t DW **216**t GDR **217**t TPL/Maximilian Stock Ltd/AGSTOCK **218**t DW **219**t GP.com/Judy White **220**t SM **221**t DW **222**t DW **223**t DW **224**t DW **225**t DF **226**t DW **227**t TE **228**t APL/ Hackenberg/Zefa **229**t GPL/John Glover **230**t WR/DW **231**t HSC **232**t DW **233**t CM **234**t DW **235**t OSF/John McCammon **236**t APL/Corbis/Robert Maass **237**t DW **238**t TPL/Wen Jia Feng **240**c GP.com/Judy White **242**t PH **243**t HSC **244**t OSF/Harold Taylor **245**t TE **246**t TE **247**t TE **248**t HSC **249**t TE **250**t IH **251**t TE **252**t TE **253**t SOM **254**t WO **255**t GPL/Mayer/Le Scanff **256**t TE **257**t APL/Corbis/Maurice Nimmo **258**t GPL/Tamara Richards **259**t GPL/Christi Carter **260**t WO/JY **261**t HSC **262**t TE **263**t TE **264**t TE **265**t TE **266**t TE **267**t PH **268**t GPL/John Glover **269**t PH **270**t SOM **271**t WO **272**t GDR **273**t GDR **274**t GDR **275**t OSF/R. F. Head **276**t HSI/Nigel Cattlin **277**t TE **278**t OSF/Bill Paton **279**t TE **280**t TE **281**t BCL/Hans Reinhard **282**t GP.com/Judy White **283**t TE **284**t SOM **285**t PH **286**t TE **287**t GDR **288**t HSC **289**t TE **290**t GDR **291**t TE **292**t DF **293**t GP.com/Judy White **294**t TE **295**t GDR **296**t DF **297**t GPL/John Glover **298**t PH **299**t PH **300**t TE **301**t SOM **302**t PH **303**t BCL/Charlie Orr **304**t GPL/John Glover **305**t TE **306**t GPL/Neil Holmes **307**t TE

Illustrations by Tony Britt-Lewis, Edwina Riddell, Barbara Rodanska, Jan Smith, Kathie Smith.

The publishers would like to thank Puddingburn Publishing Services, for compiling the index, and Bronwyn Sweeney, for proofreading.